Casenote™ Legal Briefs

ADMINISTRATIVE LAW

Adaptable to courses utilizig, **Funk, Shapiro** and **Weaver's** casebook on Administrative Procedure and Practice

NORMAN S. GOLDENBERG, SENIOR EDITOR
PETER TENEN, MANAGING EDITOR

STAFF WRITERS
DANIEL KIM
NANCY SILVER
CATHY SEMPEPOS

ISBN 0-87457-269-X

FORMAT FOR THE CASENOTE LEGAL BRIEF

PARTY ID: Quick identification of the relationship between the parties.

PALSGRAF v. LONG ISLAND R.R. CO.
Injured bystander (P) v. Railroad company (D)
N.Y. Ct. App., 248 N.Y. 339, 162 N.E. 99 (1928).

NATURE OF CASE: This section identifies the form of action (e.g., breach of contract, negligence, battery), the type of proceeding (e.g., demurrer, appeal from trial court's jury instructions) or the relief sought (e.g., damages, injunction, criminal sanctions).

NATURE OF CASE: Appeal from judgment affirming verdict for plaintiff seeking damages for personal injury.

FACT SUMMARY: This is included to refresh the student's memory and can be used as a quick reminder of the facts.

FACT SUMMARY: Helen Palsgraf (P) was injured on R.R.'s (D) train platform when R.R.'s (D) guard helped a passenger aboard a moving train, causing his package to fall on the tracks. The package contained fireworks which exploded, creating a shock that tipped a scale onto Palsgraf (P).

CONCISE RULE OF LAW: Summarizes the general principle of law that the case illustrates. It may be used for instant recall of the court's holding and for classroom discussion or home review.

CONCISE RULE OF LAW: The risk reasonably to be perceived defines the duty to be obeyed.

FACTS: This section contains all relevant facts of the case, including the contentions of the parties and the lower court holdings. It is written in a logical order to give the student a clear understanding of the case. The plaintiff and defendant are identified by their proper names throughout and are always labeled with a (P) or (D).

FACTS: Helen Palsgraf (P) purchased a ticket to Rockaway Beach from R.R. (D) and was waiting on the train platform. As she waited, two men ran to catch a train that was pulling out from the platform. The first man jumped aboard, but the second man, who appeared as if he might fall, was helped aboard by the guard on the train who had kept the door open so they could jump aboard. A guard on the platform also helped by pushing him onto the train. The man was carrying a package wrapped in newspaper. In the process, the man dropped his package, which fell on the tracks. The package contained fireworks and exploded. The shock of the explosion was apparently of great enough strength to tip over some scales at the other end of the platform, which fell on Palsgraf (P) and injured her. A jury awarded her damages, and R.R. (D) appealed.

ISSUE: The issue is a concise question that brings out the essence of the opinion as it relates to the section of the casebook in which the case appears. Both substantive and procedural issues are included if relevant to the decision.

ISSUE: Does the risk reasonably to be perceived define the duty to be obeyed?

HOLDING AND DECISION: This section offers a clear and in-depth discussion of the rule of the case and the court's rationale. It is written in easy-to-understand language and answers the issue(s) presented by applying the law to the facts of the case. When relevant, it includes a thorough discussion of the exceptions to the case as listed by the court, any major cites to other cases on point, and the names of the judges who wrote the decisions.

HOLDING AND DECISION: (Cardozo, C.J.) Yes. The risk reasonably to be perceived defines the duty to be obeyed. If there is no foreseeable hazard to the injured party as the result of a seemingly innocent act, the act does not become a tort because it happened to be a wrong as to another. If the wrong was not willful, the plaintiff must show that the act as to her had such great and apparent possibilities of danger as to entitle her to protection. Negligence in the abstract is not enough upon which to base liability. Negligence is a relative concept, evolving out of the common law doctrine of trespass on the case. To establish liability, the defendant must owe a legal duty of reasonable care to the injured party. A cause of action in tort will lie where harm, though unintended, could have been averted or avoided by observance of such a duty. The scope of the duty is limited by the range of danger that a reasonable person could foresee. In this case, there was nothing to suggest from the appearance of the parcel or otherwise that the parcel contained fireworks. The guard could not reasonably have had any warning of a threat to Palsgraf (P), and R.R. (D) therefore cannot be held liable. Judgment is reversed in favor of R.R. (D).

CONCURRENCE / DISSENT: All concurrences and dissents are briefed whenever they are included by the casebook editor.

DISSENT: (Andrews, J.) The concept that there is no negligence unless R.R. (D) owes a legal duty to take care as to Palsgraf (P) herself is too narrow. Everyone owes to the world at large the duty of refraining from those acts that may unreasonably threaten the safety of others. If the guard's action was negligent as to those nearby, it was also negligent as to those outside what might be termed the "danger zone." For Palsgraf (P) to recover, R.R.'s (D) negligence must have been the proximate cause of her injury, a question of fact for the jury.

EDITOR'S ANALYSIS: This last paragraph gives the student a broad understanding of where the case "fits in" with other cases in the section of the book and with the entire course. It is a hornbook-style discussion indicating whether the case is a majority or minority opinion and comparing the principal case with other cases in the casebook. It may also provide analysis from restatements, uniform codes, and law review articles. The editor's analysis will prove to be invaluable to classroom discussion.

EDITOR'S ANALYSIS: The majority defined the limit of the defendant's liability in terms of the danger that a reasonable person in defendant's situation would have perceived. The dissent argued that the limitation should not be placed on liability, but rather on damages. Judge Andrews suggested that only injuries that would not have happened but for R.R.'s (D) negligence should be compensable. Both the majority and dissent recognized the policy-driven need to limit liability for negligent acts, seeking, in the words of Judge Andrews, to define a framework "that will be practical and in keeping with the general understanding of mankind." The Restatement (Second) of Torts has accepted Judge Cardozo's view..

CROSS-REFERENCE TO OUTLINE: Wherever possible, following each case is a cross-reference linking the subject matter of the issue to the appropriate place in the *Casenote Law Outline*, which provides further information on the subject.

[For more information on foreseeability, see Casenote Law Outline on Torts, Chapter 8, § II. 2., Proximate Cause.]

QUICKNOTES: Conveniently defines legal terms found in the case and summarizes the nature of any statutes, codes, or rules referred to in the text.

QUICKNOTES

FORESEEABILITY - The reasonable anticipation that damage is a likely result from certain acts or omissions.

NEGLIGENCE - Failure to exercise that degree of care which a person of ordinary prudence would exercise under similiar circumstances.

PROXIMATE CAUSE - Something which in natural and continuous sequence, unbroken by any new intervening cause, produces an event, and without which the injury would not have occurred.

NOTE TO STUDENT

OUR GOAL. It is the goal of Casenotes Publishing Company, Inc. to create and distribute the finest, clearest and most accurate legal briefs available. To this end, we are constantly seeking new ideas, comments and constructive criticism. As a user of *Casenote Legal Briefs,* your suggestions will be highly valued. With all correspondence, please include your complete name, address, and telephone number, including area code and zip code.

THE TOTAL STUDY SYSTEM. Casenote Legal Briefs are just one part of the Casenotes TOTAL STUDY SYSTEM. Most briefs are (wherever possible) cross-referenced to the appropriate *Casenote Law Outline,* which will elaborate on the issue at hand. By purchasing a Law Outline together with your Legal Brief, you will have both parts of the Casenotes TOTAL STUDY SYSTEM. (See the advertising in the front of this book for a list of Law Outlines currently available.)

A NOTE ABOUT LANGUAGE. Please note that the language used in *Casenote Legal Briefs* in reference to minority groups and women reflects terminology used within the historical context of the time in which the respective courts wrote the opinions. We at Casenotes Publishing Co., Inc. are well aware of and very sensitive to the desires of all people to be treated with dignity and to be referred to as they prefer. Because such preferences change from time to time, and because the language of the courts reflects the time period in which opinions were written, our case briefs will not necessarily reflect contemporary references. We appreciate your understanding and invite your comments.

A NOTE REGARDING NEW EDITIONS. As of our press date, this Casenote Legal Brief is current and includes briefs of all cases in the current version of the casebook, divided into chapters that correspond to that edition of the casebook. However, occasionally a new edition of the casebook comes out in the interim, and sometimes the casebook author will make changes in the sequence of the cases in the chapters, add or delete cases, or change the chapter titles. Should you be using this Legal Brief in conjuction with a casebook that was issued later than this book, you can receive all of the newer cases, which are available free from us, by sending in the "Supplement Request Form" in this section of the book (please follow all instructions on that form). The Supplement(s) will contain all the missing cases, and will bring your Casenote Legal Brief up to date.

EDITOR'S NOTE. Casenote Legal Briefs are intended to supplement the student's casebook, not replace it. There is no substitute for the student's own mastery of this important learning and study technique. If used properly, *Casenote Legal Briefs* are an effective law study aid that will serve to reinforce the student's understanding of the cases.

REF.#1268-97-800

SUPPLEMENT REQUEST FORM

At the time this book was printed, a brief was included for every major case in the casebook and for every existing supplement to the casebook. However, if a new supplement to the casebook (or a new edition of the casebook) has been published since this publication was printed and if that casebook supplement (or new edition of the casebook) was available for sale at the time you purchased this Casenote Legal Briefs book, we will be pleased to provide you the new cases contained therein AT NO CHARGE when you send us a stamped, self-addressed envelope.

TO OBTAIN YOUR FREE SUPPLEMENT MATERIAL, **YOU MUST FOLLOW THE INSTRUCTIONS BELOW PRECISELY** OR YOUR REQUEST WILL NOT BE ACKNOWLEDGED!

1. Please check if there is in fact an existing supplement and, if so, that the cases are not already included in your Casenote Legal Briefs. Check the main table of cases as well as the supplement table of cases, if any.
2. **REMOVE THIS ENTIRE PAGE FROM THE BOOK.** You MUST send this ORIGINAL page to receive your supplement. This page acts as your proof of purchase and contains the reference number necessary to fill your supplement request properly. No photocopy of this page or written request will be honored or answered. Any request from which the reference number has been removed, altered or obliterated will not be honored.
3. Prepare a STAMPED self-addressed envelope for return mailing. Be sure to use a FULL SIZE (9 X 12) ENVELOPE (MANILA TYPE) so that the supplement will fit and AFFIX ENOUGH POSTAGE TO COVER 3 OZ. **ANY SUPPLEMENT REQUEST NOT ACCOMPANIED BY A STAMPED SELF-ADDRESSED ENVELOPE WILL ABSOLUTELY NOT BE FILLED OR ACKNOWLEDGED.**
4. MULTIPLE SUPPLEMENT REQUESTS: If you are ordering more than one supplement, we suggest that you enclose a stamped, self-addressed envelope for each supplement requested. If you enclose only one envelope for a multiple request, your order may not be filled immediately should any supplement which you requested still be in production. In other words, your order will be held by us until it can be filled completely.
5. Casenotes prints two kinds of supplements. A "New Edition" supplement is issued when a new edition of your casebook is published. A "New Edition" supplement gives you all major cases found in the new edition of the casebook which did not appear in the previous edition. A regular "supplement" is issued when a paperback supplement to your casebook is published. If the box at the lower right is stamped, then the "New Edition" supplement was provided to your bookstore and is *not* available from Casenotes; however, Casenotes will still send you any regular "supplements" which have been printed either before or after the new edition of your casebook appeared and which, according to the reference number at the top of this page, have not been included in this book. If the box is not stamped, Casenotes will send you any supplements, "New Edition" and/or regular, needed to completely update your Casenote Legal Briefs.

 ***NOTE:* REQUESTS FOR SUPPLEMENTS WILL NOT BE FILLED UNLESS THESE INSTRUCTIONS ARE COMPLIED WITH!**

6. Fill in the following information:

Full title of CASEBOOK **ADMINISTRATIVE LAW** ____________

CASEBOOK author's name **Funk, Shapiro and Weaver** ____________

Copyright year of new edition or new paperback supplement ____________

Name and location of bookstore where this Casenote Legal Brief was purchased ____________

Name and location of law school you attend ____________

Any comments regarding Casenote Legal Briefs ____________

NOTE: IF THIS BOX IS STAMPED, NO NEW EDITION SUPPLEMENT CAN BE OBTAINED BY MAIL.

PUBLISHED BY CASENOTES PUBLISHING CO., INC. 1640 5th ST, SUITE 208 SANTA MONICA, CA 90401

PLEASE PRINT

NAME ____________ **PHONE** ________ **DATE** ____________

ADDRESS/CITY/STATE/ZIP ____________

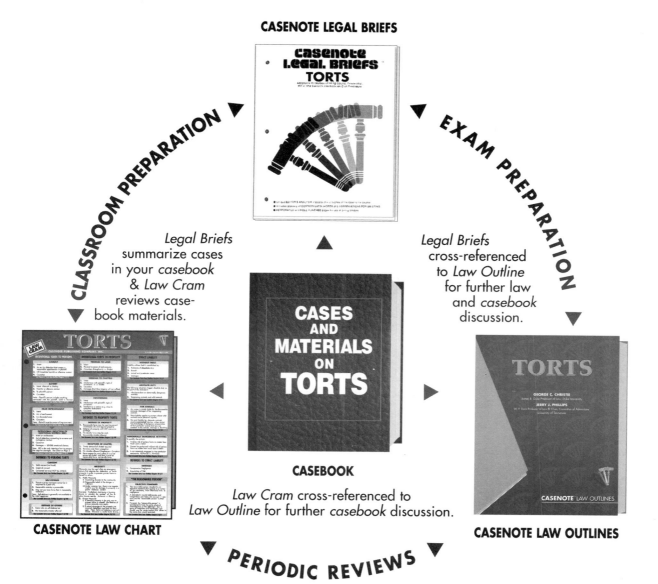

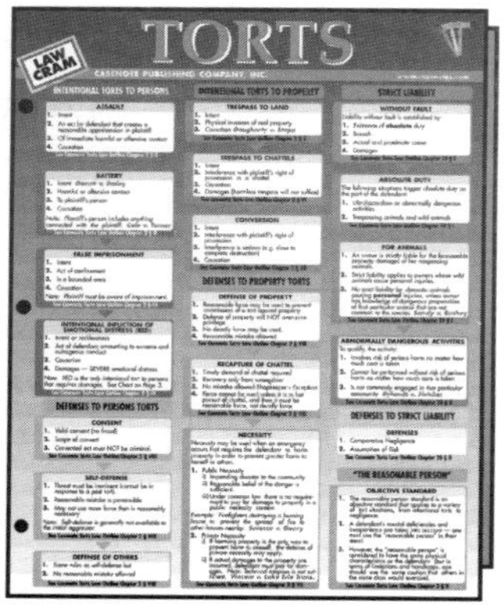

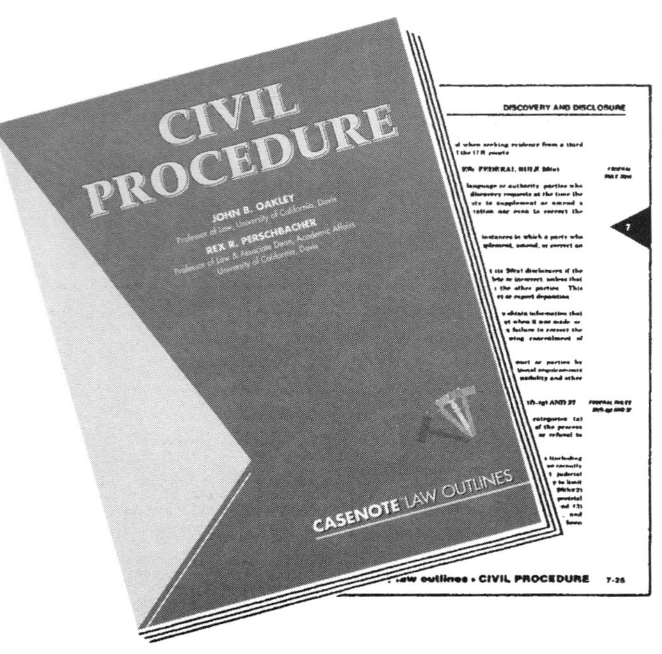

the Ultimate Outline

- *RENOWNED AUTHORS: Every **Casenote Law Outline** is written by highly respected, nationally recognized professors.*
- *KEYED TO **CASENOTE LEGAL BRIEF** BOOKS: In most cases, **Casenote Law Outlines** work in conjunction with the **Casenote Legal Briefs** so that you can see how each case in your textbook relates to the entire subject area. In addition, **Casenote Law Outlines** are cross-referenced to most major casebooks.*
- *FREE SUPPLEMENT SERVICE: As part of being the most up-to-date legal outline on the market, whenever a new supplement is published, the corresponding outline can be updated for free using the supplement request form found in this book.*

ADMINISTRATIVE LAW (1999) **$21.95**
Charles H. Koch, Jr., Dudley W. Woodbridge Professor of Law, College of William and Mary
Sidney A. Shapiro, John M. Rounds Professor of Law, University of Kansas

CIVIL PROCEDURE (1999) **$22.95**
John B. Oakley, Professor of Law, University of California, Davis School of Law
Rex R. Perschbacher, Professor and Dean of University of California, Davis School of Law

COMMERCIAL LAW (see SALES ● SECURED TRANSACTIONS ● NEGOTIABLE INSTRUMENTS & PAYMENT SYSTEMS)

CONFLICT OF LAWS (1996) **$21.95**
Luther L. McDougal, III, W.R. Irby Professor of Law, Tulane University
Robert L. Felix, James P. Mozingo, III, Professor of Law, University of South Carolina

CONSTITUTIONAL LAW (1997) **$24.95**
Gary Goodpaster, Professor of Law, University of California, Davis School of Law

CONTRACTS (1999) **$21.95**
Daniel Wm. Fessler, Professor of Law, University of California, Davis School of Law

CORPORATIONS (2000) **$24.95**
Lewis D. Solomon, Arthur Selwin Miller Research Professor of Law, George Washington University
Daniel Wm. Fessler, Professor of Law, University of California, Davis School of Law
Arthur E. Wilmarth, Jr., Associate Professor of Law, George Washington University

CRIMINAL LAW (1999) **$21.95**
Joshua Dressler, Professor of Law, McGeorge School of Law

CRIMINAL PROCEDURE (1999) **$20.95**
Joshua Dressler, Professor of Law, McGeorge School of Law

ESTATE & GIFT TAX (2000) **$22.95**
Joseph M. Dodge, W.H. Francis Professor of Law, University of Texas at Austin

EVIDENCE (1996) **$23.95**
Kenneth Graham, Jr., Professor of Law, University of California, Los Angeles School of Law

FEDERAL COURTS (1997) **$22.95**
Howard P. Fink, Isadore and Ida Topper Professor of Law, Ohio State University
Linda S. Mullenix, Bernard J. Ward Centennial Professor of Law, University of Texas

FEDERAL INCOME TAXATION (1998) **$22.95**
Joseph M. Dodge, W.H. Francis Professor of Law, University of Texas at Austin

LEGAL RESEARCH (1996) **$21.95**
Nancy L. Schultz, Professor of Law, Chapman University
Louis J. Sirico, Jr., Professor of Law, Villanova University

NEGOTIABLE INSTRUMENTS & PAYMENT SYSTEMS (1995) **$22.95**
Donald B. King, Professor of Law, Saint Louis University
Peter Winship, James Cleo Thompson, Sr. Trustee Professor, SMU

PROPERTY (1999) **$22.95**
Sheldon F. Kurtz, Percy Bordwell Professor of Law, University of Iowa
Patricia Cain, Professor of Law, University of Iowa

SALES (2000) **$22.95**
Robert E. Scott, Dean and Lewis F. Powell, Jr. Professor of Law, University of Virginia
Donald B. King, Professor of Law, Saint Louis University

SECURED TRANSACTIONS (1995 w/ '96 supp.) **$20.95**
Donald B. King, Professor of Law, Saint Louis University

TORTS (1999) **$22.95**
George C. Christie, James B. Duke Professor of Law, Duke University
Jerry J. Phillips, W.P. Toms Professor of Law, University of Tennessee

WILLS, TRUSTS, & ESTATES (1996) **$22.95**
William M. McGovern, Professor of Law, University of California, Los Angeles School of Law

CASENOTE LEGAL BRIEFS

PRICE LIST — EFFECTIVE JULY 1, 2000 ● PRICES SUBJECT TO CHANGE WITHOUT NOTICE

Ref. No.	Course	Adaptable to Courses Utilizing	Retail Price
1265	ADMINISTRATIVE LAW	ASIMOW, BONFIELD & LEVIN	21.00
1263	ADMINISTRATIVE LAW	BREYER, STEWART & SUNSTEIN	22.00
1266	ADMINISTRATIVE LAW	CASS, DIVER & BEERMAN	20.00
1260	ADMINISTRATIVE LAW	GELLHORN, B., S., R. & F.	20.00
1268	ADMINISTRATIVE LAW	FUNK, SHAPIRO & WEAVER	22.00
1264	ADMINISTRATIVE LAW	MASHAW, MERRILL & SHANE	21.50
1267	ADMINISTRATIVE LAW	REESE	20.00
1262	ADMINISTRATIVE LAW	SCHWARTZ	21.00
1350	AGENCY & PARTNERSHIP (ENT.ORG)	CONARD, KNAUSS & SIEGEL	24.00
1351	AGENCY & PARTNERSHIP	HYNES	24.00
1281	ANTITRUST (TRADE REGULATION)	HANDLER, P., G. & W.	20.50
1283	ANTITRUST	SULLIVAN & HOVENKAMP	21.00
1611	BANKING LAW	MACEY & MILLER	20.00
1305	BANKRUPTCY	JORDAN, WARREN & BUSSELL	20.00
1058	BUSINESS ASSOCIATIONS (CORPORATIONS)	KLEIN, RAMSEYER & BAINBRIDGE	22.00
1059	BUSINESS ORGANIZATIONS (CORPORATIONS)	SODERQUIST, S., C., & S.	24.00
1040	CIVIL PROCEDURE	COUND, F., M. & S	21.00
1043	CIVIL PROCEDURE	FIELD, KAPLAN & CLERMONT	23.00
1049	CIVIL PROCEDURE	FREER & PERDUE	19.00
1041	CIVIL PROCEDURE	HAZARD, TAIT & FLETCHER	22.00
1047	CIVIL PROCEDURE	MARCUS, REDISH & SHERMAN	22.00
1044	CIVIL PROCEDURE	ROSENBERG, S. & D.	23.00
1046	CIVIL PROCEDURE	YEAZELL	20.00
1311	COMM'L LAW	FARNSWORTH, H., R., H. & M.	22.00
1312	COMM'L LAW	JORDAN, WARREN & WALT	22.00
1310	COMM'L LAW (SALES/SEC.TR./PAY.LAW [Sys.])	SPEIDEL, SUMMERS & WHITE	24.00
1313	COMM'L LAW (SALES/SEC.TR./PAY.LAW)	WHALEY	23.00
1314	COMMERCIAL TRANSACTIONS	LOPUKI, W., K. & M.	22.00
1320	COMMUNITY PROPERTY	BIRD	20.50
1630	COMPARATIVE LAW	SCHLESINGER, B., D., H.& W.	19.00
1048	COMPLEX LITIGATION	MARCUS & SHERMAN	20.00
1072	CONFLICTS	BRILMAYER	20.00
1071	CONFLICTS	CRAMTON, C. K., & K.	20.00
1070	CONFLICTS	HAY, WEINTRAUB & BORCHER	23.00
1073	CONFLICTS	SYMEONIDES, P., & M.	23.00
1086	CONSTITUTIONAL LAW	BREST, LEVINSON, B.& A.	21.00
1082	CONSTITUTIONAL LAW	COHEN & VARAT	24.00
1088	CONSTITUTIONAL LAW	FARBER, ESKRIDGE & FRICKEY	21.00
1080	CONSTITUTIONAL LAW	GUNTHER & SULLIVAN	21.00
1081	CONSTITUTIONAL LAW	LOCKHART, K., C., S. & F.	21.00
1085	CONSTITUTIONAL LAW	ROTUNDA	23.00
1089	CONSTITUTIONAL LAW (FIRST AMENDMENT)	SHIFFRIN & CHOPER	18.00
1087	CONSTITUTIONAL LAW	STONE, S., S. & T.	22.00
1103	CONTRACTS	BARNETT	24.00
1102	CONTRACTS	BURTON	23.00
1017	CONTRACTS	CALAMARI, PERILLO & BENDER	26.00
1101	CONTRACTS	CRANDALL & WHALEY	23.00
1014	CONTRACTS	DAWSON, HARVEY & H.	22.00
1010	CONTRACTS	FARNSWORTH & YOUNG	20.00
1011	CONTRACTS	FULLER & EISENBERG	24.00
1013	CONTRACTS	KESSLER, GILMORE & KRONMAN	26.00
1016	CONTRACTS	KNAPP & CRYSTAL	23.50
1012	CONTRACTS	MURPHY & SPEIDEL	25.00
1015	CONTRACTS	ROSETT	24.00
1019	CONTRACTS	VERNON	23.00
1502	COPYRIGHT	GOLDSTEIN	21.00
1504	COPYRIGHT	JOYCE, PETRY, L. & J.	20.00
1501	COPYRIGHT	NIMMER, M., M. & N.	22.50
1218	CORPORATE TAXATION	LIND, S. L. & R	17.00
1050	CORPORATIONS	CARY & EISENBERG	22.00
1054	CORPORATIONS	CHOPER, COFFEE, & GILSON	24.50
1350	CORPORATIONS (ENTERPRISE ORG.)	CONARD, KNAUSS & SIEGEL	24.00
1053	CORPORATIONS	HAMILTON	22.00
1058	CORPORATIONS (BUSINESS ASSOCIATIONS	KLEIN, RAMSEYER & BAINBRIDGE	22.00
1057	CORPORATIONS	O'KELLEY & THOMPSON	21.00
1059	CORPORATIONS (BUSINESS ORG.)	SODERQUIST, S., C. & S.	24.00
1056	CORPORATIONS	SOLOMON, S., B. & W.	22.00
1052	CORPORATIONS	VAGTS	21.00
1300	CREDITOR'S RIGHTS (DEBTOR-CREDITOR)	RIESENFELD	24.00
1550	CRIMINAL JUSTICE	WEINREB	21.00
1029	CRIMINAL LAW	BONNIE, C., J. & L.	20.00
1020	CRIMINAL LAW	BOYCE & PERKINS	25.00
1028	CRIMINAL LAW	DRESSLER	24.00
1027	CRIMINAL LAW	JOHNSON	22.00
1021	CRIMINAL LAW	KADISH & SCHULHOFER	22.00
1026	CRIMINAL LAW	KAPLAN, WEISBERG & BINDER	21.00
1205	CRIMINAL PROCEDURE	ALLEN, KUHNS & STUNTZ	20.00
1206	CRIMINAL PROCEDURE	DRESSLER & THOMAS	25.00
1202	CRIMINAL PROCEDURE	HADDAD, Z., S. & B.	23.00
1200	CRIMINAL PROCEDURE	KAMISAR, LAFAVE & ISRAEL	22.00
1204	CRIMINAL PROCEDURE	SALTZBURG & CAPRA	20.00
1300	DEBTOR-CREDITOR (CREDITORS RIGHTS)	RIESENFELD	24.00
1304	DEBTOR-CREDITOR	WARREN & WESTBROOK	22.00
1224	DECEDENTS ESTATES (TRUSTS)	RITCHIE, A, & E.(DOBRIS/STERK).	24.00
1222	DECEDENTS ESTATES	SCOLES, HALBACH, L. & R.	24.50
	DOMESTIC RELATIONS (*see* FAMILY LAW)		
3000	EDUCATION LAW (COURSE OUTLINE)	AQUILA & PETZKE	28.50
1670	EMPLOYMENT DISCRIMINATION	FRIEDMAN & STRICKLER	20.00
1671	EMPLOYMENT DISCRIMINATION	ZIMMER, SULLIVAN, R. & C.	21.00
1660	EMPLOYMENT LAW	ROTHSTEIN, KNAPP & LIEBMAN	22.50
1342	ENVIRONMENTAL LAW	ANDERSON, MANDELKER & T.	19.00
1341	ENVIRONMENTAL LAW	FINDLEY & FARBER	21.00
1345	ENVIRONMENTAL LAW	MENELL & STEWART	20.00
1344	ENVIRONMENTAL LAW	PERCIVAL, MILLER, S. & L.	21.00
1343	ENVIRONMENTAL LAW	PLATER, A., G. & G.	20.00
1217	ESTATE & GIFT TAXATION	BITTKER, CLARK & McCOUCH	18.00
	ETHICS (*see* PROFESSIONAL RESPONSIBILITY)		
1063	EVIDENCE	LEMPERT, GROSS & LIEBMAN	TBA
1066	EVIDENCE	MUELLER & KIRKPATRICK	20.00
1064	EVIDENCE	STRONG, BROUN & M..	25.50
1062	EVIDENCE	WELLBORN	25.00
1061	EVIDENCE	WALTZ & PARK	21.00
1060	EVIDENCE	WEINSTEIN, M., A. & B.	25.50
1244	FAMILY LAW (DOMESTIC RELATIONS)	AREEN	25.00
1242	FAMILY LAW (DOMESTIC RELATIONS)	CLARK & ESTIN	22.00
1245	FAMILY LAW (DOMESTIC RELATIONS)	ELLMAN, KURTZ & BARTLETT	23.00
1246	FAMILY LAW (DOMESTIC RELATIONS)	HARRIS, T. & W.	22.00
1243	FAMILY LAW (DOMESTIC RELATIONS)	KRAUSE, O., E. & G.	27.00
1240	FAMILY LAW (DOMESTIC RELATIONS)	WADLINGTON & O'BRIEN	23.00
1247	FAMILY LAW (DOMESTIC RELATIONS)	WEISBERG & APPLETON	22.00
1360	FEDERAL COURTS	FALLON, M. & S. (HART & W.)	22.00
1360	FEDERAL COURTS	HART & WECHSLER (FALLON)	22.00
1363	FEDERAL COURTS	LOW & JEFFRIES	19.00
1361	FEDERAL COURTS	McCORMICK, C. & W.	23.00
1364	FEDERAL COURTS	REDISH & SHERRY	20.00
1690	FEDERAL INDIAN LAW	GETCHES, W. & W.	23.00
1089	FIRST AMENDMENT (CONSTITUTIONAL LAW)	SHIFFRIN & CHOPER	18.00
1700	GENDER AND LAW (SEX DISCRIMINATION)	BARTLETT & HARRIS	22.00
1510	GRATUITOUS TRANSFERS	CLARK, L., M., A., & M.	21.00
1651	HEALTH CARE LAW	CURRAN, H., B. & O.	24.00
1650	HEALTH LAW	FURROW, J., J. & S.	20.50
1640	IMMIGRATION LAW	ALEINIKOFF, MARTIN & M.	19.00
1641	IMMIGRATION LAW	LEGOMSKY	22.00
1690	INDIAN LAW	GETCHES, W. & W.	23.00
1373	INSURANCE LAW	ABRAHAM	23.00
1371	INSURANCE LAW	KEETON	24.00
1370	INSURANCE LAW	YOUNG & HOLMES	20.00
1503	INTELLECTUAL PROPERTY	MERGES, M.& J.	22.00
1394	INTERNATIONAL BUSINESS TRANSACTIONS	FOLSOM, GORDON & SPANOGLE	18.00
1393	INTERNATIONAL LAW	CARTER & TRIMBLE	19.00
1392	INTERNATIONAL LAW	HENKIN, P., S. & S.	20.00
1390	INTERNATIONAL LAW	OLIVER, F., B., S. & W.	25.00
1331	LABOR LAW	COX, BOK, GORMAN & FINKIN	22.00
1471	LAND FINANCE (REAL ESTATE TRANS.)	BERGER & JOHNSTONE	21.00
1620	LAND FINANCE (REAL ESTATE TRANS.)	NELSON & WHITMAN	21.00
1452	LAND USE	CALLIES, FREILICH & ROBERTS	20.00
1421	LEGISLATION	ESKRIDGE, FRICKEY & GARRETT	18.00
1480	MASS MEDIA	FRANKLIN & ANDERSON	18.00
1312	NEGOTIABLE INSTRUMENTS (COMM. LAW)	JORDAN, WARREN & WALT	22.00
1541	OIL & GAS	KUNTZ., L., A., S. & P..	21.00
1540	OIL & GAS	MAXWELL, WILLIAMS, M. & K.	21.00
1561	PATENT LAW	ADELMAN, R., T. & W.	25.00
1560	PATENT LAW	FRANCIS & COLLINS	26.00
1310	PAYMENT LAW [SYST.][COMM. LAW]	SPEIDEL, SUMMERS & WHITE	25.00
1313	PAYMENT LAW (COMM.LAW / NEG. INST.)	WHALEY	23.00
1431	PRODUCTS LIABILITY	OWEN, MONTGOMERY & K.	25.00
1091	PROF. RESPONSIBILITY (ETHICS)	GILLERS	16.00
1093	PROF. RESPONSIBILITY (ETHICS)	HAZARD, KONIAK, & CRAMTON	21.00
1092	PROF. RESPONSIBILITY (ETHICS)	MORGAN & ROTUNDA	16.00
1094	PROF. RESPONSIBILITY (ETHICS)	SCHWARTZ, W. & P.	16.00
1030	PROPERTY	CASNER & LEACH -(by F., K. & V.	24.00
1031	PROPERTY	CRIBBET, J., F. & S.	24.50
1037	PROPERTY	DONAHUE, KAUPER & MARTIN	21.00
1035	PROPERTY	DUKEMINIER & KRIER	20.00
1034	PROPERTY	HAAR & LIEBMAN	23.50
1036	PROPERTY	KURTZ & HOVENKAMP	21.00
1033	PROPERTY	NELSON, STOEBUCK, & W.	23.50
1032	PROPERTY	RABIN & KWALL	23.00
1038	PROPERTY	SINGER	21.50
1621	REAL ESTATE TRANSACTIONS	GOLDSTEIN & KORNGOLD	21.00
1471	REAL ESTATE TRANS. & FIN. (LAND FINANCE)	BERGER & JOHNSTONE	21.00
1620	REAL ESTATE TRANSFER & FINANCE	NELSON & WHITMAN	21.00
1254	REMEDIES (EQUITY)	LAYCOCK	23.00
1253	REMEDIES (EQUITY)	LEAVELL, L., N. & K-F.	24.00
1252	REMEDIES (EQUITY)	RE & RE	26.00
1255	REMEDIES (EQUITY)	SHOBEN & TABB	25.50
1250	REMEDIES (EQUITY)	RENDLEMAN	28.00
1310	SALES (COMM. LAW)	SPEIDEL, SUMMERS & WHITE	25.00
1313	SALES (COMM. LAW)	WHALEY	23.00
1312	SECURED TRANS. (COMMERICIAL LAW)	JORDAN, WARREN & WALT	22.00
1310	SECURED TRANS.	SPEIDEL, SUMMERS & WHITE	25.00
1313	SECURED TRANS. (COMMERCIAL LAW)	WHALEY	23.00
1272	SECURITIES REGULATION	COX, HILLMAN, LANGEVOORT	21.00
1270	SECURITIES REGULATION	JENNINGS, M., C. & S.	21.00
1680	SPORTS LAW	WEILER & ROBERTS	20.50
1217	TAXATION (ESTATE & GIFT)	BITTKER, CLARK & McCOUCH	18.00
1219	TAXATION (INDIV. INCOME)	BURKE & FRIEL	22.00
1212	TAXATION (FEDERAL INCOME)	FREELAND, L., S. & L.	21.00
1211	TAXATION (FEDERAL INCOME)	GRAETZ & SCHENK	20.00
1210	TAXATION (FEDERAL INCOME)	KLEIN, BANKMAN & SHAVIRO	21.00
1218	TAXATION (CORPORATE)	LIND, S., L. & R.	17.00
1006	TORTS	DOBBS	22.00
1003	TORTS	EPSTEIN	23.50
1004	TORTS	FRANKLIN & RABIN	20.50
1001	TORTS	HENDERSON, P. & S.	23.50
1000	TORTS	PROSSER, W., S., K. & P.	25.00
1005	TORTS	SHULMAN, JAMES & GRAY	25.00
1281	TRADE REGULATION (ANTITRUST)	HANDLER, P., G. & W.	20.50
1410	U.C.C.	EPSTEIN, MARTIN, H. & N.	18.00
1510	WILLS/TRUSTS (GRATUITOUS TRANSFER)	CLARK, L., M., A., & M.	21.00
1223	WILLS, TRUSTS & ESTATES	DUKEMINIER & JOHANSON	22.00
1220	WILLS	MECHEM & ATKINSON	23.00

ABBREVIATIONS FOR BRIEFING

The following list of abbreviations will assist you in the process of briefing and provide an illustration of the technique of formulating functional personal abbreviations for commonly encountered words, phrases, and concepts.

acceptance .... acp
affirmed .... aff
answer .... ans
assumption of risk .... a/r
attorney .... atty
beyond a reasonable doubt .... b/r/d
bona fide purchaser .... BFP
breach of contract .... br/k
cause of action .... c/a
common law .... c/l
Constitution .... Con
constitutional .... con
contract .... K
contributory negligence .... c/n
cross x
cross-complaint .... x/c
cross-examination .... x/ex
cruel and unusual punishment .... c/u/p
defendant .... D
dismissed .... dis
double jeopardy .... d/j
due process .... d/p
equal protection .... e/p
equity .... eq
evidence .... ev
exclude .... exc
exclusionary rule .... exc/r
felony .... f/m
freedom of speech .... f/s
good faith .... g/f
habeas corpus .... h/c
hearsay .... hr
husband .... H
in loco parentis .... ILP
injunction .... inj
inter vivos .... I/v
joint tenancy .... j/t
judgment .... judgt
jurisdiction .... jur
last clear chance LCC
long-arm statute .... LAS
majority view .... maj
meeting of minds .... MOM
minority view .... min
Miranda warnings .... Mir/w
Miranda rule .... Mir/r
negligence .... neg
notice .... mtc
nuisance .... nus
obligation .... ob
obscene .... obs
offer .... O
offeree .... OE
offeror .... OR
ordinance .... ord
pain and suffering .... p/s
parol evidence .... p/e
plaintiff .... P
prima facie .... p/f
probable cause .... p/c
proximate cause .... px/c
real property .... r/p
reasonable doubt .... r/d
reasonable man .... r/m
rebuttable presumption .... rb/p
remanded .... rem
res ipsa loquitur .... RIL
respondent superior .... r/s
Restatement .... RS
reversed .... rev
Rule Against Perpetuities .... RAP
search and seizure .... s/s
search warrant .... s/w
self-defense .... s/d
specific performance .... s/p
statute of limitations .... S/L
statute of frauds .... S/F
statute .... S
summary judgment .... s/j
tenancy in common .... t/c
tenancy at will .... t/w
tenant .... t
third party .... TP
third party beneficiary .... TPB
transferred intent .... TI
unconscionable .... uncon
unconstitutional .... unconst
undue influence .... u/e
Uniform Commercial Code .... UCC
unilateral .... uni
vendee .... VE
vendor .... VR
versus v
void for vagueness .... VFV
weight of the evidence .... w/e
weight of authority .... w/a
wife .... W
with .... w/
within .... w/I
without prejudice .... w/o/p
without .... w/o
wrongful death .... wr/d

GLOSSARY

COMMON LATIN WORDS AND PHRASES ENCOUNTERED IN LAW

A FORTIORI: Because one fact exists or has been proven, therefore a second fact that is related to the first fact must also exist.

A PRIORI: From the cause to the effect. A term of logic used to denote that when one generally accepted truth is shown to be a cause, another particular effect must necessarily follow.

AB INITIO: From the beginning; a condition which has existed throughout, as in a marriage which was void ab initio.

ACTUS REUS: The wrongful act; in criminal law, such action sufficient to trigger criminal liability.

AD VALOREM: According to value; an ad valorem tax is imposed upon an item located within the taxing jurisdiction calculated by the value of such item.

AMICUS CURIAE: Friend of the court. Its most common usage takes the form of an amicus curiae brief, filed by a person who is not a party to an action but is nonetheless allowed to offer an argument supporting his legal interests.

ARGUENDO: In arguing. A statement, possibly hypothetical, made for the purpose of argument, is one made arguendo.

BILL QUIA TIMET: A bill to quiet title (establish ownership) to real property.

BONA FIDE: True, honest, or genuine. May refer to a person's legal position based on good faith or lacking notice of fraud (such as a bona fide purchaser for value) or to the authenticity of a particular document (such as a bona fide last will and testament).

CAUSA MORTIS: With approaching death in mind. A gift causa mortis is a gift given by a party who feels certain that death is imminent.

CAVEAT EMPTOR: Let the buyer beware. This maxim is reflected in the rule of law that a buyer purchases at his own risk because it is his responsibility to examine, judge, test, and otherwise inspect what he is buying.

CERTIORARI: A writ of review. Petitions for review of a case by the United States Supreme Court are most often done by means of a writ of certiorari.

CONTRA: On the other hand. Opposite. Contrary to.

CORAM NOBIS: Before us; writs of error directed to the court that originally rendered the judgment.

CORAM VOBIS: Before you; writs of error directed by an appellate court to a lower court to correct a factual error.

CORPUS DELICTI: The body of the crime; the requisite elements of a crime amounting to objective proof that a crime has been committed.

CUM TESTAMENTO ANNEXO, ADMINISTRATOR (ADMINISTRATOR C.T.A.): With will annexed; an administrator c.t.a. settles an estate pursuant to a will in which he is not appointed.

DE BONIS NON, ADMINISTRATOR (ADMINISTRATOR D.B.N.): Of goods not administered; an administrator d.b.n. settles a partially settled estate.

DE FACTO: In fact; in reality; actually. Existing in fact but not officially approved or engendered.

DE JURE: By right; lawful. Describes a condition that is legitimate "as a matter of law," in contrast to the term "de facto," which connotes something existing in fact but not legally sanctioned or authorized. For example, de facto segregation refers to segregation brought about by housing patterns, etc., whereas de jure segregation refers to segregation created by law.

DE MINIMUS: Of minimal importance; insignificant; a trifle; not worth bothering about.

DE NOVO: Anew; a second time; afresh. A trial de novo is a new trial held at the appellate level as if the case originated there and the trial at a lower level had not taken place.

DICTA: Generally used as an abbreviated form of obiter dicta, a term describing those portions of a judicial opinion incidental or not necessary to resolution of the specific question before the court. Such nonessential statements and remarks are not considered to be binding precedent.

DUCES TECUM: Refers to a particular type of writ or subpoena requesting a party or organization to produce certain documents in their possession.

EN BANC: Full bench. Where a court sits with all justices present rather than the usual quorum.

EX PARTE: For one side or one party only. An ex parte proceeding is one undertaken for the benefit of only one party, without notice to, or an appearance by, an adverse party.

EX POST FACTO: After the fact. An ex post facto law is a law that retroactively changes the consequences of a prior act.

EX REL.: Abbreviated form of the term ex relatione, meaning, upon relation or information. When the state brings an action in which it has no interest against an individual at the instigation of one who has a private interest in the matter.

FORUM NON CONVENIENS: Inconvenient forum. Although a court may have jurisdiction over the case, the action should be tried in a more conveniently located court, one to which parties and witnesses may more easily travel, for example.

GUARDIAN AD LITEM: A guardian of an infant as to litigation, appointed to represent the infant and pursue his/her rights.

HABEAS CORPUS: You have the body. The modern writ of habeas corpus is a writ directing that a person (body) being detained (such as a prisoner) be brought before the court so that the legality of his detention can be judicially ascertained.

IN CAMERA: In private, in chambers. When a hearing is held before a judge in his chambers or when all spectators are excluded from the courtroom.

IN FORMA PAUPERIS: In the manner of a pauper. A party who proceeds in forma pauperis because of his poverty is one who is allowed to bring suit without liability for costs.

INFRA: Below, under. A word referring the reader to a later part of a book. (The opposite of supra.)

IN LOCO PARENTIS: In the place of a parent.

IN PARI DELICTO: Equally wrong; a court of equity will not grant requested relief to an applicant who is in pari delicto, or as much at fault in the transactions giving rise to the controversy as is the opponent of the applicant.

IN PARI MATERIA: On like subject matter or upon the same matter. Statutes relating to the same person or things are said to be in pari materia. It is a general rule of statutory construction that such statutes should be construed together, i.e., looked at as if they together constituted one law.

IN PERSONAM: Against the person. Jurisdiction over the person of an individual.

IN RE: In the matter of. Used to designate a proceeding involving an estate or other property.

IN REM: A term that signifies an action against the res, or thing. An action in rem is basically one that is taken directly against property, as distinguished from an action in personam, i.e., against the person.

INTER ALIA: Among other things. Used to show that the whole of a statement, pleading, list, statute, etc., has not been set forth in its entirety.

INTER PARTES: Between the parties. May refer to contracts, conveyances or other transactions having legal significance.

INTER VIVOS: Between the living. An inter vivos gift is a gift made by a living grantor, as distinguished from bequests contained in a will, which pass upon the death of the testator.

IPSO FACTO: By the mere fact itself.

JUS: Law or the entire body of law.

LEX LOCI: The law of the place; the notion that the rights of parties to a legal proceeding are governed by the law of the place where those rights arose.

MALUM IN SE: Evil or wrong in and of itself; inherently wrong. This term describes an act that is wrong by its very nature, as opposed to one which would not be wrong but for the fact that there is a specific legal prohibition against it (malum prohibitum).

MALUM PROHIBITUM: Wrong because prohibited, but not inherently evil. Used to describe something that is wrong because it is expressly forbidden by law but that is not in and of itself evil, e.g., speeding.

MANDAMUS: We command. A writ directing an official to take a certain action.

MENS REA: A guilty mind; a criminal intent. A term used to signify the mental state that accompanies a crime or other prohibited act. Some crimes require only a general mens rea (general intent to do the prohibited act), but others, like assault with intent to murder, require the existence of a specific mens rea.

MODUS OPERANDI: Method of operating; generally refers to the manner or style of a criminal in committing crimes, admissible in appropriate cases as evidence of the identity of a defendant.

NEXUS: A connection to.

NISI PRIUS: A court of first impression. A nisi prius court is one where issues of fact are tried before a judge or jury.

N.O.V. (NON OBSTANTE VEREDICTO): Notwithstanding the verdict. A judgment n.o.v. is a judgment given in favor of one party despite the fact that a verdict was returned in favor of the other party, the justification being that the verdict either had no reasonable support in fact or was contrary to law.

NUNC PRO TUNC: Now for then. This phrase refers to actions that may be taken and will then have full retroactive effect.

PENDENTE LITE: Pending the suit; pending litigation underway.

PER CAPITA: By head; beneficiaries of an estate, if they take in equal shares, take per capita.

PER CURIAM: By the court; signifies an opinion ostensibly written "by the whole court" and with no identified author.

PER SE: By itself, in itself; inherently.

PER STIRPES: By representation. Used primarily in the law of wills to describe the method of distribution where a person, generally because of death, is unable to take that which is left to him by the will of another, and therefore his heirs divide such property between them rather than take under the will individually.

PRIMA FACIE: On its face, at first sight. A prima facie case is one that is sufficient on its face, meaning that the evidence supporting it is adequate to establish the case until contradicted or overcome by other evidence.

PRO TANTO: For so much; as far as it goes. Often used in eminent domain cases when a property owner receives partial payment for his land without prejudice to his right to bring suit for the full amount he claims his land to be worth.

QUANTUM MERUIT: As much as he deserves. Refers to recovery based on the doctrine of unjust enrichment in those cases in which a party has rendered valuable services or furnished materials that were accepted and enjoyed by another under circumstances that would reasonably notify the recipient that the rendering party expected to be paid. In essence, the law implies a contract to pay the reasonable value of the services or materials furnished.

QUASI: Almost like; as if; nearly. This term is essentially used to signify that one subject or thing is almost analogous to another but that material differences between them do exist. For example, a quasi-criminal proceeding is one that is not strictly criminal but shares enough of the same characteristics to require some of the same safeguards (e.g., procedural due process must be followed in a parol hearing).

QUID PRO QUO: Something for something. In contract law, the consideration, something of value, passed between the parties to render the contract binding.

RES GESTAE: Things done; in evidence law, this principle justifies the admission of a statement that would otherwise be hearsay when it is made so closely to the event in question as to be said to be a part of it, or with such spontaneity as not to have the possibility of falsehood.

RES IPSA LOQUITUR: The thing speaks for itself. This doctrine gives rise to a rebuttable presumption of negligence when the instrumentality causing the injury was within the exclusive control of the defendant, and the injury was one that does not normally occur unless a person has been negligent.

RES JUDICATA: A matter adjudged. Doctrine which provides that once a court of competent jurisdiction has rendered a final judgment or decree on the merits, that judgment or decree is conclusive upon the parties to the case and prevents them from engaging in any other litigation on the points and issues determined therein.

RESPONDEAT SUPERIOR: Let the master reply. This doctrine holds the master liable for the wrongful acts of his servant (or the principal for his agent) in those cases in which the servant (or agent) was acting within the scope of his authority at the time of the injury.

STARE DECISIS: To stand by or adhere to that which has been decided. The common law doctrine of stare decisis attempts to give security and certainty to the law by following the policy that once a principle of law as applicable to a certain set of facts has been set forth in a decision, it forms a precedent which will subsequently be followed, even though a different decision might be made were it the first time the question had arisen. Of course, stare decisis is not an inviolable principle and is departed from in instances where there is good cause (e.g., considerations of public policy led the Supreme Court to disregard prior decisions sanctioning segregation).

SUPRA: Above. A word referring a reader to an earlier part of a book.

ULTRA VIRES: Beyond the power. This phrase is most commonly used to refer to actions taken by a corporation that are beyond the power or legal authority of the corporation.

ADDENDUM OF FRENCH DERIVATIVES

IN PAIS: Not pursuant to legal proceedings.

CHATTEL: Tangible personal property.

CY PRES: Doctrine permitting courts to apply trust funds to purposes not expressed in the trust but necessary to carry out the settlor's intent.

PER AUTRE VIE: For another's life; in property law, an estate may be granted that will terminate upon the death of someone other than the grantee.

PROFIT A PRENDRE: A license to remove minerals or other produce from land.

VOIR DIRE: Process of questioning jurors as to their predispositions about the case or parties to a proceeding in order to identify those jurors displaying bias or prejudice.

Notes

TABLE OF CASES

Continued on next page.

Notes

TABLE OF CASES (Continued)

CHAPTER 1
ADMINISTRATIVE LAW PRACTICE

QUICK REFERENCE RULES OF LAW

1. **Law Practice.** [No rule is provided, the case in the textbook gives only the facts and issues to show example of an administrative law case]. (Fund for Animals, Inc. v. Rice)

FUND FOR ANIMALS, INC. v. RICE

Public interest group (P) v. Government agency (D)

85 F.3d 535 (11th Cir. 1996).

NATURE OF CASE: Action seeking injunction against agency decision.

FACT SUMMARY: Fund for Animals (P) challenged the Fish and Wildlife Service's (D) decision to issue a permit for a landfill on a site they claimed would threaten endangered species.

CONCISE RULE OF LAW: [No rule is provided, the case in the textbook gives only the facts and issues to show example of an administrative law case].

FACTS: Sarasota County applied for a permit to build a landfill with the United States Army Corps of Engineers (D). The Corps (D) could only grant a permit if the proposed project was consistent with the rules of the Environmental Protection Agency (D) and did not adversely affect a species covered under the Endangered Species Act. Accordingly, the Fish and Wildlife Service (FWS) (D) was required to conduct an environmental assessment of Sarasota's proposed landfill. The FWS (D) gave its approval to the project but the Fund for Animals (P) complained that they hadn't considered the affect on the endangered Florida panther and Eastern Indigo snake. The FWS then issued a Biological Opinion that addressed concerns over those species and concluded that the project was unlikely to jeopardize the panther and snake. The opinion did include recommendations for certain preservation measures. The Fund for Animals (P) then filed suit against all of the agencies involved with approving the permit. After some modifications, the permit was approved on April 13, 1995 and the Fund (P) amended their complaint and sought injunctive relief. The district court ruled against the Fund (P) and they appealed.

ISSUE: (n/a)

HOLDING AND DECISION: (Dubina, J.) The district court did not act arbitrarily or capriciously in approving the permit for the Sarasota project or in relying on the Biological Opinion of the FWS (D). Affirmed.

EDITOR'S ANALYSIS: This is a standard case in terms of the parties involved. Government agencies usually make decisions that affect private parties differently. When it reaches the stage of litigation, one party seeks to overturn the decision and another desires to uphold it.

QUICKNOTES

INJUNCTIVE RELIEF - A court order issued as a remedy, requiring a person to do, or prohibiting that person from doing, a specific act.

NOTES:

CHAPTER 2
RULEMAKING

QUICK REFERENCE RULES OF LAW

1. **Petitions for Rulemaking: Agency Inaction.** Unreasonable agency delays are subject to interlocutory appeals and may warrant mandamus under certain circumstances. (Telecommunications Research & Action Center v. Federal Communications Commission)

2. **Petitions for Rulemaking: Denial of a Petition.** Courts will compel agencies to institute rulemaking proceedings only in extremely rare circumstances. (Arkansas Power & Light Co. v. Interstate Commerce Commission)

3. **Petitions for Rulemaking: Denial of a Petition.** Agency action is arbitrary and capricious where the agency has failed to articulate a satisfactory explanation for its action, including a rational connection between the decision and the factual record. (Northern Spotted Owl v. Hodel)

4. **APA Rulemaking Procedures: Exceptions from Notice and Comment.** The requirement of notice and an opportunity for comment does not apply to interpretative rules, general statements of policy, or rules of agency organization, procedure, or practice. (American Hospital Assn. v. Bowen)

   [For more information on rulemaking exceptions, see Casenote Law Outline on Administrative Law, Chapter 7, Rulemaking Processes, §X, Categoric and Subject Matter Exceptions.]

5. **APA Rulemaking Procedures: Exceptions from Notice and Comment.** The promulgation of regulations governing the adjudication of administrative civil penalty actions is not exempt from the requirements of notice and comment. (Air Transport Association of America v. Department of Transportation)

   [For more information on rulemaking exceptions, see Casenote Law Outline on Administrative Law, Chapter 7, Rulemaking Processes, §X, Categoric and Subject Matter Exceptions.]

6. **APA Rulemaking Procedures: Exceptions from Notice and Comment.** Rules of agency organization, procedure and practice are exempt from the general notice and comment rulemaking requirements. (JEM Broadcasting Company, Inc. v. Federal Communications Commission)

7. **Formal, Informal, or Hybrid Rulemaking.** Informal rulemaking is permitted where the governing statute does not require that rules be made on the record. (United States v. Allegheny-Ludlum Steel Corp.)

8. **Formal, Informal, or Hybrid Rulemaking.** ICC need not hold a formal hearing prior to establishing rules with respect to car service by common carriers. (United States v. Florida East Coast Railroad Co.)

   [For more information on hybrid rulemaking, see Casenote Law Outline on Administrative Law, Chapter 7, § V, Some Rules Must Be Promulgated Through Formal Procedures.]

9. **Formal, Informal, or Hybrid Rulemaking.** The adequacy of the record in rulemaking proceeding does not depend on the type of procedural devices employed but turns on whether the agency has followed the statutory mandate of the Administrative Procedure Act. (Vermont Yankee Nuclear Power Corp. v. Natural Resources Defense Council, Inc.)

   [For more information on hybrid rulemaking, see Casenote Law Outline on Administrative Law, Chapter 7, § V, Some Rules Must Be Promulgated Through Formal Procedures.]

10. **APA Rulemaking Procedures: Informal Rulemaking Requirements.** The notice in the Federal Register that an agency must give of a proposed rulemaking must contain either the terms or substance of the proposed rule or a description of the subjects and issues involved. (Chocolate Manufacturers Association v. Block)

[For more information on Public Participation in Rulemaking, see Casenote Law Outline on Administrative Law, Chapter 7, § III, The Procedural Norm is "Notice and Comment" Rulemaking.]

11. **APA Rulemaking Procedures: Opportunity for Comment.** The public record must reflect the representations made to an agency so that relevant information supporting or refuting those representations may be brought to the attention of the reviewing courts by persons participating in agency proceedings. (Home Box Office v. Federal Communications Commission)

[For more information on ex parte communications in rulemaking, see Casenote Law Outline on Administrative Law, Chapter 8, Integrity of Internal Decision-making Processes, § IV, Ex Parte Communications Between Agency Decision-makers and "Interested Persons" Are Generally Prohibited.]

12. **APA Rulemaking Procedures: Opportunity for Comment.** *The Clean Air Amendments of 1977 provide that all relevant documents that become available after a proposed rule has been published shall be placed in the docket as soon as possible after their availability. (Sierra Club v. Costle)*

[For more information on Public Participation in Rulemaking Procedures, see Casenote Law Outline on Administrative Law, Chapter 8, § V, Administrative Processes Should Be Sensitive to Public Opinion.]

13. **Judicial Review: Statutory Interpretation.** Where Congress has left an open question in its legislation, judicial review of an agency's interpretation of that question must be limited to whether the agency's construction is legitimate. (Chevron v. Natural Resources Defense Council, Inc.)

[For more information on judicial review of questions of law, see Casenote Law Outline on Administrative Law, Chapter 9, § IV, Level of Review Determined by the Nature of the Controverted Issues.]

14. **Substantive Decisions: Adequate Explanation.** When an agency modifies or rescinds a previously promulgated rule, it is required to supply a satisfactory, rational analysis supporting its decision. (Motor Vehicle Manufacturers Assoc. v. State Farm Mutual Automobile Ins. Co.)

[For more information on judicial review of administrative policy, see Casenote Law Outline on Administrative Law, Chapter 9, § IV, Level of Review Determined by the Nature of the Controverted Issues.]

TELECOMMUNICATIONS RESEARCH & ACTION CENTER v. FEDERAL COMMUNICATIONS COMMISSION

Consumer group (P) v. Government agency (D)

750 F.2d 70 (D.C. Cir. 1984).

NATURE OF CASE: Action challenging agency's failure to make a decision.

FACT SUMMARY: The FCC (D) hadn't made a decision five years after being petitioned to decide whether AT&T had overcharged its customers.

CONCISE RULE OF LAW: Unreasonable agency delays are subject to interlocutory appeals and may warrant mandamus under certain circumstances.

FACTS: The Telecommunications Research & Action Center (TRAC) (P) petitioned the FCC (D) in 1979 to decide whether AT&T had overcharged its customers. After periodically claiming that a decision was forthcoming, the FCC (D) still hadn't decided the issue five years later. TRAC (P) filed suit to compel the FCC (D) to decide and, while the case was pending, the FCC (D) indicated that it would resolve the matter by November 1984.

ISSUE: Are claims of unreasonable agency delays subject to interlocutory appeals?

HOLDING AND DECISION: (Edwards, J.) Yes. Unreasonable agency delays are subject to interlocutory appeals and may warrant mandamus under certain circumstances. Generally, appeals can only be taken of final actions by agencies. By waiting for final action, an administrative agency will have developed a factual record and piecemeal appeals are avoided. However, the agency's expertise and preparation of a factual record is not a factor where the agency never takes action. Thus, claims of unreasonable delay must be subject to interlocutory appeal. Furthermore, statutes expressly require agencies to decide matters within a reasonable time. The first stage of judicial inquiry is to consider whether the delay is so egregious as to warrant mandamus. There is no single standard for this determination, but the time agencies take to make decision must be governed by a rule of reason. The key factors include any express Congressional requirements, the effect of the delay on other agencies, and the resulting prejudice to interested parties. A delay can be unreasonable even without impropriety behind the delay. In the present case, the delays are very serious but the FCC (D) has assured the court that a final decision is imminent. Accordingly, the court will not resort to mandamus, but will retain jurisdiction over the case until the FCC (D) does decide the issue.

EDITOR'S ANALYSIS: The court acknowledged that delay in agency proceedings can deprive parties of important economic opportunities. However, the court plainly stated that decisions affecting health and welfare would be judged more closely in terms of delay. Even where the law lays out a timetable, agencies often ignore the deadlines and must be sued in order to prompt decisions.

QUICKNOTES

INTERLOCUTORY APPEAL - The appeal of an issue that does not resolve the disposition of the case, but is essential to a determination of the parties' legal rights.

MANDAMUS - A court order issued commanding a public or private entity, or an official thereof, to perform a duty required by law.

NOTES:

ARKANSAS POWER & LIGHT CO. v. INTERSTATE COMMERCE COMMISSION

Utility company (P) v. Government agency (D)

725 F.2d 716 (D.C. Cir. 1984).

NATURE OF CASE: Appeal from agency rejection of petition for rulemaking.

FACT SUMMARY: Arkansas Power & Light (P) petitioned the ICC (D) to collect certain data so that it could review rates that railroads charged for certain shippers.

CONCISE RULE OF LAW: Courts will compel agencies to institute rulemaking proceedings only in extremely rare circumstances.

FACTS: Arkansas Power & Light (P) and other utility companies wanted review of rates that "captive" shippers were charged by railroads. They petitioned the ICC (D) to institute rulemaking to collect data so that the rates could be approved. The ICC (D) concluded that development of a nationwide data base was unnecessary, not required by statute and too burdensome. The ICC (D) decided to retain a system whereby companies could obtain the needed data on an individual basis for rate approvals. Arkansas Power (P) filed suit to compel the rulemaking and collection of a data base.

ISSUE: Will courts commonly compel agencies to institute rulemaking proceedings?

HOLDING AND DECISION: (Edwards, J.) No. Courts will compel agencies to institute rulemaking proceedings only in extremely rare circumstances. Review of agency decisions is limited to ensuring that the agency has adequately explained the facts and policy concerns it relied on and that the facts have some factual basis. In the present case, the ICC (D) clearly decided that there were important reasons for not instituting rulemaking to collect data from all carriers. The reasons had a factual basis and were not arbitrary. Accordingly, there is absolutely no basis for the court to step in and compel agency action in this matter. The ICC's (D) decision not to engage in rulemaking is affirmed.

EDITOR'S ANALYSIS: The ICC (D) apparently believed that making decisions on rates was best handled on an individual case basis. The agency (D) thought that the plaintiff utility companies would have adequate information available without an established data base for the entire nation. Given the narrow standard of review, this explanation was more than adequate for the court.

QUICKNOTES

RULEMAKING - The promulgation of a rule governing a particular activity by an administrative agency, acting within the scope of its power pursuant to statute.

NOTES:

NORTHERN SPOTTED OWL v. HODEL

Environmental groups (P) v. Government agency (D)

716 F. Supp. 479 (W.D. Wash. 1988).

NATURE OF CASE: Cross summary judgment motions in a challenge to an agency decision.

FACT SUMMARY: Environmental protection groups (P) complained that the Fish and Wildlife Service (D) arbitrarily decided not to list the Spotted Owl under the Endangered Species Act.

CONCISE RULE OF LAW: Agency action is arbitrary and capricious where the agency has failed to articulate a satisfactory explanation for its action, including a rational connection between the decision and the factual record.

FACTS: In January 1987, the Fish and Wildlife Service (D) was petitioned to include the northern Spotted Owl on the Endangered Species list. The Service's (D) role was to assess the technical and scientific data in the administrative record against the criteria of the statute and to exercise its expert discretion. Public comment was sought and biologists were charged with reviewing the data. The biologists determined that the Spotted Owl's habitat could be threatened by the cutting down of old growth trees on public lands and that it should be placed on the Endangered Species list. Despite these opinions, the Service (D) announced that it was not listing the Spotted Owl. Several environmental protection groups (P) filed suit against the Service (D) and each side moved for summary judgment.

ISSUE: Is agency action arbitrary and capricious where the agency has failed to articulate a satisfactory explanation for its action, including a rational connection between the decision and the factual record?

HOLDING AND DECISION: (Zilly, J.) Yes. Agency action is arbitrary and capricious where the agency has failed to articulate a satisfactory explanation for its action including a rational connection between the decision and the factual record. An agency's action is reviewable under the arbitrary and capricious standard of the Administrative Procedure Act. This standard is very narrow and presumes that the agency action is valid. However, it does not mean that agency decisions are rubber-stamped. Courts will reject conclusory assertions of agency expertise where the agency rejects unrebutted expert opinions without providing a credible alternative explanation. In the present case, the Service (D) disregarded all the expert opinions and failed to provide any of its own or other expert analysis supporting its conclusions. Instead, it merely asserted that the Spotted Owl was not facing extinction without any factual support. The only reference to an actual opinion in its report was a mischaracterization of a biologist's real conclusion. Accordingly, the Service's (D) decision not to list the northern Spotted Owl was arbitrary and capricious and contrary to law. The matter was remanded to the Service (D) to provide an analysis for its decision within 90 days.

EDITOR'S ANALYSIS: The court did not require that the Service (D) list the Spotted Owl as endangered. Such a remedy, where agency rulemaking is compelled, is very rare and courts resort to it only under extreme circumstances. The end result here is far more common, although it can often result in further litigation.

QUICKNOTES

ENDANGERED SPECIES ACT - Prohibits the destruction of the habitat of endangered species.

ADMINISTRATIVE PROCEDURE ACT - Provides the standard for judicial review of agency rules.

ARBITRARY AND CAPRICIOUS STANDARD - Standard imposed in reviewing the decision of an agency or court that the decision was made in disregard of the facts or law.

NOTES:

AMERICAN HOSPITAL ASSOCIATION. v. BOWEN

Trade organization (P) v. Regulatory department (D)

834 F.2d 1037 (D.C. Cir. 1987).

NATURE OF CASE: Not stated in the casebook excerpt.

FACT SUMMARY: The Department of Health and Human Services (D) promulgated regulations concerning Peer Review Organizations without following notice and comment procedures.

CONCISE RULE OF LAW: The requirement of notice and an opportunity for comment does not apply to interpretative rules, general statements of policy, or rules of agency organization, procedure, or practice.

FACTS: The Department of Health and Human Services (HHS) (D) contracted with Peer Review Organizations (PROs) to oversee the expenditure of Medicare dollars by doctors and hospitals. PROs determined whether the hospitals and doctors were performing in accordance with various standards. If they were not so performing, HHS (D) would deny them Medicare reimbursement funds or impose other sanctions. HHS (D) promulgated its regulations concerning the organization of PROs, their activities, and their enforcement powers without following notice and comment procedures.

ISSUE: Does the requirement of notice and an opportunity for comment apply to interpretative rules, general statements of policy, or rules of agency organization, procedure, or practice?

HOLDING AND DECISION: (Wald, C.J.) No. The requirement of notice and an opportunity for comment does not apply to interpretative rules, general statements of policy, or rules of agency organization, procedure, or practice. (See §553 of the Administrative Procedure Act (APA)). The rules in question are procedural in nature, and impose no direct substantive obligations upon the hospitals they are intended to regulate. While the terms of the contracts between the PROs and the HHS (D) set forth "rules" and "regulations," they also appear to set goals rather than impose definite standards. They are thus "statements of policy" and exempt from the procedural requirements. The perimeters of the exemptions for interpretative announcements and general statements of policy are fuzzy, and turn on the facts of each case. Substantive rules are ones which grant rights, impose obligations, or produce other significant effects on private interests, or which effect a change in existing law or policy. Interpretative rules merely clarify or explain existing law or regulations, while general statements of policy only announce what an agency seeks to establish as policy. An exemption for interpretative rules allows agencies to explain ambiguous terms in legislative enactments without having to undertake cumbersome proceedings, and the exemption for general policy statements allows agencies to announce their tentative intentions for the future without binding themselves. The purpose of the exemption for rules of agency organization, procedure, or practice ensures that agencies retain latitude in organizing their internal operations.

EDITOR'S ANALYSIS: While it may appear under this ruling that exemptions remove all control from agency actions involving interpretative rules, general statements of policy, or rules of agency organization, procedure, or practice, such is not the case. Many other statutes, court decisions, and regulations control government contracts, sometimes more strictly than the APA. Note, also, that agencies are free to provide notice and comment even where the APA does not require it.

[For more information on rulemaking exceptions, see Casenote Law Outline on Administrative Law, Chapter 7, Rulemaking Processes, §X, Categoric and Subject Matter Exceptions.]

QUICKNOTES

RULEMAKING - The promulgation of a rule by an administrative agency, acting within the scope of its power pursuant to statute, enacting a rule governing a particular activity.

INTERPRETIVE RULES - A rule issued by an administrative agency for the purpose of explaining or interpreting a statute.

NOTES:

AIR TRANSPORT ASSOCIATION OF AMERICA v. DEPARTMENT OF TRANSPORTATION

Trade association (P) v. Federal agency (D)

900 F.2d 369 (D.C. Cir. 1990)

NATURE OF CASE: Not stated in the casebook excerpt.

FACT SUMMARY: In December of 1987, Congress enacted a series of amendments to the Federal Aviation Act relating to civil penalties.

CONCISE RULE OF LAW: The promulgation of regulations governing the adjudication of administrative civil penalty actions is not exempt from the requirements of notice and comment.

FACTS: Of the amendments to the Federal Aviation Act, pertaining to civil penalties, one raised the maximum penalty for a single violation of aviation safety standards to $10,000. Another established a "demonstration program" authorizing the Federal Aviation Administration (FAA) (D) to prosecute and adjudicate administrative penalty actions involving less than $50,000. Because the prior method of handling disputed penalties resulted in few prosecutions, Congress sought to close the holes in the FAA's (D) safety net by raising the maximum penalty and giving the FAA the power to prosecute penalty actions administratively. Approximately nine months after Congress enacted the amendments, the FAA (D) promulgated the Penalty Rules, establishing a schedule of civil penalties and a comprehensive adjudicatory scheme providing for formal notice, settlement procedures, discovery, an adversary hearing before an Administrative Law Judge (ALJ), and an administrative appeal. The FAA (D) argued that the Penalty Rules were exempt as "rules of organization, procedure, or practice" because they established "procedures" for adjudicating civil penalty actions.

ISSUE: Is the promulgation of regulations governing the adjudication of administrative civil penalty actions exempt from the requirements of notice and comment?

HOLDING AND DECISION: (Edwards, J.) No. The promulgation of regulations governing the adjudication of administrative civil penalty actions is not exempt from the requirements of notice and comment. Cases interpreting § 553(b)(A) of the Administrative Procedure Act (APA) have long emphasized that a rule does not fall within the scope of the exception merely because it is capable of bearing the label "procedural." Where nominally procedural rules contain a substantial value judgment, or substantially alter the rights or interest of regulated parties, the rules must be preceded by notice and comment. The Penalty Rules fall outside the scope of §553(b)(A) because they substantially affect a civil penalty defendant's right to an administrative adjudication. Therefore, members of the aviation community had a legitimate interest in participating in the rulemaking process.

DISSENT: (Silberman, J.) The Penalty Rules deal with enforcement or adjudication of claims of violations of the substantive norm, but do not purport to affect the substantive norm. These kinds of rules are, therefore, clearly procedural. Of course, procedure impacts on outcomes and thus can virtually always be described as affecting substance, but to pursue this line of analysis results in the obliteration of the distinction that Congress demanded.

EDITOR'S ANALYSIS: Courts will consider the label an agency puts on its own rules, but, as in this case, such labels are not determinative as to the ruling of the court. Rather, courts will also consider whether rules go "beyond formality and substantially affect the rights of those over whom the agency exercises authority." Pickus v. United States Board of Parole, 507 F.2d 1107 (D.C. Cir. 1974). Thus, a rule will not be considered procedural if it has a substantive effect on the regulated parties to whom it applies.

[For more information on rulemaking exceptions, see Casenote Law Outline on Administrative Law, Chapter 7, Rulemaking Processes, §X, Categoric and Subject Matter Exceptions.]

QUICKNOTES

RULEMAKING - The promulgation of a rule by an administrative agency, acting within the scope of its power pursuant to statute, enacting a rule governing a particular activity.

PROCEDURAL RULE - Rule relating to the process of carrying out a lawsuit and not to the substantive rights asserted by the parties.

NOTES:

JEM BROADCASTING COMPANY, INC. v. FEDERAL COMMUNICATIONS COMMISSION

Radio station (P) v. Government agency (D)

22 F.3d 320 (D.C. Cir. 1994).

NATURE OF CASE: Appeal from denial of license application.

FACT SUMMARY: JEM (P) submitted a radio license application containing inconsistent information to the FCC (D) who refused to allow correction of the error.

CONCISE RULE OF LAW: Rules of agency organization, procedure and practice are exempt from the general notice and comment rulemaking requirements.

FACTS: In July 1988 JEM (P) submitted a license application for a radio station in Arkansas. When the FCC (D) reviewed the application, it determined that JEM (P) had provided inconsistent information that could not be resolved from the application documents. Therefore, the FCC (D) used its 1985 "hard look" regulations, which established a fixed filing window for substantially complete applications. Those applications that did not include the requisite information were returned without any opportunity to fix the errors under the hard look rules. JEM (P) contended that the hard look rules should not be applied because they were not promulgated with notice and comment in violation of the APA.

ISSUE: Are rules of agency organization, procedure and practice exempt from the general notice and comment rulemaking requirements?

HOLDING AND DECISION: (Edwards, J.) Yes. Rules of agency organization, procedure and practice are exempt from the general notice and comment rulemaking requirements. The Administrative Procedure Act generally requires notice and comment before new regulations are promulgated. However, there is an exception to this general rule for procedural regulations, as opposed to substantive rules that alter the rights and interests of parties affected by the regulations. In the present case, it is unquestioned that the FCC (D) can set a deadline for applications. Although the hard look rules are significant, they do not change the substantive standards by which the FCC (D) evaluates applications. Thus, they are mostly procedural and are not required to go through notice and comment before being adopted.

EDITOR'S ANALYSIS: The court considered JEM's (P) argument that the hard look regulations were substantive because they sacrificed applications with minor errors for the sake of efficiency. However, they held that this view would swallow up the procedural exception. A previous decision that seemed to support this argument is no longer good law.

QUICKNOTES

RULEMAKING - The promulgation of a rule by an administrative agency, acting within the scope of its power pursuant to statute, enacting a rule governing a particular activity.

ADMINISTRATIVE PROCEDURE ACT - Provides the standard for judicial review of agency rules.

NOTES:

UNITED STATES v. ALLEGHENY-LUDLUM STEEL CORP.

Government (D) v. Shipper (P)

406 U.S. 742 (1972).

NATURE OF CASE: Challenge to agency regulation.

FACT SUMMARY: Allegheny-Ludlum (P) complained that the Interstate Commerce Commission (D) should have held hearings before promulgating rules regarding railroad rates.

CONCISE RULE OF LAW: Informal rulemaking is permitted where the governing statute does not require that rules be made on the record.

FACTS: The Interstate Commerce Commission (ICC) (D) regulated railroad rates. Congress passed the Esch Car Service Act, which allowed the ICC (D) to establish reasonable rules and regulations on its own initiative without requiring that they be inside "on the record." The ICC (D) used informal rulemaking to set some rates and Allegheny-Ludlum (P), a shipper, sought judicial review, complaining that a hearing should have been held.

ISSUE: Is informal rulemaking permitted where the governing statute does not require that rules be made on the record?

HOLDING AND DECISION: (Rehnquist, J.) Yes. Informal rulemaking is permitted where the governing statute does not require that rules be made on the record. According to 5 U.S.C. §§ 556 and 557, rulemaking procedure includes a hearing before the promulgation of the new regulation. However, these sections only apply when the statute requires rules be made "on the record." In the present case, the Esch Act does not absolutely require that the rules be made on the record. While the precise words "on the record" are not the only factor to be considered, the language of the Esch Act does not indicate that formal rulemaking was to be involved.

EDITOR'S ANALYSIS: The formal rulemaking procedures of §§ 556 and 557 include a trial-type proceeding. A hybrid type of rulemaking has also arisen where Congress has expressly required it. Hybrid rulemaking is more burdensome than informal rulemaking, but less burdensome than the formal type.

QUICKNOTES

5 U.S.C. §§556, 557 - Provides for certain procedures in agency rulemaking.

RULEMAKING - The promulgation of a rule by an administrative agency, acting within the scope of its power pursuant to statute, enacting a rule governing a particular activity.

NOTES:

UNITED STATES v. FLORIDA EAST COAST RAILROAD CO.
Government (D) v. Railroad company (P)
410 U.S. 224 (1973).

NATURE OF CASE: Appeal of nullification of certain boxcar compensation rules.

FACT SUMMARY: The ICC (D) adopted rules regarding per diem charges on boxcars following an informal conference.

CONCISE RULE OF LAW: The ICC need not hold a formal hearing prior to establishing rules with respect to car service by common carriers.

FACTS: Amendments to the Interstate Commerce Act empowered the ICC (D) to adopt rules with respect to car service by common carriers and particularly to the compensation to be paid car owners for borrowed boxcars. The ICC (D) obtained data on freight-car demand from various carriers. In response to concerns expressed by various carriers, the ICC (D) held an informal conference. The ICC (D) subsequently published rule proposals inviting criticism. The proposals were then adopted. The ICC's (D) actions were challenged for failure to hold a formal hearing. The lower court invalidated the ICC's (D) actions.

ISSUE: Must the ICC (D) hold a formal hearing prior to establishing rules with respect to car service by common carriers?

HOLDING AND DECISION: (Rehnquist, J.) No. The ICC (D) need not hold a formal hearing prior to establishing rules with respect to car service by common carriers. The Administrative Procedure Act states the evidentiary requirements for formal hearings but does not mandate that formal hearings always be held. When a statute does not expressly require a formal hearing, the agency in question may, when conducting rulemaking, take evidence by written submission if the agency believes a formal hearing unnecessary. Here, the ICC (D) took extensive steps to obtain evidence through written submission. Since this Court has already held that the Interstate Commerce Act does not require hearings, the ICC's (D) actions were proper. Reversed.

DISSENT: (Douglas, J.) The Act should be interpreted to require a hearing.

EDITOR'S ANALYSIS: The Court's opinion here took a very narrow view of the necessity for formal hearings. The Interstate Commerce Act amendment in question did contain language suggesting a hearing would be necessary, but the Court found the language insufficient to trigger the requirement of a hearing. It would seem that only statutes clearly spelling out the requirement of a hearing will bring the Administrative Procedure Act's rules for formal hearings into play.

[For more information on formal rulemaking requirements, see Casenote Law Outline on Administrative Law, Chapter 7, § V, Some Rules Must Be Promulgated Through Formal Procedures.]

QUICKNOTES

INTERSTATE COMMERCE ACT § 1 (14) - Allows the Commission to prescribe per diem charges for the use of railroad cars owned by another.

PRETERMINATION HEARING - A hearing held prior to the termination of a property interest.

APA § 553 - Establishes the minimum requirements of public rulemaking procedure.

RULEMAKING - The promulgation of a rule by an administrative agency, acting within the scope of its power pursuant to statute, enacting a rule governing a particular activity.

NOTES:

VERMONT YANKEE NUCLEAR POWER CORP. v. NATURAL RESOURCES DEFENSE COUNCIL, INC.

Nuclear power plant (D) v. Environmental group (P)

435 U.S. 519 (1978).

NATURE OF CASE: Appeal in connection with review of agency rulemaking procedure.

FACT SUMMARY: The Nuclear Regulatory Commission (Commission) (D) promulgated a rule on nuclear wastes, which was struck down on review because of alleged procedural defects.

CONCISE RULE OF LAW: The adequacy of the record in rulemaking proceeding does not depend on the type of procedural devices employed, but turns on whether the agency has followed the statutory mandate of the Administrative Procedure Act.

FACTS: In connection with a grant of a permit to build a nuclear power plant to Vermont Yankee Nuclear Power Corp. (D) and its receipt of an operating license therefor, an issue concerning disposal of toxic nuclear wastes arose. Although this issue was excluded from consideration in the Commission's (D) hearings on the operating license, the Commission (D) subsequently promulgated a rule concerning the waste problem. National Resources Defense Council, Inc. (NRDC) (P) appealed from both the Commission's (D) adoption of the rule and its decision to grant Vermont Yankee's (D) license to the Court of Appeals for the District of Columbia Circuit. The court remanded the question of Vermont Yankee's (D) license for further proceedings. The court then invalidated the rulemaking proceedings despite the fact that it appeared that the agency employed all the procedures required by the Administrative Procedure Act. Vermont Yankee (D) argued that the Commission (D) may grant a license to operate a nuclear reactor without any consideration of waste disposal and fuel reprocessing, although the Commission (D) considered this issue includable in individual license proceedings. The rulemaking proceedings were reviewed on the basis of the record only.

ISSUE: Does the adequacy of the record in an agency rulemaking proceeding depend on the type of procedural devices employed, but turns on whether the agency has followed the statutory mandate of the Administrative Procedure Act?

HOLDING AND DECISION: (Rehnquist, J.) Yes. The adequacy of the record in an agency rulemaking proceeding is not correlated directly to the type of procedural devices employed, but turns on whether the agency has followed the statutory mandate of the Administrative Procedure Act. Vermont Yankees' (D) contention fails because the Commission (D) was well within its authority on the waste disposal and fuel reprocessing issues as they applied in individual license proceedings. However, the court of appeals was incorrect in its invalidation of the Commission's (D) rulemaking proceeding. Absent constitutional restraints or extremely compelling circumstances, the administrative agencies should be free to fashion their own rules of procedure and to pursue methods of inquiry capable of permitting them to discharge their duties. There are three compelling reasons why the agencies' discretion should be determinative. First, if courts continually review agency proceedings to determine whether the agency employed procedures which were what the court perceived to be the best or correct results, judicial review would be totally unpredictable. Second, the fact that the court looked only at the record and not at information available to the Commission (D) when it decided to structure the proceedings in a certain way is an example of Monday morning quarterbacking which would compel the agency to conduct all rulemaking proceedings with the full panoply of procedural devices normally associated only with adjudicatory hearings. Finally, and perhaps most importantly, this type of review misconceives the standard for judicial review of an agency rule; rulemaking need not be based solely on the transcript of a hearing. In fact, in a case like this, there need not be a formal hearing. Reversed and remanded.

EDITOR'S ANALYSIS: Executive Order 12044 concerned President Carter's directive to the agencies to "adopt procedures to improve existing and future regulations." 43 Fed. Reg. 12661. The order called for greater involvement by the public. This consisted, in part, of suggestions concerning published notice, conferences, hearings, and direct mailing. Gellhorn, W., Admin. Law, 203-204.

[For more information on hybrid rulemaking, see Casenote Law Outline on Administrative Law, Chapter 7, § V, Some Rules Must Be Promulgated Through Formal Procedures.]

QUICKNOTES

5 U.S.C. § 553 - Establishes minimum requirements of public rulemaking procedure.

JUDICIAL REVIEW - The authority of the courts to review decisions, actions or omissions committed by another agency or branch of government.

ADJUDICATORY PROCEEDING - A hearing conducted by an administrative agency resulting in a final judgment regarding the rights of the parties involved.

CHOCOLATE MANUFACTURERS ASSOCIATION v. BLOCK

Trade group (P) v. Federal agency (D)

755 F.2d 1098 (4th Cir. 1985).

NATURE OF CASE: Appeal from decision denying relief from an administrative rule.

FACT SUMMARY: The Chocolate Manufacturers Association (CMA) (P) challenged, on inadequate-notice grounds, a USDA (D) rule that prohibited the use of chocolate-flavored milk in the federally funded Special Supplemental Food Program for Women, Infants, and Children (WIC).

CONCISE RULE OF LAW: The notice in the Federal Register that an agency must give of a proposed rulemaking must contain either the terms or substance of the proposed rule or a description of the subjects and issues involved.

FACTS: WIC was established by Congress in 1972 to assist pregnant, postpartum, and breastfeeding women, infants, and children from families with inadequate income whose physical and mental health was in danger because of inadequate nutrition or health care. In 1979, Congress extended the WIC Program and redefined the term "supplemental foods" that the program was established to provide. This redefinition stated that the USDA (D) must assure that the fat, sugar, and salt content of foods prescribed by the WIC were appropriate. The USDA (D) then published for comment the proposed rule at issue here, which proposed a maximum sugar content for authorized cereals but did not discuss sugar in relation to flavoring in milk. The USDA (D) notice allowed sixty days for comment and specifically invited comment on the entire scope of the proposed rule. Of the over 1,000 comments received, 78 recommended that flavored milk be deleted from the WIC list of approved foods. The USDA (D) did delete flavored milk from the list, and the CMA (P) challenged the rule on the grounds that it did not provide that the disallowance of flavored milk would be considered. The lower court denied the CMA (P) any reliefs and it appealed.

ISSUE: Must the notice in the Federal Register that an agency must give of a proposed rulemaking contain either the terms or substance of the proposed rule or a description of the subjects and issues involved?

HOLDING AND DECISION: (Sprouse, J.) Yes. Section 4 of the Administrative Procedure Act requires that the notice in the Federal Register that an agency must give of a proposed rulemaking contain either the terms or substance of the proposed rule or a description of the subjects and issues involved. The purpose of the notice-and-comment procedure is both to allow the agency to benefit from the experience and input of the parties who file comments and to see to it that the agency maintains a flexible and open-minded attitude toward its own rules. There is no question that an agency may promulgate a final rule that differs in some particulars from its proposal, but it does not have carte blanche to establish a rule contrary to its original proposal simply because it receives suggestions to alter it during the comment period. If the final rule materially alters the issues involved in the rulemaking or if it substantially departs from the terms or substance of the proposed rule, the notice is inadequate. Here, the final rule was an outgrowth of the original rule proposed, but perhaps not a logical outgrowth. In all of the activities setting out and discussing food packaging, including the proposed rule and its preamble, the USDA (D) never suggested that flavored milk be removed from the WIC Program. At the time of the proposed rulemaking, neither the CMA (P) nor the general public could have any indication that flavored milk was not part of the WIC Program acceptable diet. Reversed and remanded.

EDITOR'S ANALYSIS: Section 553 of the Administrative Procedure Act has been and remains the foremost example of federal rulemaking. Section 553's provisions detail the procedure an agency must follow in promulgating a rule. These provisions state that the general public must be given a chance to comment in writing or orally about the rule to be promulgated, and that the agency promulgating the rule must incorporate in the final rule a statement of its basis and purpose.

[For more information on public participation in Rulemaking, see Casenote Law Outline on Administrative Law, Chapter 7, § III, The Procedural Norm is "Notice and Comment" Rulemaking.]

QUICKNOTES

APA § 4 - Requires notice in the Federal Register about proposed rules.

NOTES:

HOME BOX OFFICE, INC. v. FEDERAL COMMUNICATIONS COMMISSION

Television network (P) v. Government agency (D)

567 F.2d 9 (D.C. Cir. 1977).

NATURE OF CASE: Review of an informal rulemaking procedure.

FACT SUMMARY: Ex parte comments were received in connection with an informal rulemaking procedure.

CONCISE RULE OF LAW: The public record must reflect the representations made to an agency so that relevant information supporting or refuting those representations may be brought to the attention of the reviewing courts by persons participating in agency proceedings.

FACTS: Ex parte comments were received in connection with an informal rulemaking proceeding dealing with subscription television. A participant in the proceeding, and an amicus before the court, Geller (P), filed a petition with the Federal Communications Commission (D) to disclose ex parte communications during the proceedings. The FCC (D) took no action and Geller (P) sought judicial review of the FCC's (D) order promulgating four amendments regulating subscription television. The court of appeals sua sponte ordered the FCC (D) to disclose the ex parte contacts. The FCC (D) did so and showed that the competing industry representatives had a great voice in the outcome of the proceedings.

ISSUE: Must the public record reflect what representations were made to an agency so that relevant information supporting or refuting those representations may be brought to the attention of the reviewing courts by persons participating in agency proceedings?

HOLDING AND DECISION: [Per curiam.] Yes. The public record must reflect the representations made to an agency so that relevant information supporting or refuting those representations may be brought to the attention of the reviewing courts by persons participating in agency proceedings. Here, the evidence is consistent with the claim of undue industry influence over the FCC (D) proceedings. The presence of secrecy makes it difficult to judge the truth even when later disclosed by the FCC (D). Secrecy is inconsistent with fundamental notions of fairness implicit in due process. Therefore, once a notice of proposed rulemaking has been issued, discussion with interested parties should be prohibited, and if made, a written document or a summary of any oral communications must be placed in the public file immediately after the communication so that interested parties may comment. Remanded to FCC (D).

EDITOR'S ANALYSIS: The courts encouraged agencies to use an informal rulemaking procedure. However, they became afraid that this informal procedure would fall victim to too much political pressure. Therefore, the courts currently are demanding that these procedures become more judicial in nature. Gellhorn, quoting Robinson, 64 Va. L. Rev. 227-230 (1978).

[For more information on ex parte communications in rulemaking, see Casenote Law Outline on Administrative Law, Chapter 8, Integrity of Internal Decision-Making Processes, § IV, Ex Parte Communications Between Agency Decision-Makers and "Interested Persons" Are Generally Prohibited.]

QUICKNOTES

EX PARTE - A proceeding commenced by one party without providing any opposing parties with notice or which is uncontested by an adverse party.

SUA SPONTE - An action taken by the court by its own motion and without the suggestion of one of the parties.

DUE PROCESS - The constitutional mandate requiring the courts to protect and enforce individuals' rights and liberties consistent with prevailing principals of fairness and justice and prohibiting the federal and state governments from such activities that deprive its citizens of a life, liberty or property interest.

AMICUS BRIEF - A brief submitted by a third party, not a party to the action, that contains information for the court's consideration in conformity with its position.

NOTES:

SIERRA CLUB v. COSTLE

Environmental protection group (P) v.
Environmental agency (D)
657 F.2d 298 (D.C. Cir. 1981).

NATURE OF CASE: Appeal from decision denying relief in a challenge to an agency rule.

FACT SUMMARY: The Sierra Club (P) and the Environmental Defense Fund (EDF) (P) challenged the EPA's (D) adoption of the 1.2 lbs./MBtu standard for power plants using coal fuel to generate power.

CONCISE RULE OF LAW: The Clean Air Amendments of 1977 provide that all relevant documents that become available after a proposed rule has been published shall be placed in the docket as soon as possible after their availability.

FACTS: The EDF (P) and the Sierra Club (P) challenged a rule promulgated by Costle (D) and the EPA (D) that adopted a 1.2 lbs/MBtu standard for power plants using coal fuel to generate power. The EDF (P) objected that comments regarding the adopted standard were filed after the close of the official comment period, and that meetings between EPA (D) officials and various government and private parties interested in the outcome of the final rule took place after the close of the comment period. The EDF (P) alleged that such "late" comments, mostly from representatives of the coal or utility industries, and the meetings persuaded the EPA (D) to back away from adopting a .55 lb./MBtu limit and instead to adopt the more lenient 1.2 lbs./MBtu standard. The EDF (P) also alleged that some post-comment communications were not docketed by the EPA (D) in violation of the Clean Air Amendments of 1977 (Act) and that, therefore, the EDF (P) was not able to adequately respond to those documents before the 1.2 lbs./MBtu standard was adopted. The lower court ruled in favor of the EPA (D), and the EDF (P) appealed.

ISSUE: Do the Clean Air Amendments of 1977 provide that all documents that become available after a proposed rule has been published and which the Administrator determines are of central relevance to the rulemaking shall be placed in the docket as soon as possible after their availability?

HOLDING AND DECISION: (Wald, J.) Yes. The Clean Air Amendments of 1977 provide that all relevant documents that become available after a proposed rule has been published shall be placed in the docket as soon as possible after their availability. This provision is not limited to the comment period, and it apparently allows the EPA (D) not only to put documents in the record after the comment period is over, but also to define which documents are "of central relevance" so as to require that they be placed in the docket. EPA (D) thus has the authority to place post-comment documents into the docket, but it need not do so in all instances. The Act does not expressly treat the issue of post-comment period meetings with individuals outside the EPA (D). Oral face-to-face discussions are not prohibited anywhere, anytime, in the Act. But at least some adequate summary of them must be made in order to preserve the integrity of the rulemaking docket. Docketing of such summaries may be needed to give practical effect to the provisions of the Act that demand that all documents of central relevance to the rulemaking shall be placed in the docket post-haste. It was not unlawful in this case for EPA (D) not to docket a meeting since EPA (D) makes no effort to base the rule on any information arising from that meeting. In sum, EPA's (D) adoption of the 1.2 lbs/MBtu emissions ceiling was free from procedural error. Affirmed.

EDITOR'S ANALYSIS: In the above case, the comment period regarding the proposed emissions ceiling ran from September 19, 1978 to January 15, 1979. After January 15, the EPA (D) received almost 300 written submissions on the proposed rule that were accepted by the EPA (D) and entered on its administration docket. EPA (D) did not officially reopen the comment period, and it did not notify the public through the Federal Register that it had received and was entering "late" comments. Of the late comments, the EDF (P) claimed that at least 30 were from representatives of the coal or utility industries and 22 were submitted by Congressmen as advocates of those interests. The EDF (P) characterized such comments and meetings that took place after the comment-period closed as an "ex parte blitz" by the coal industry to force the EPA to adapt a higher emissions ceiling.

[For more information on public participation in rulemaking procedures, see Casenote Law Outline on Administrative Law, Chapter 8, § V, Administrative Processes Should Be Sensitive to Public Opinion.]

QUICKNOTES

CLEAN AIR ACT § 307 - Requires that documents relevant to rulemaking under the Act be docketed.

NOTES:

CHEVRON v. NATURAL RESOURCES DEFENSE COUNCIL, INC.

Parties not identified.

467 U.S. 837 (1984).

NATURE OF CASE: Appeal from review of an EPA (D) regulation.

FACT SUMMARY: The EPA (D) passed a regulation incorporating a broader definition of an air pollution "source" than it had used previously.

CONCISE RULE OF LAW: Where Congress has left an open question in its legislation, judicial review of an agency's interpretation of that question must be limited to whether the agency's construction is legitimate.

FACTS: In the Clean Air Act Amendments of 1977, Congress limited the issuance of permits to stationary sources of air pollution to those meeting strict requirements. The legislation was unclear as to what the term "stationary source" meant. The EPA (D) passed a regulation applying the strict standard to each individual emitting source. The EPA (D) later revised the regulation to allow all emitting sources in a single plant to be treated as a single source for the purposes of the legislation. The Natural Resources Defense Council, Inc. (P) filed a petition for review of this regulation. The court of appeals found the EPA's (D) interpretation inconsistent with the policy of the legislation. The EPA (D) appealed, and the Supreme Court granted certiorari.

ISSUE: Must judicial review of an agency's interpretation of a question left open in legislation by Congress be limited to whether the agency's construction is legitimate?

HOLDING AND DECISION: (Stevens, J.) Yes. Where Congress has left an open question in legislation, judicial review of the agency's interpretation of that question must be limited to whether the agency's construction is legitimate. In this case Congress did not clearly define "stationary source." The legislative history is not clear as to whether "stationary source" should have a plantwide definition. The EPA's (D) construction is reasonable in light of the plain English of the statute as well as the competing interests involved. The judiciary may not review an agency's authority in light of the policy of the statute but only based on the reasonableness of the language. Reversed.

EDITOR'S ANALYSIS: In a 1989 law review article, Justice Scalia delineated two categories of congressional ambiguity, each requiring a different standard of review by the judiciary. Where Congress clearly intended a certain result, but was unclear about it, the court must resolve the issue as a question of law. On the other hand, where congressional vagueness was intentionally meant to delegate authority to an agency, the standard of Chevron must apply. See Scalia, Judicial Deference to Administrative Interpretations of Law, 1989 Duke L.J. 511, 516.

[For more information on judicial review of questions of law, see Casenote Law Outline on Administrative Law, Chapter 9, § IV, Level of Review Determined by the Nature of the Controverted Issues.]

QUICKNOTES

JUDICIAL REVIEW - The authority of the courts to review decisions, actions or omissions committed by another agency or branch of government.

NOTES:

MOTOR VEHICLE MANUFACTURERS ASSOC. v. STATE FARM MUTUAL AUTOMOBILE INS. CO.

Parties not identified.

463 U.S. 29 (1983).

NATURE OF CASE: Appeal from decision finding agency action arbitrary and capricious.

FACT SUMMARY: The National Highway Traffic Safety Administration (NHTSA) (D) appealed from a decision of the court of appeals, finding that the revocation of the requirement that new motor vehicles produced after September 1982 be equipped with passive restraints to protect occupants in the event of a collision was arbitrary and capricious.

CONCISE RULE OF LAW: When an agency modifies or rescinds a previously promulgated rule, it is required to supply a satisfactory, rational analysis supporting its decision.

FACTS: Standard 208 is a rule promulgated by the Dept. of Transportation dealing with motor vehicle occupant safety. Since originally issued in 1967, the standard has been subject to constant rescission, modification, and amendment. In 1969, the standard first formally proposed to include a passive restraint requirement. Between 1976-1980, a mandatory passive restraint requirement was issued. The two systems that would satisfy the standard would be an air bag system or a passive seat belt system, with the choice of system being left up to the manufacturer. It was assumed that manufacturers would install approximately 60% air bags and 40% passive belts. By 1981, the manufacturers planned to produce 99% of their cars equipped with passive belts. In 1981, even though studies, surveys, and other empirical evidence indicated that the use rate associated with the passive belts was more than double that associated with manual belts, the NHTSA (D) concluded that the safety benefits associated with the standard's implementation did not justify the costs of implementing the standard. In that same year, the NHTSA (D), without considering the possible use of air bags, rescinded the passive restraint requirement. From a court of appeals decision finding revocation of the passive restraint requirement arbitrary and capricious, the NHTSA (D) appealed.

ISSUE: When an agency rescinds or modifies a previously promulgated rule, is it required to supply a satisfactory, rational analysis supporting its decision?

HOLDING AND DECISION: (White, J.) Yes. When an agency rescinds or modifies a previously promulgated rule, it is required to supply a satisfactory, rational analysis supporting its decision. A change or rescission is akin to the promulgation of the rule itself and is subject to the same arbitrary and capricious standard. The agency may be required to more fully justify its decision than if the agency had not acted in the first instance. The agency must show a rational connection between the facts found and the decision rendered. If an agency relies on improper facts or fails to consider important aspects of the problem or renders a decision that runs contrary to the evidence, its decision may be considered arbitrary and capricious. The National Traffic and Motor Vehicle Safety Act of 1966 (Act) mandates the achievement of traffic safety. Given the conceded effectiveness of air bags, the logical response to the manufacturers' actions would have been to require air bags. Not only was this not done, it appears that the NHTSA (D) did not even consider it. A rational rescission decision cannot be made without the consideration of technologically feasible alternatives of proven value. Further, the empirical evidence runs counter to the agency's determination that the safety aspects associated with the use of passive belts could not be determined. The empirical evidence indicates that there is a doubling of use over the use of manual belts, and the safety benefits associated with the increased use of safety belts is unquestioned. Finally, the NHTSA (D) has failed to articulate a basis for not requiring nondetachable passive belts. By failing to consider feasible, logical alternatives and dismissing the safety benefits associated with passive restraints in light of the evidence, the NHTSA (D) has failed to present an adequate basis or explanation for rescinding the mandatory passive restraint requirement. Vacated and remanded.

EDITOR'S ANALYSIS: Standard setting by the NHTSA (D) has proved most troublesome. Initial promulgation of standards were in large part mere adoptions of already existing standards. The promulgation of new standards is associated with a whole host of problems, including the problem of obtaining accurate information and the problem of enforcement and the problems that may be encountered in negotiating such standards with industry and other interest groups.

[For more information on judicial review of administrative policy, see Case note Law Outline on Administrative Law, Chapter 9, § IV, Level of Review Determined by the Nature of the Controverted Issues.]

QUICKNOTES

5 U.S.C. § 706 - Authorizes judicial review of all orders establishing Federal motor vehicle safety standards.

ARBITRARY AND CAPRICIOUS STANDARD - Standard imposed in reviewing the decision of an agency or court that the decision was made in disregard of the facts or law.

CHAPTER 3
ADJUDICATION

QUICK REFERENCE RULES OF LAW

1. **Formal or Informal Adjudication.** Unless otherwise specified, an administrative adjudicatory hearing that is subject to judicial review must be on the record. (Seacoast Anti-Pollution League v. Costle)

   [For more information on basic procedural law, see Casenote Law Outline on Administrative Law, Chapter 4, Internal Decisionmaking Processes, § V, Statutes Also Assure an "Opportunity to be Heard" in Many Administrative Programs.]

2. **Formal or Informal Adjudication.** A formal adjudication is necessary when an agency is required by statute to conduct a hearing through on-the-record proceedings. (City of West Chicago v. U.S. Nuclear Regulatory Commission)

3. **Formal or Informal Adjudication.** Where a statutory provision is ambiguous, regulations that represent a reasonable interpretation of that provision are not inconsistent with the requirement of due process. (Chemical Waste Management, Inc. v. U.S. Environmental Protection Agency)

   [For more information on informal rulemaking, see Casenote Law Outline on Administrative Law, Chapter 7, Rulemaking Processes, § III, The Procedural Norm is "Notice and Comment" Rulemaking.]

4. **State Adjudication.** The Administrative Procedure Act (APA) requires that there be adequate notice, argument and evidence before an administrative law judge makes a decision. (Natural Labor Relations Board v. Local Union No. 35 International Brotherhood of Electrical Workers)

5. **State Adjudication.** The notice requirement of the Administrative Procedure Act is satisfied where parties understood the relevant issues and were afforded a full opportunity to justify their conduct. (Southwest Sunsites, Inc. v. Federal Trade Commission)

6. **State Adjudication.** Agencies may summarily withdraw approval for applications after providing the party with due notice. (John D. Copanos and Sons, Inc. v. Food and Drug Administration)

7. **State Adjudication.** Agencies may not make adjudications based on post-hearing reports that are not subject to cross-examination. (Wallace v. Bowen)

8. **Ex Parte Communications.** Ex parte communications concerning the merits of a case are not permitted in an adversary administrative hearing. (Camero v. United States)

9. **Ex Parte Communications.** Undisclosed improper ex parte communications during agency proceedings do not necessarily void an agency decision. (Professional Air Traffic Controllers Organization v.Federal Labor Relations Authority)

10. **Due Process Hearing.** Due process requires that before a tax set by an agency becomes irrevocably fixed, the taxpayer be afforded notice and an opportunity to participate in an oral evidentiary hearing. (Londoner v. Denver)

    [For more information on the adjudication requirement, see Casenote Law Outline on Administrative Law, Chapter 4, Internal Decisionmaking Processes, §I, The First Step in Analyzing a Question About Internal Process.]

11. **Due Process Hearings: Individualized Decisionmaking.** Where an agency rule will apply to a vast number of people, the Constitution does not require that each be given an opportunity to be heard directly for the purpose of arguing in favor of or against its adoption. (Bi-Metallic Investment Company v. State Board of Equalization)

[For more information on the rulemaking process, see Casenote Law Outline on Administrative Law, Chapter 4, Internal Decisionmaking Processes, §I, The First Step in Analyzing a Question About Internal Process.]

12. **Protected Interests: Property Interests.** The state need not hold hearings or offer reasons for its employment decisions. (Board of Regents v. Roth)

[For more information on opportunity to be heard, see Casenote Law Outline on Administrative Law, Chapter 4,Internal Decisionmaking Processes, § III, The Due Process Clause Establishes a Constitutional Right to an "Opportunity to be Heard."]

13. **Protected Interests: Liberty Interest.** In enacting 42 U.S.C. § 1983, Congress should not be understood to have attempted to make all torts of state officials federal crimes. (Paul v. Davis)

[For more information on adjudication and due process hearing rights, see Casenote Law Outline on Administrative Law, Chapter 4, Internal Decisionmaking Processes, § III, The Due Process Clause estatblishes a constitutional right to an "Opportunity to be Heard."]

14. **Protected Interests: Liberty Interest.** Hearings mandated by the Due Process Clause are only required when there is a clear factual dispute. (Codd v. Velger)

15. **Protected Interests: Liberty Interest.** Government employees are entitled to procedural due process in connection with employment discharges only when they have been deprived of a constitutionally protected liberty or property interest. (Shands v. City of Kennett)

16. **What Hearing Procedures must be Used?** The Due Process Clause does not require a hearing prior to termination of disability benefits. (Mathews v. Eldridge)

[For more information on due process requirements, see Casenote Law Outline on Administrative Law, Chapter 4, Internal Decisionmaking Processes, § IV, Due Process Requires "Some Kind of Hearing."]

17. **What Hearing Procedures must be Used?** A formal hearing is not required to dismiss a student for unsatisfactory performance based on the academic judgment of school officials. (Board of Curators of the University of Missouri v. Horowitz)

[For more information on how much process is due, see Casenote Law Outline on Administrative Law, Chapter 4, § IV, Due Process Requires "Some Kind of Hearing."]

18. **What Hearing Procedures must be Used?** There is no constitutional right to counsel in student disciplinary proceedings. (Osteen v. Henley)

19. **Neutral Decisionmaker.** The performance of both prosecutorial and adjudicative functions by the same agency officials is not per se a denial of due process. (Withrow v. Larkin)

[For more information on the "separation of functions" doctrine, see Casenote Law Outline on Administrative Law, Chapter 8, Integrity of the Internal Decisionmaking Processes, §III, The Doctrine of "Separation of Functions."]

20. **Judicial Review: Substantial Evidence and the ALJ's Credibility Findings.** Reviewing courts should review more critically an agency's findings of fact if they are contrary to those of the administrative law judge whose findings are based on a witness's demeanor. (Panasquitos Village, Inc. v. National Labor Relations Board)

[For more information on findings of fact, see Casenote Law Outline on Administrative Law, Chapter 9, Judicial Control of the Administrative Process, § IV, Level of Review Determined by the Nature of the Controverted Issues.]

21. **Judicial Review: Substantial Evidence and the ALJ's Credibility Findings.** Findings by an ALJ that reflect an evaluation of witness demeanor are entitled to more weight on review. (Kopack v. National Labor Relations Board)

22. **Judicial Review: Substantial Evidence and the ALJ's Credibility Findings.** A board must articulate sound reasons, based on the record of evidence, when its evaluation of testimony is contrary to that of the presiding official. (Jackson v. Veterans Administration)

23. **Judicial Review: Mixed Questions of Law and Fact.** A reviewing court must accept an agency's application of a broad statutory term if such application is supported in the record and has a reasonable basis in law. (National Labor Relations Board v. Hearst)

[For more information on covert review of mixed questions of law and fact, see Casenote Law Outline on Administrative Law, Chapter 9, Judicial Control of the Administrative Processes, §IV, Level of Review Determined by the Nature of the Controverted Issues.]

24. **Judicial Review: Mixed Questions of Law and Fact.** Decisions by Administrative Law Judges should be upheld on judicial review, unless they are irrational or unsupported by substantial evidence on the record. (Evening Star Newspaper Company v. Kemp)

25. **Judicial Review: Mixed Questions of Law and Fact.** Employees need not be engaged directly in an activity to the benefit of the employer at the time of an injury to be entitled to workers compensation. (Durrah v. Washington Metropolitan Area Transit Authority)

26. **Informal Adjudication.** When reviewing administrative decisions which are not supported by formal factual findings, courts should determine the scope of the appropriate official's authority, whether that authority was abused, and whether all applicable procedural requisites have been observed. (Citizens to Preserve Overton Park v. Volpe)

[For more information on standards of review, see Casenote Law Outline on Administrative Law, Chapter 9,Judicial Control of the Administrative Processes, § II, "Standards of Review."]

27. **"Consistency".** Agencies must offer reasoned explanations for their rulings, even if the ruling appears reasonable and plausible. (Yepes-Prado v. U.S. Immigration and Naturalization)

28. **"Consistency".** Agencies are prohibited from adopting inconsistent policies that result in conflicting lines of precedent governing identical situations. (Davila-Bardales v. U.S. Immigration and Naturalization)

SEACOAST ANTI-POLLUTION LEAGUE v. COSTLE

Advocacy group (P) v. Discharge permit grantee (D)

572 F.2d 872 (1st Cir. 1978).

NATURE OF CASE: Appeal from ruling upholding issuance of a pollution discharge permit.

FACT SUMMARY: An EPA administrator decided to grant Costle (D) a permit to discharge heated water into an estuary by relying on information not validated by a hearing.

CONCISE RULE OF LAW: Unless otherwise specified, an administrative adjudicatory hearing that is subject to judicial review must be on the record.

FACTS: After an administrator for the EPA reviewed the record of a prior administrative decision to deny Costle (D) a permit for discharging heated water into an estuary, he reversed the decision and granted Costle (D) a permit. In reaching this subsequent decision, the administrator relied on information not validated by a hearing and on expert evidence additional to that provided in the record. Seacoast (P), an environmental watchdog organization, appealed a lower court ruling in favor of Costle (D).

ISSUE: Unless otherwise specified, must an administrative adjudicatory hearing that is subject to judicial review be on the record?

HOLDING AND DECISION: (Coffin, C. J.) Yes. Unless otherwise specified, an administrative adjudicatory hearing that is subject to judicial review must be on the record. This rule naturally follows from the plain language of § 554(a) of the APA, which applies "in every case of adjudication required by statute to be determined on the record after opportunity for an agency hearing." Indeed, the crucial portion of the statute's limiting language necessarily requires a hearing as a precursor for administrative decisions. Moreover, the statute presumably dictates that such hearings be on the record. In the instant case, since the administrator failed to hold a hearing to receive relevant decisional information and utilized evidence from agency experts above and beyond that provided in the record, he must reconsider the issues in order to take more appropriate actions within his power which are consistent with this opinion. Remanded.

EDITOR'S ANALYSIS: Section 301(a) of the F.W.P.C.A., 33 U.S.C. § 1311(a), prohibits the discharge of any pollutant unless the discharger has obtained an EPA permit. In deciding to grant this permit, the EPA must be careful not to implement or prescribe law but must decide specific factual questions (5 U.S.C. § 551(4)). Moreover, the bases for the resolution of these questions must be on a reviewable record to survive judicial review. This requirement insures that administrative decisions have some grounds of reasonableness.

[For more information on basic procedural law, see Casenote Law Outline on Administrative Law, Chapter 4, Internal Decisionmaking Processes, § V, Statutes Also Assure an "Opportunity to be Heard" in Many Administrative Programs.]

QUICKNOTES

APA, § 554 - Provides that adjudicatory hearings must be on the record.

APA, § 556 - Provides that the testimony transcript the exclusive record.

FWCPA, § 301 - Prohibits discharge of pollutants by parties not permitted.

NOTES:

CITY OF WEST CHICAGO v. U.S. NUCLEAR REGULATORY COMMISSION

City (P) v. Federal agency (D)

701 F.2d 632 (7th Cir. 1983).

NATURE OF CASE: Appeal from administrative agency order issuing an amendment to a source materials license.

FACT SUMMARY: The City of West Chicago (P) challenged an order issued by the Nuclear Regulatory Commission (NRC) (D) granting Kerr-McGee Corporation permission to receive and store contaminated radioactive waste material.

CONCISE RULE OF LAW: A formal adjudication is necessary when an agency is required by statute to conduct a hearing through on-the-record proceedings.

FACTS: The NRC (D) is a federal agency that regulates the nuclear industry. Kerr-McGee operated a thorium milling plant pursuant to an NRC (D) license. Kerr-McGee applied to the NRC (D) for permission to destroy six of its buildings and to receive and store contaminated radioactive waste material. The NRC (D) granted the license amendment permitting the storage, which the City (P) of West Chicago challenged.

ISSUE: Is a formal adjudication necessary when an agency is required by statute to conduct a hearing through on-the-record proceedings?

HOLDING AND DECISION: (Cummings, C. J.) Yes. A formal adjudication is necessary when an agency is required by statute to conduct a hearing through on-the-record proceedings. In contrast, an informal adjudication refers to all administrative agency actions that are not pursuant to the agency's rulemaking function, and for which on-the-record proceedings are not required. Section 198(a) of the Atomic Energy Act (AEA) requires the NRC (D) to grant a hearing upon request for the grant, suspension, revocation or amendment of a license or construction permit. The City (P) contends that the AEA § 198(a) invoked the formal hearing provisions of the Administrative Procedure Act (APA). APA § 554 requires a formal hearing if the agency's governing statute requires the adjudication to be determined "on the record" following a hearing. A formal hearing is also required, in the absence of such language, if the legislature's intent indicates a desire to invoke the APA's formal hearing provisions. Although the NRC (P) has traditionally held formal hearings in respect to reactor cases pursuant to the same code section, that does not mean that the legislature intended formal hearings to apply to all actions brought under that section. Since the legislative history of the AEA is silent as to such an intent in respect to materials license cases, a formal hearing was not required. In addition, the NRC's (D) informal hearing did not violate the City's (P) due process rights since the City (P) was provided with an opportunity to argue why the materials license amendment should have been denied. Affirmed.

EDITOR'S ANALYSIS: Note that in order for the formal hearings provisions of the APA to be invoked, the federal statute must require the agency hearing to be "on the record." This does not simply mean that a record of the hearing must be kept, but rather that only such evidence that has been admitted at the hearing may be considered by the agency in making its final determination. The Supreme Court has held that when an agency acts pursuant to its rulemaking function, the applicable statute must specify that the hearing be conducted "on the record." However, when the agency acts in an adjudicatory capacity, statutory language simply requiring a hearing may be sufficient.

NOTES:

CHEMICAL WASTE MANAGEMENT, INC. v. ENVIRONMENTAL PROTECTION AGENCY

Private company (P) v. Federal agency (D)

873 F.2d 1477 (D.C. Cir. 1989).

NATURE OF CASE: Petition for review of federal agency regulations establishing informal procedures for administrative hearings.

FACT SUMMARY: Chemical Waste Management (P) sought review of regulations promulgated by the EPA (D) establishing informal administrative procedures for administrative hearings concerning the issuance of corrective action orders under § 3008(h) of RCRA.

CONCISE RULE OF LAW: Where a statutory provision is ambiguous, regulations that represent a reasonable interpretation of that provision are not inconsistent with the requirement of due process.

FACTS: The EPA (D) established informal procedures for administrative hearings concerning the issuance of corrective action orders under § 3008(h) of the Resource Conservation and Recovery Act (RCRA) as modified by the Hazardous and Solid Waste Amendments of 1984. Chemical Waste Management (P) sought review of the regulations, arguing that informal procedures were inconsistent with the intent of Congress in enacting and amending § 3008 and that the requirement in § 3008 of a "public hearing" indicated an intent that formal adjudicatory procedures be held.

ISSUE: Where a statutory provision is ambiguous, are regulations that represent a reasonable interpretation of that provision inconsistent with the requirement of due process?

HOLDING AND DECISION: (Ginsburg, J.) No. Where a statutory provision is ambiguous, regulations that represent a reasonable interpretation of that provision are not inconsistent with the requirement of due process. The analysis of CWM's (P) contentions requires a two-step process. First, where Congress has directly spoken to the precise question at issue, effect must be given to the unambiguously expressed intent of Congress. Here, the statutory language, taken alone, does not show that Congress has directly spoken to the precise question at issue. Subsection (b) requires a public hearing but does not indicate whether Congress intended that formal or informal hearing procedures be used. Second, where the statute is silent or ambiguous with respect to the specific issue, the court must ask whether the agency's answer is based on a permissible construction of the statute. If so, then the court must defer to the agency's construction. Because the agency has provided a reasonable explanation for its choice of informal procedures, the petition for review is denied.

EDITOR'S ANALYSIS: The two-step analysis utilized by the court was decreed by the Supreme Court in Chevron, U.S.A., Inc. v. Natural Resources Defense Council, Inc., 467 U.S. 837 (1984). That decision established that it was the prerogative of the agency to bring its own expertise to bear upon the resolution of ambiguities in the statute Congress charged it to administer. An agency that reasonably reads a simple requirement that it hold a hearing to allow for informal hearing procedures must prevail under the second step of Chevron.

[For more information on informal rulemaking, see Casenote Law Outline on Administrative Law, Chapter 7, Rulemaking Processes, § III, The Procedural Norm is "Notice and Comment" Rulemaking.]

QUICKNOTES

DUE PROCESS - The constitutional mandate requiring the courts to protect and enforce individuals' rights and liberties consistent with prevailing principals of fairness and justice and prohibiting the federal and state governments from such activities that deprive its citizens of a life, liberty or property interest.

NOTES:

NATIONAL LABOR RELATIONS BOARD v. LOCAL UNION NO. 25, INTERNATIONAL BROTHERHOOD OF ELECTRICAL WORKERS

Government agency (P) v. Labor union (D)

586 F.2d 959 (2d. Cir. 1978).

NATURE OF CASE: Petition for enforcement of order invalidating a collective bargaining agreement.

FACT SUMMARY: An administrative law judge ruled that the union (D) had engaged in unfair labor practices and that a provision of the collective bargaining agreement was illegal.

CONCISE RULE OF LAW: The Administrative Procedure Act (APA) requires that there be adequate notice, argument and evidence before an administrative law judge makes a decision.

FACTS: Flores filed a complaint with the NLRB (P) that the union (D) failed to provide him with job referrals because he was not a union member. The administrative law judge hearing the case agreed and found that the union (D) had engaged in unfair labor practices. The judge then went beyond the NLRB (P) complaint and found that a provision of the collective bargaining agreement at issue was illegal and invalidated it. The union (D) claimed that they were denied a fair hearing on this issue because there was no notice, argument or evidence presented on the legality of the agreement's clause.

ISSUE: Does the Administrative Procedure Act (APA) require that there be adequate notice, argument and evidence before an administrative law judge makes a decision?

HOLDING AND DECISION: (Lumbard, J.) Yes. The Administrative Procedure Act (APA) requires that there be adequate notice, argument and evidence before an administrative law judge makes a decision. APA § 554 requires that there be notice to the parties before an administrative law judge rules on an issue. In the present case, the judge hearing the NLRB's (P) complaint on behalf of Flores went ahead and ruled on the validity of the collective bargaining agreement even though the issue was not raised in the complaint or in oral argument, nor was there any evidence presented. Accordingly, the union (D) did not receive the requisite notice and the decision cannot be enforced.

EDITOR'S ANALYSIS: Different states handle administrative law judges in various manners. In some, the judges are hired by the agencies themselves. In others, there are central panels of judges not controlled by the agency.

QUICKNOTES

COLLECTIVE BARGAINING - Negotiations between an employer and employee that are mediated by a specified third party.

APA § 554 - Provides for procedures in agency adjudications.

NOTES:

SOUTHWEST SUNSITES, INC. v. FEDERAL TRADE COMMISSION

Land developer (P) v. Government agency (D)

785 F.2d 1431 (9th Cir. 1986).

NATURE OF CASE: Appeal from agency cease and desist order.

FACT SUMMARY: Southwest Sunsites (P) complained that the FTC (D) had applied a new standard with regard to deceptive practices without advance notice.

CONCISE RULE OF LAW: The notice requirement of the Administrative Procedure Act is satisfied where parties understood the relevant issues and were afforded a full opportunity to justify their conduct.

FACTS: Southwest Sunsites (P) sold undeveloped land in rural west Texas to out-of-state purchasers. The FTC (D) filed a complaint against Southwest (P) contending that they were engaged in untold and deceptive practices with regard to the sales. The complaint argued that Southwest (P) misrepresented the investment potential of the land and its suitability for use and value. An administrative law judge (ALJ) dismissed the complaint, finding that the representations did not have the tendency and capacity to mislead. The FTC (D), applying a different standard, found that the representations were likely to mislead reasonable consumers, and reversed and issued a cease and desist order. Southwest (P) appealed.

ISSUE: Is the notice requirement of the Administrative Procedure Act satisfied where parties understood the relevant issues and were afforded a full opportunity to justify their conduct?

HOLDING AND DECISION: (Beezer, J.) Yes. The notice requirement of the Administrative Procedure Act is satisfied where parties understood the relevant issues and were afforded a full opportunity to justify their conduct. The APA requires that parties involved in agency complaints be "timely informed of the matters of fact and law asserted." In the present case, the standard used by the FTC (D) was different than that used by the judge, but it imposed a greater burden on the agency since probable deception and detriment to the consumer had to be expressly proved. Thus, the ALJ's finding was based on a standard that was more narrow, and completely subsumed by the FTC's (D) new standard. Accordingly, Southwest (P) had a more than adequate opportunity to respond to the complaint. The FTC's (D) cease and desist order is affirmed.

EDITOR'S ANALYSIS: This case involves an unusual situation. The court correctly ruled that the "likely" standard applied by the FTC (D) was harder to reach than the "tendency" standard used by the ALJ. Thus, the ALJ and the agency must have had wildly different views of the facts involved to come to opposite conclusions.

QUICKNOTES

ADMINISTRATIVE PROCEDURE ACT - Provides the standard for judicial review of agency rules.

NOTICE AND COMMENT - Informal rulemaking.

CEASE AND DESIST ORDER - An order from a court or administrative agency prohibiting a person or business from continuing a particular course of conduct.

NOTES:

JOHN D. COPANOS AND SONS, INC. v. FOOD AND DRUG ADMINISTRATION

Drug manufacturer (P) v. Government agency (D)

854 F.2d 510 (D.C. Cir. 1988).

NATURE OF CASE: Petition for review of agency's rejection of application.

FACT SUMMARY: The FDA (D) withdrew its approval of Kanasco's (P) drug applications due to a record of manufacturing violations.

CONCISE RULE OF LAW: Agencies may summarily withdraw approval for applications after providing the party with due notice.

FACTS: John D. Copanos & Sons and Kanasco (P) manufactured and distributed human and veterinary drugs. In March 1987, the FDA (D) published a Notice of Opportunity for a Hearing proposing to withdraw Kanasco's (P) applications for new drugs on the grounds that Kanasco's (P) manufacturing was sub-standard. Over a three-year period, periodic inspections of Kanasco's (P) facilities had resulted in numerous violations and evidence that false records were submitted to cover up other violations. Kanasco (P) requested a hearing, but in August 1987, the FDA (D) summarily withdrew the applications. Kanasco (P) petitioned for review on the ground that it had not received adequate notice of the basis for the action.

ISSUE: May agencies summarily withdraw approval for applications after providing the party with due notice?

HOLDING AND DECISION: (Ginsburg, J.) Yes. Agencies may summarily withdraw approval for applications after providing the party with due notice. The Federal Drug and Cosmetic Act prohibits the introduction of new drugs without prior FDA (D) approval. The Act also established procedures whereby the FDA (D) can withdraw approval after due notice to the applicant. One of the grounds for withdrawal is sub-standard manufacturing by the applicant. This provision does not guarantee an applicant a hearing in all circumstances since the agency may summarily withdraw approval where there is no "genuine and substantial issue of fact that requires a hearing." Thus, notice being critical, it must contain enough information to provide the applicant with a genuine opportunity to identify the material issues of fact in the context of the action. In the present case, Kanasco (P) was not confronted with any significant ambiguity regarding the type of information that would warrant an agency hearing. Considering the context of the prior proceedings and violations, the hearing notice certainly advised Kanasco (P) of the type of information it would need to submit to command a hearing. Even without specific instructions telling Kanasco (P) what to produce, they have failed to identify any evidence that might have been presented but for lack of notice. Accordingly, the petition for review is denied.

EDITOR'S ANALYSIS: The narrow grounds for Kanasco's (P) petition for review should be noted. In this case, they were not challenging the FDA's (D) finding directly, but arguing only that the lack of proper notice had invalidated the subsequent summary decision. The court did take the FDA (D) to task for not making it easier to more clearly identify the exact violations that formed the basis for the approval withdrawal.

QUICKNOTES

FEDERAL DRUG AND COSMETIC ACT - Prohibits the sale of new drugs without approval from the FDA.

NOTES:

WALLACE v. BOWEN

Social security applicant (P) v. Government agency (D)

869 F.2d 187 (3d Cir. 1989).

NATURE OF CASE: Petition for review of agency denial of benefits.

FACT SUMMARY: Wallace (P) appealed his denial of social security disability benefits, based on reports that were not available for cross-examination at the hearing, claiming violations of his statutory and constitutional due process rights and that one ALJ's decision was not supported by sustantial evidence.

CONCISE RULE OF LAW: Agencies may not make adjudications based on post-hearing reports that are not subject to cross-examination.

FACTS: In February 1985, Wallace (P) suffered a heart attack while working and a stroke a month later. The stroke may have resulted in the loss of vision in one eye. Wallace (P) applied for disability benefits and supplemental security income based on his condition. After his claims were denied, Wallace (P) was granted a hearing before an ALJ in which he introduced doctors' reports about his ailments. After the hearing, the ALJ sent Wallace (P) to two doctors, both of whom reported back that his impairments did not meet the required criteria. Thus, the ALJ ruled that Wallace (P) was not disabled under the terms of the Social Security Act. Wallace (P) sought review, arguing that he did not have an opportunity to cross-examine the two post-hearing reports.

ISSUE: May agencies make adjudications based on post-hearing reports that are not subject to cross-examination?

HOLDING AND DECISION: (Sloviter, J.) No. Agencies may not make adjudications based on post-hearing reports that are not subject to cross-examination. Section 205 of the Social Security Act provides that upon denial of a claim, applicants are entitled to a hearing where a decision will be based on evidence adduced at the hearing. A full disclosure of the facts at a hearing requires the opportunity for cross-examination, which is an element of fundamental fairness to the applicant. Even where an opinion is wholly medical, cross-examination could reveal what evidence a doctor considered or failed to consider in formulating a conclusion. Accordingly, an applicant must have the opportunity to cross-examine any post-hearing reports that are relied upon by the ALJ when such cross-examination may be required for a full and accurate disclosure of the facts. Therefore, Wallace's petition for review is upheld; the judgment is vacated and the case is remanded.

EDITOR'S ANALYSIS: The court found that the two post-hearing reports by the doctors in this case were substantially relied upon by the ALJ. The judge even had remarked in the opinion that he had relied "in particular" on the report of the doctor who ruled that Wallace's visual impairment was not sufficient to qualify. Thus, there was little question that cross-examination could have affected the result here.

QUICKNOTES

SOCIAL SECURITY ACT §205 - Reasonable notice and an opportunity for a hearing must be given to an applicant who requests it after an unfavorable determination of claim.

NOTES:

CAMERO v. UNITED STATES

Former government employee (P) v. Employer (D)

375 F.2d 777 (Ct. Claims 1967).

NATURE OF CASE: Appeal from agency adjudication regarding employment decision.

FACT SUMMARY: Camero (P), a government employee, was terminated during a proceeding in which the attorney representing the employer had ex parte communications with the Commissioner making the decision.

CONCISE RULE OF LAW: Ex parte communications concerning the merits of a case are not permitted in an adversary administrative hearing.

FACTS: Camero (P) was a supervisory inspector at Army's military clothing agency. He was removed from his position on charges including bribery, fraud and undue familiarity with contractors. Camero (P) protested his removal and a hearing was held before the Grievance Committee with an attorney, Kostos, representing the agency. The Committee recommended that he not be removed, but the General Counsel of the agency, Wolverton, submitted an opinion to the commander that Camero (P) be dismissed notwithstanding the recommendation and the commander sustained the removal. Later Camero (P) became aware that attorney Kostos had discussed the case with Wolverton prior to his opinion. Camero (P) then filed suit for wrongful removal claiming that the ex parte communications were unfair.

ISSUE: Are ex parte communications concerning the merits of a case permitted in an adversary administrative hearing?

HOLDING AND DECISION: (Collins, J.) No. Ex parte communications concerning the merits of a case are not permitted in an adversary administrative hearing. Employee grievance hearings that arise out of an adverse agency action are evidentiary hearings where the agency representative acts similarly to a prosecutor. The employee is in the position of a defendant. One of the fundamental premises inherent in the concept of an adversary hearing is that neither party be permitted to engage in ex parte communications regarding the merits of the case with those responsible for the decision. There are few more serious incursions on the fairness of the process, and such conduct effectively renders the hearing meaningless. In the present case, the discussion of Camero's (P) case between Kostos and Wolverton after the hearing and prior to Wolverton's opinion for the commander was unfair to the process and invalidates the decision. Camero (P) is entitled to back pay from the date of his removal, less any salary he may have received from other employment.

EDITOR'S ANALYSIS: The court claimed that it believed Wolverton had made an independent decision on Camero's (P) case. If that is truly the case, then the overturning of the decision based on a talk with Kostos and other attorneys seems to favor process over substance. This case points up the problems that can arise when agency lawyers who work together also play the roles of judge and prosecutor in some situations.

QUICKNOTES

EX PARTE - A proceeding commenced by one party without providing any opposing parties with notice or which is uncontested by an adverse party.

NOTES:

PROFESSIONAL AIR TRAFFIC CONTROLLERS ORG. v. FEDERAL LABOR RELATIONS AUTHORITY

Union (D) v. Government agency (P)

685 F.2d 547 (D.C. Cir. 1982).

NATURE OF CASE: Evidentiary hearing to determine nature, extent and effect of ex parte communications in unfair labor practice case.

FACT SUMMARY: While Federal Labor Relations Authority (FRLA) (P) was deciding a case involving PATCO (D), board members had ex parte contacts with some interested parties.

CONCISE RULE OF LAW: Undisclosed improper ex parte communications during agency proceedings do not necessarily void an agency decision.

FACTS: PATCO (D) was the exclusive bargaining representative for air traffic controllers when negotiations over a new contract stalled in 1981. PATCO (D) struck the Federal Aviation Administration (FAA) on August 3, 1981. The government obtained a restraining order against the strike and then fired 11,000 controllers who failed to return to work two days later. The FAA also filed an unfair labor practice charge against PATCO (D) with the FRLA (P) alleging that the strike was unfair and seeking revocation of PATCO's (D) certification as the bargaining representative for the controllers. While the FRLA (P) was hearing the case, Board members who were deciding the case had brief encounters with interested parties to the case and did not disclose them. After PATCO's (D) certification was revoked, it sought to invalidate the decision based on the ex parte communications. The court ordered that an evidentiary hearing be held.

ISSUE: Do undisclosed improper ex parte communications during agency proceedings necessarily void an agency decision?

HOLDING AND DECISION: (Edwards, J.) No. Undisclosed improper ex parte communications during agency proceedings do not necessarily void an agency decision. The Civil Service Reform Act requires that FRLA (D) hearings be conducted in accordance with the Administrative Procedure Act. As such, ex parte communications with interested parties during agency adjudications are prohibited if they are not made public and are relevant to the merits of the proceeding. Disclosure of ex parte communications can usually solve any problems that may arise since it prevents the appearance of any impropriety. Thus, it is often the first remedy. If it isn't sufficient, the violating party may have to show cause why the proceeding should not be dismissed or denied on account of the violation. Thus, agency proceedings that have been blemished by ex parte communications are voidable based on whether the process was irrevocably tainted so as to make the ultimate judgment unfair. There are no mechanical rules to apply; rather, each case must be looked at given the surrounding circumstances. In the present case, there is insufficient reason to vacate the FRLA decision. While the ex parte communications at issue should have been disclosed, there does not appear to be any evidence that the proceedings were prejudiced against PATCO (D). Authority's decision affirmed.

EDITOR'S ANALYSIS: The court looked closely at three contacts with the FRLA (P) board members. As it turned out, the court had the most problem with a dinner between a different union's leader who tried to convince the board member not to severely punish the union. The court found this totally unacceptable behavior but obviously found that no party had benefitted from this contact.

QUICKNOTES

EX PARTE - A proceeding commenced by one party without providing any opposing parties with notice or which is uncontested by an adverse party.

ADMINISTRATIVE PROCEDURE ACT § 557(D) - Governs ex parte communications in agency proceedings.

CIVIL SERVICE REFORM ACT - Requires that the FRLA conduct hearings in accordance with the APA.

NOTES:

LONDONER v. DENVER

Property owner (P) v. City council (D)

210 U.S. 373 (1908).

NATURE OF CASE: Appeal of a tax assessment.

FACT SUMMARY: Londoner (P) contended the Denver City Council (D) denied him due process by imposing an assessment of paving costs without notice and an evidentiary hearing.

CONCISE RULE OF LAW: Due process requires that before a tax set by an agency becomes irrevocably fixed, the taxpayer be afforded notice and an opportunity to participate in an oral evidentiary hearing.

FACTS: The Denver City Council (D), under statutory authority, approved an assessment on Londoner's (P) property for the costs of paving a public street. Before approving the assessment the Council (D) gave notice to Londoner and afforded an opportunity to file written objections to the assessment. Londoner's (P) objections consisted of allegations that the hearing procedures, precluding the presentation of evidence, denied due process. The Colorado courts rejected Londoner's (P) contentions, and the Supreme Court took jurisdiction.

ISSUE: Does due process require that before a tax is irrevocably set by an agency the taxpayers be afforded notice and an opportunity to participate in an oral evidentiary hearing?

HOLDING AND DECISION: (Moody, J.) Yes. Due process requires that before a tax is set by an agency the taxpayers be afforded notice and an opportunity to participate in an evidentiary hearing. While there are few constitutional restrictions on a state legislature's power to tax, there are limitations imposed where this power is delegated to an administrative agency. In such a case, as here, more than an opportunity to tender written objections to the tax is required by due process. The taxpayer must be allowed to present evidence in support of his allegations, and an opportunity to participate in oral argument. The failure to afford such opportunities in this case renders the assessments invalid as adopted through a denial of due process. Reversed.

EDITOR'S ANALYSIS: This case illustrates the general requirement that agencies exercising taxation or economic regulation follow formal procedures. This requirement can have several sources including the agency's enabling statute, its own procedural requirements, the Administrative Procedure Act, federal common law, and judicial decisions.

[For more information on the adjudication requirement, see Casenote Law Outline on Administrative Law, Chapter 4, Internal Decisionmaking Processes, §I, The First Step in Analyzing a Question About Internal Process.]

QUICKNOTES

PROCEDURAL DUE PROCESS - The constitutional mandate that if the state or federal government acts so as to deny a citizen of a life, liberty or property interest the individual is first entitled to notice and the right to be heard.

NOTICE - Communication of information to a person by an authorized person or an otherwise proper source.

EVIDENTIARY HEARING - Hearing pertaining to the evidence of the case.

NOTES:

BI-METALLIC INVESTMENT COMPANY v. STATE BOARD OF EQUALIZATION

Property owner (P) v. State board (D)

239 U.S. 441 (1915).

NATURE OF CASE: Suit to enjoin enforcement of administrative order.

FACT SUMMARY: Bi-Metallic Investment Co. (P) sued Colorado (D) to enjoin enforcement of an order increasing property taxes in Denver. Bi-Metallic (P) argued that it was entitled to an opportunity to be heard in opposition to the order.

CONCISE RULE OF LAW: Where an agency rule will apply to a vast number of people, the Constitution does not require that each be given an opportunity to be heard directly for the purpose of arguing in favor of or against its adoption.

FACTS: The Colorado Tax Commission (D) and the State Board of Equalization (D) ordered a 41% increase in the valuation of all taxable property in the city of Denver. Bi-Metallic Investment Co. (P), the owner of certain real estate in Denver, sought to enjoin enforcement of the order. It argued that it had been afforded no opportunity to be heard in opposition to the order, and was thus threatened with deprivation of property without due process of law. The Supreme Court of Colorado ordered dismissal of Bi-Metallic's (P) claim, and Bi-Metallic (P) appealed to the United States Supreme Court.

ISSUE: Are all property owners entitled to an opportunity to be heard prior to adoption of an administrative order which increases property taxes?

HOLDING AND DECISION: (Holmes, J.) No. Agency orders and rules which will affect vast numbers of people may be adopted without affording every interested party a direct opportunity to be heard. In cases such as the present one, it would be impractical to allow all individuals affected to offer a direct voice in support of or in opposition to an order. Thus, the Constitution is satisfied by the fact that, as voters, the taxpayers involved exercise power, remote or direct, over those responsible for the order. Accordingly, the judgment of the state supreme court dismissing this suit must be affirmed.

EDITOR'S ANALYSIS: The result of this case is opposite to that reached in Londoner v. Denver. However, the apparent conflict between the two cases is explained by the observation that Bi-Metallic involved so-called "legislative" facts whereas Londoner was a case which presented an issue requiring evaluation of "adjudicative" facts. "Legislative" facts are those which primarily involve determinations of broad policies or principles of general application, e.g., whether every tract of land in a large city has been under-assessed for property tax purposes. In resolving issues pertaining to "legislative" as opposed to "adjudicative" facts, administrative agencies may dispense with the practice of according every interested party an opportunity to be heard.

[For more information on the rulemaking process, see Casenote Law Outline on Administrative Law, Chapter 4, Internal Decisionmaking Processes, §I, The First Step in Analyzing a Question About Internal Process.]

QUICKNOTES

RULEMAKING - The promulgation of a rule governing a particular activity by an administrative agency, acting within the scope of its power pursuant to statute.

ADMINISTRATIVE ORDER - The final disposition of an administrative hearing or the interpretation or application of a statute.

NOTES:

BOARD OF REGENTS v. ROTH

School administrator (D) v. Professor (P)

408 U.S. 564 (1972).

NATURE OF CASE: Suit to set aside an action of a state agency.

FACT SUMMARY: Roth's (P) contract as a college professor was not renewed by the Wisconsin Board of Regents of State Colleges (D).

CONCISE RULE OF LAW: The state need not hold hearings or offer reasons for its employment decisions.

FACTS: Roth (P) was hired to a one-year term of employment as an assistant professor at Wisconsin State University — Oshkosh. At the conclusion of that one year, he was informed by that university's president that his contract would not be renewed. According to state law, nontenured professors such as Roth (P) could be terminated without any hearing or explanation, and it was by this summary procedure that he was dismissed. Roth (P), however, filed suit against the Board of Regents of State Colleges (D), alleging that he was entitled by the Constitution to a pretermination hearing and statement of the reasons for his dismissal. In addition, he contended that he had been terminated solely because of his exercise of his right to free speech. The district court sustained Roth's (P) contention that he was entitled to the requisites of procedural due process. The court of appeals affirmed, whereupon the Supreme Court granted certiorari.

ISSUE: Are state employees entitled to a hearing and a statement of the reasons for the state's employment decisions?

HOLDING AND DECISION: (Stewart, J.) No. A state employee may not insist that the state hold hearings or offer reasons for its failure to rehire him after his initial term of employment has expired. Due process must be accorded only when an individual is threatened with deprivation of either liberty or property. Failure to rehire an employee does not abridge his liberty, unless, of course, in so doing, his employer stigmatizes him in such fashion as will restrict his freedom to seek employment elsewhere. Similarly, a contract of employment for a specific term confers upon an employee no legitimate claim to subsequent employment sufficient to constitute a property right. Accordingly, Roth (P) has made no showing that either his property or his liberty was at stake when the Board (D) acted. Therefore, he has failed to establish a right to the guarantees of procedural due process.

EDITOR'S ANALYSIS: The government may fire or refuse to hire an employee, unless, in so doing, it stigmatizes him in a way which seriously forecloses future employment opportunities or deprives him of employment to which he had shown himself entitled as a matter of right, contractual or otherwise. It is doubtful, however, whether the government may dispense with the elements of due process when its basis for firing or not hiring an employee is itself unconstitutional, i.e., when it is related to the applicant's race, sex, religion, etc. In this connection, it may be noted that the Court expressly declined to consider whether the petitioner would have merited a hearing on the contention that he had been discharged for exercising his right to free speech, an issue which the Supreme Court believed itself to be foreclosed from considering.

[For more information on opportunity to be heard, see Casenote Law Outline on Administrative Law, Chapter 4, Internal Decisionmaking Process § III, The Due Process Clause Establishes a Constitutional Right to an "Opportunity to be Heard."]

QUICKNOTES

DUE PROCESS - The constitutional mandate requiring the courts to protect and enforce individuals' rights and liberties consistent with prevailing principals of fairness and justice and prohibiting the federal and state governments from such activities that deprive its citizens of a life, liberty or property interest.

NOTES:

PAUL v. DAVIS

Police chief (D) v. Alleged shoplifter (P)

424 U.S. 693 (1976).

NATURE OF CASE: Appeal from decision in a claim under 42 U.S.C. § 1983 of the Fourteenth Amendment of the United States Constitution.

FACT SUMMARY: Davis (P) sued Paul (D), the police chief of Louisville, Kentucky, and McDaniel (D), the police chief in Jefferson County, Kentucky, seeking redress for an alleged violation of his constitutional rights.

CONCISE RULE OF LAW: In enacting 42 U.S.C. § 1983, Congress should not be understood to have attempted to make all torts of state officials federal crimes.

FACTS: Police Chiefs Paul (D) and McDaniel (D) alerted local area merchants to possible shoplifters who might be operating during the 1972 Christmas season. They distributed a flyer to approximately 800 merchants in the Louisville area that consisted of five pages of "mug shot" photos of active shoplifters. Davis's (P) picture appeared in the flyer because on June 14, 1971, he had been arrested in Louisville on a shoplifting charge. Davis (P) was arraigned on the charge, pled not guilty, and the charge was filed away with leave to reinstate, which left the charge outstanding. Thus, at the time Paul (D) circulated the flyer, Davis (P) had been charged with shoplifting, but his guilt or innocence had not been resolved. Shortly after circulation of the flyer, the charge against Davis (P) was dismissed. Davis (P) then sued Paul (D) and McDaniel (D) in U.S. district court, alleging a § 1983 violation of his constitutional rights. Davis (P) sought damages as well as declaratory and injunctive relief. The Sixth Circuit Court of Appeals concluded that he had set forth a § 1983 claim because he alleged facts that constituted a denial of due process of law. Paul (D) and McDaniel (D) appealed.

ISSUE: In enacting 42 U.S.C. § 1983, should Congress be understood to have attempted to make all torts of state officials federal crimes?

HOLDING AND DECISION: (Rehnquist, J.) No. In enacting 42 U.S.C. § 1983, Congress should not be understood to have attempted to make all torts of state official's federal crimes. Davis (P) asserts that the flyer impermissibly deprived him of some "liberty" protected by the Fourteenth Amendment. He contends that the designation "active shoplifter" that was applied to him in the flyer would inhibit him from entering business establishments for fear of being suspected of shoplifting, and, if apprehended, would seriously impair his future employment opportunities. Davis (P) would appear to state a classical claim for defamation actionable in the courts of almost every state. Imputing criminal behavior to an individual is generally considered defamation per se and actionable without proof of special damages. Davis (P), however, brought this action in federal district court and claimed deprivation of Fourteenth Amendment rights. A study of our decisions convinces us that they do not support Davis's (P) claim. Davis (P) has pointed to no specific constitutional guarantees safeguarding the interest he asserts to have been invaded and apparently believes that the Due Process Clause of the Fourteenth Amendment should, by its own force, extend to him a right to be free of injury wherever the State may be characterized as the tortfeasor. We disagree. The words "liberty" and "property" as used in the Fourteenth Amendment do not single out reputation as a candidate for special protection, and we hold that the interest in reputation asserted here is neither "liberty" nor "property" guaranteed by against state deprivation without due process of law. Reversed.

DISSENT: (Brennan, J.) The stark fact here is that the police have officially imposed on Davis (P) the stigmatizing label "criminal" without the salutary and constitutionally mandated safeguards of a criminal trial. Our precedents clearly mandate that a person's interest in his good name and reputation is cognizable as a liberty interest within the meaning of the Due Process Clause, and the Court has simply failed to distinguish those precedents in any rational manner in holding that no invasion of a "liberty" interest was effected in the official stigmatizing of Davis (P) as a criminal without any "process" whatsoever.

EDITOR'S ANALYSIS: The majority opinion above noted that there existed a variety of interests that were difficult to define but were still comprehended within the meaning of either "liberty" or "property" as meant by the Due Process Clause. These interests attained their constitutional status because they had been initially recognized and protected by state law and that the U.S. Supreme Court had repeatedly ruled that the procedural guarantees of the Fourteenth Amendment applied whenever the State sought to remove or significantly alter that protected status. In each of these cases, as a result of the state action complained of, a right or status previously recognized by state law was distinctly altered or extinguished, and it was this official removal of the interest from the recognition and protection previously afforded by the State that invoked the procedural guarantees in the Due Process Clause of the Fourteenth Amendment.

[For more information on adjudication and due process hearing rights, see Casenote Law Outline on Administrative Law, Chapter 4, Internal Decisionmaking Processes, § III, The Doctine of "Separation of Functions."]

NOTES:

CODD v. VELGER

Employer (D) v. Employee (P)
429 U.S. 624 (1977).

NATURE OF CASE: Appeal from denial of agency employment hearing.

FACT SUMMARY: Velger (P) was dismissed as a police officer and claimed he was due a hearing because of stigmatizing information placed in his file.

CONCISE RULE OF LAW: Hearings mandated by the Due Process Clause are only required when there is a clear factual dispute.

FACTS: Velger (P) was a police officer in New York City in a probationary position. He was dismissed, apparently because he had put a gun to his head in a suicide attempt. Velger (P) then obtained a job with the Penn-Central Railroad Police Department, but was dismissed when a Penn-Central officer was shown his New York City file. Velger (P), who ordinarily wasn't entitled to a hearing as probationary employee, claimed that a hearing was required because of the stigmatizing information in his file that prevented him from finding similar employment. The court decided that Velger (P) did not prove that he had been stigmatized and Velger (P) appealed. The court of appeals held that the finding of no stigma was clearly erroneous. This court granted certiorari.

ISSUE: Are hearings mandated by the Due Process Clause only required when there is a clear factual dispute?

HOLDING AND DECISION: [Per curiam.] Yes. Hearings mandated by the Due Process Clause are only required when there is a clear factual dispute. Whether the report in Velger's (P) file was stigmatizing need not be determined in this case because Velger (P) has failed to prove another essential element. Nowhere in the pleadings is there any assertion that the report of the suicide attempt is substantially false. The absence of this allegation is fatal to any claim or request for a hearing. If there is no factual dispute at issue, the hearing usually required by the Due Process Clause would be rendered meaningless. Thus, Velger (P) is not entitled to a hearing.

DISSENT: (Stewart, J.) The purpose of a hearing is two-fold. First, it is to establish the truth or falsity of the charges, and second, to also provide a basis for deciding what action is warranted. Even if the charge is clearly true, procedural safeguards still must be observed.

EDITOR'S ANALYSIS: The dissent made a valid point when it said that the government should carry the burden in these instances. Justice Stewart argued that the agency employer should at least have to show that the denial of due process was harmless error. It is unclear from the majority opinion just how much Velger (P) would have to allege regarding the facts in order to sufficiently justify the hearing.

QUICKNOTES

DUE PROCESS CLAUSE - Clauses found in the Fifth and Fourteenth Amendments to the United States Constitution providing that no person shall be deprived of "life, liberty, or property, without due process of law."

NOTES:

SHANDS v. CITY OF KENNETT

Volunteer fireman (P) v. City government (D)
993 F.2d 1337 (8th Cir. 1993).

NATURE OF CASE: Appeal from judgment notwithstanding the verdict in action for deprivation of due process.

FACT SUMMARY: Several volunteer firemen (P) were dismissed from their positions and claimed they were deprived of their constitutional rights without due process.

CONCISE RULE OF LAW: Government employees are entitled to procedural due process in connection with employment discharges only when they have been deprived of a constitutionally protected liberty or property interest.

FACTS: The Kennett City Council (D) dismissed several volunteer firemen (P) when they undermined the authority of the Fire Chief with respect to another employment decision. At a city council (D) meeting, the dismissed firemen told their side of the case and were allowed to question some witnesses. Still, the council (D) voted not to reinstate them and released a statement that the men (P) had not been dismissed for any illegal or immoral activities but rather, as the result of personnel matters. The dismissed firemen (P) then filed suit alleging that there had been false and stigmatizing statements made against them to the media and that they were entitled to a fair hearing in order to clear their names. The firemen (P) earned a favorable verdict but the court granted Kennett's (D) motion for judgment notwithstanding the verdict and the firemen (P) appealed.

ISSUE: Are government employees entitled to procedural due process in connection with employment discharges only when they have been deprived of a consttitutionally protected liberty or property interest?

HOLDING AND DECISION: (Wollman, J.) Yes. Government employees are entitled to procedural due process in connection with employment discharges only when they have been deprived of a constitutionally protected liberty or property interest. To establish a protected liberty interest, a dismissed government employee must show that an official publicly made untrue charges that would stigmatize him so as to seriously damage the employee's standing in the community or prevent further employment. In the present case, the only public statements on the record about the dismissed firemen (P) expressly said that the dismissals were for "personnel" reasons and for being "insubordinate" to an order of city policy. These statements did not create the level of stigma that implicates a constitutionally protected liberty interest. The requisite stigma has generally been found in cases involving accusations of dishonesty, immorality, criminality or racism. A mere charge of insubordination is insufficient. Accordingly, the dismissed firemen (P) were not entitled to a hearing regarding their dismissal. Affirmed.

EDITOR'S ANALYSIS: There are often two steps to the due process claim. If a court decides that a hearing was required, it must then be decided what that entails. Sometimes, an administrative hearing is necessary. Other times, the courts have found that a fuller trial-type proceeding with notice and evidentiary rulings is required.

QUICKNOTES

DUE PROCESS - The constitutional mandate requiring the courts to protect and enforce individuals' rights and liberties consistent with prevailing principals of fairness and justice and prohibiting the federal and state governments from such activities that deprive its citizens of a life, liberty or property interest.

JUDGMENT NOTWITHSTANDING THE VERDICT - A judgment entered by the trial judge reversing a jury verdict if the jury's determination has no basis in law or fact.

NOTES:

MATHEWS v. ELDRIDGE
Social security administration (D) v.
Disability benefits recipient (P)
424 U.S. 319 (1976).

NATURE OF CASE: Appeal concerning constitutional validity of procedures on termination of disability benefits.

FACT SUMMARY: Eldridge (P) had his disability benefits terminated and brought suit.

CONCISE RULE OF LAW: The Due Process Clause does not require a hearing prior to termination of disability benefits.

FACTS: The state agency and the Social Security Administration (D) terminated Eldridge's (P) disability benefits. The relevant administrative procedure was the provision of the opportunity for a claimant to assert his claim prior to any administrative action, a right to an evidentiary hearing, and subsequent judicial review before the claim became final. Instead of requesting reconsideration, Eldridge (P) commenced an action challenging the constitutional validity of the administrative procedures. The district court held that the administrative procedures pursuant to which Eldridge's (P) benefits had been terminated abridged his right to procedural due process. The court of appeals affirmed. The dispute centered on what kind of procedure was required when benefits were initially terminated, pending review. The courts below held that due process required an evidentiary hearing prior to termination.

ISSUE: Does the Due Process Clause require a hearing prior to termination of disability benefits?

HOLDING AND DECISION: (Powell, J.) No. The Due Process Clause does not require a hearing prior to termination of disability benefits. Only in Goldberg v. Kelly, 397 U.S. 254 (1970), has this Court held that due process requires an evidentiary hearing prior to a temporary deprivation because in that case it was emphasized that welfare assistance is given to persons on the very margin of subsistence. Eligibility for disability benefits, on the other hand, is not based on financial need. The probable value of additional procedural safeguards is not that great because termination of disability benefits turn on the routine medical reports of physicians. In considering the public interest, experience with the constitutionalizing of government procedures suggests that the ultimate additional cost in terms of money and administrative burden would be substantial. The judgment of the court of appeals is reversed.

EDITOR'S ANALYSIS: The Supreme Court took on the issue of what due process procedures apply in the case of the revocation of a driver's license according to the three factors weighed in Mathews above. It held that: (1) a driver's license is not as important as welfare; (2) the possibility of a mistake where there is no hearing before revocation is small; (3) a prior hearing would not be administratively efficient and thus is probably contrary to the public interest. Held: no prior hearing required. Gellhorn, W., Admin. Law, at 508-509.

[For more information on due process requirements, see Casenote Law Outline on Administrative Law, Chapter 4, Internal Decisionmaking Process, § IV, Due Process Requires "Some Kind of Hearing."]

QUICKNOTES

DUE PROCESS - The constitutional mandate requiring the courts to protect and enforce individuals' rights and liberties consistent with prevailing principals of fairness and justice and prohibiting the federal and state governments from such activities that deprive its citizens of a life, liberty or property interest.

NOTES:

BOARD OF CURATORS OF THE UNIVERSITY OF MISSOURI v. HOROWITZ

State university (D) v. Medical school student (P)

435 U.S. 78 (1978).

NATURE OF CASE: Appeal from reinstatement of action protesting a student's dismissal from school.

FACT SUMMARY: When Horowitz (P) was dismissed from medical school for unsatisfactory performance, she filed suit, alleging that the Board of Curators (D) had not accorded her procedural due process.

CONCISE RULE OF LAW: A formal hearing is not required to dismiss a student for unsatisfactory performance based on the academic judgement of school officials.

FACTS: As Horowitz (P) progressed through medical school, several faculty members expressed dissatisfaction with her clinical performance during her first year. Faculty dissatisfaction with her performance continued during the following year. The Council on Evaluation finally recommended that, absent radical improvement, Horowitz (P) be dropped from school. Horowitz (P) was permitted to take a set of oral and practical examinations as an "appeal" of the eventual decision not to permit her to graduate. Only two of seven practicing physicians in the area who evaluated Horowitz (P) recommended that she be graduated on schedule. Following her dismissal, Horowitz (P) filed suit, alleging she had not been accorded procedural due process prior to that dismissal. After a trial, the district court dismissed her complaint. The court of appeals reversed. The University's Board of Curators (D) appealed.

ISSUE: Is a formal hearing required to dismiss a student for unsatisfactory performance based on the academic judgement of school officials?

HOLDING AND DECISION: (Rehnquist, J.) No. A formal hearing is not required to dismiss a student for unsatisfactory performance based on the academic judgement of school officials. The ultimate decision to dismiss Horowitz (P) was careful and deliberate. These procedures were sufficient under the Due Process Clause of the Fourteenth Amendment. The determination whether to dismiss a student for academic reasons requires an expert evaluation of cumulative information and is not readily adapted to the procedural tools of judicial or administrative decision-making. There is no reason to further enlarge the judicial presence in the academic community and thereby risk deterioration of many beneficial aspects of the faculty-student relationship. Reversed.

EDITOR'S ANALYSIS: The Court referred to its prior decision in Gos. v. Lopez, 419 U.S. 565 (1975), in making a distinction between students who are dismissed for disciplinary purposes and those who are dismissed for academic reasons. In Goss, the Court felt that suspensions of students for disciplinary reasons have a sufficient resemblance to traditional judicial and administrative factfinding to call for a "hearing" before the relevant school authority. Even in the context of a school disciplinary proceeding, however, the Court stopped short of requiring a formal hearing.

[For more information on how much process is due, see Casenote Law Outline on Administrative Law, Chapter 4, Internal Decisionmaking Processes, § IV, Due Process Requires "Some Kind of Hearing."]

QUICKNOTES

FOURTEENTH AMENDMENT - Declares that no state shall make or enforce any law which shall abridge the privileges and immunities of citizens of the United States.

PROCEDURAL DUE PROCESS - The constitutional mandate that if the state or federal government acts so as to deny a citizen of a life, liberty or property interest the individual is first entitled to notice and the right to be heard.

NOTES:

OSTEEN v. HENLEY

Student (P) v. University (D)

13 F.3d 221 (7th Cir. 1993).

NATURE OF CASE: Appeal from school's decision to expel student.

FACT SUMMARY: Osteen (P) was expelled for two years from Northern Illinois University (D) for fighting.

CONCISE RULE OF LAW: There is no constitutional right to counsel in student disciplinary proceedings.

FACTS: Osteen (P), a football player at Northern Illinois University (D), hit two students and broke their noses after an argument involving his friends. Osteen (P) admitted his guilt to the charges at a meeting with the University's (D) judicial officer, but requested a hearing regarding the proposed sanction. At the hearing, Osteen (P) was represented by a student advocate, but the appeals board approved the recommended two-year expulsion, as did the University's (D) vice-president. Osteen (P) sought judicial review of this decision.

ISSUE Is there a constitutional right to counsel in student disciplinary hearings?

HOLDING AND DECISION: (Posner, C.J.) No. There is no constitutional right to counsel in student disciplinary proceedings. The application of the Due Process Clause to student disciplinary hearings has not been resolved definitively by the courts. However, it is at least arguable that when faced with serious charges, a student is entitled to consult with a lawyer. But there does not seem to be any right to have a lawyer perform the traditional functions of a trial lawyer at the proceeding. To recognize that right would force disciplinary hearings into the mold of adversary litigation and would severely increase their cost and complexity. Since there is no real danger that schools will engage in unwarranted expulsions without this right, there is no reason to think that students' rights will be violated. Furthermore, the consequence to a student such as Osteen (P), who may still enroll in other colleges, is not so severe as to entitle him to litigation-type procedural protections. Therefore, Osteen's (P) claim for review is denied.

EDITOR'S ANALYSIS: The court went on to note that it doubted that any student disciplinary hearing could rise to the level requiring the right of counsel. The decision also rejected Osteen's (P) claim that the interruption of himself and his advocate at the hearing by the board was a denial of due process. The court found that the interruptions only related to times where Osteen (P) was attempting to revisit the issue of guilt.

QUICKNOTES

DUE PROCESS CLAUSE - Clauses found in the Fifth and Fourteenth Amendments to the United States Constitution providing that no person shall be deprived of "life, liberty, or property, without due process of law."

NOTES:

WITHROW v. LARKIN

Medical board (D) v. Physician (P)

421 U.S. 35 (1975).

NATURE OF CASE: Appeal from a license revocation order.

FACT SUMMARY: The district court held that the Wisconsin Medical Examining Board's (D) suspension of Larkin's medical license at its own hearing on charges evolving from its own investigation constituted a denial of procedural due process as the agency was performing both adjudicative and investigative functions on the same case.

CONCISE RULE OF LAW: The performance of both prosecutorial and adjudicative functions by the same agency officials is not per se a denial of due process.

FACTS: The Wisconsin Medical Examining Board (D) held an investigative hearing to determine whether Larkin (P) had committed certain proscribed acts within his medical practice. As a result of the investigation, the Board (D) notified Larkin (P) that it would hold a contested hearing to determine whether his medical license should be suspended. Larkin (P) brought suit to enjoin the contested hearing on the basis that it was improper for the Board (D) to adjudicate the same case it had investigated. The district court granted the injunction holding that the Board (D) could not properly rule on the same charges it investigates. The Board (D) appealed.

ISSUE: Is the performance of both investigatory and adjudicative functions by the same agency officials per se a denial of due process?

HOLDING AND DECISION: (White, J.) No. The performance of both investigatory and adjudicative functions by the same agency officials is not per se a denial of due process. There is a presumption of honesty and integrity in adjudications. As a result, the performance of these two functions is not a denial of due process unless this presumption is overcome by a showing of bias on the part of those performing the dual functions of investigation and adjudication. Such bias will not be implied merely by the performance of these functions by the same entity. In this case, the only evidence offered of the impropriety of the contested hearing was the performance of both functions by the same officials. This was insufficient to constitute a denial of due process. Reversed and remanded.

EDITOR'S ANALYSIS: Some commentators argue that combining adjudicatory and prosecutorial functions, even if not inherently unconstitutional, is fundamentally unfair. An empirical study conducted by Professor Richard Posner, The Behavior of Administrative Agencies, 1 J. Legal Stud. 305 (1972), found that dismissal rates did not reflect a reluctance of agencies to dismiss complaints when performing both prosecutorial and adjudicative functions. Regardless of this empirical evidence, veteran administrators continue to argue that dual functions inhibit an agency from reaching a just conclusion.

[For more information on the "separation of functions" doctrine, see Casenote Law Outline on Administrative Law, Chapter 8, Integrity of the Internal Decisionmaking Processes, §III, The Doctrine of "Separation of Functions."]

QUICKNOTES

PROCEDURAL DUE PROCESS - The constitutional mandate that if the state or federal government acts so as to deny a citizen of a life, liberty or property interest the individual is first entitled to notice and the right to be heard.

LICENSE - A right that is granted to a person allowing him or her to conduct an activity that without such permission he or she could not lawfully do, and which is unassignable and revocable at the will of the licensor.

PER SE - An activity that is so inherently obvious that it is unnecessary to examine its underlying validity.

NOTES:

PENASQUITOS VILLAGE, INC. v. NATIONAL LABOR RELATIONS BOARD

Employer (P) v. Union (D)
565 F.2d 1074 (9th Cir. 1977).

NATURE OF CASE: Petition to review and set aside the reversal of an administrative law judge's decision in an action for wrongful discharge.

FACT SUMMARY: The NLRB (D) reversed an administrative law judge's finding that Penasquitos (P) had not engaged in coercive interrogation or wrongful discharge of employees.

CONCISE RULE OF LAW: Reviewing courts should review more critically an agency's findings of fact if they are contrary to those of the administrative law judge whose findings are based on a witness's demeanor.

FACTS: An administrative law judge found that Penasquitos (P) had not engaged in coercive interrogation of employees in violation of § 8(a)(1) of the National Labor Relations Act, 9 U.S.C. § 158(a)(1), and had not wrongfully discharged employees in violation of the Act. The NLRB (D) reversed. Penasquitos (P) petitioned the court of appeals for review, asking that the NLRB's (D) order be set aside, alleging that it was not supported by substantial evidence. The NLRB (D) cross-petitioned for enforcement.

ISSUE: Should reviewing courts review more critically an agency's findings of fact if they are contrary to those of the administrative law judge whose findings are based on a witness's demeanor?

HOLDING AND DECISION: (Wallace, J.) Yes. Reviewing courts should review more critically an agency's findings of fact if they are contrary to those of the administrative law judge whose findings are based on a witness's demeanor. All aspects of the witness's demeanor, including the expression of his countenance, how he sits or stands, whether he is inordinately nervous, his coloration during critical cross-examination, the modulation or pace of his speech and other nonverbal communication are available to the observing fact-finder for credibility determinations. These important factors are not available to the entity reviewing the transcript. The NLRB's (D) rejection of the ALJ's testimonial inferences was not supported by substantial evidence in the record. Thus, enforcement is denied and the order set aside.

CONCURRENCE AND DISSENT: (Duniway, J.) Much that is thought and said about the trier of fact as a lie detector is myth or folklore. It is not unusual for an accomplished liar to fool a jury, or even a trial judge, into believing him because his demeanor is so convincing. Anyone who really believes that he can infallibly determine credibility solely on the basis of observed demeanor is naive. The Board (D) should have more leeway in making its own findings, and in rejecting findings of its trial examiner, than this court has in reviewing the Board's (D) findings or those of a trial judge or jury.

EDITOR'S ANALYSIS: Judge Wallace made a distinction between credibility determinations based on demeanor, or what he referred to as testimonial inferences, and those based on inferences drawn from the evidence itself, derivative inferences. Judge Duniway suggested that such a dichotomy is actually based on unsupported folklore. Judge Duniway was properly concerned that decisions based on these alleged testimonial inferences would become unassailable.

[For more information on findings of fact, see Casenote Law Outline on Administrative Law, Chapter 9, Judicial Control of the Administrative Processes, § IV, Level of Review Determined by the Nature of the Controverted Issues.]

NOTES:

KOPACK v. NATIONAL LABOR RELATIONS BOARD

Truck driver (P) v. Government agency (D)

668 F.2d 946 (7th Cir. 1982).

NATURE OF CASE: Petition for review of NLRB (D) order.

FACT SUMMARY: Kopack (P) was fired for poor driving and filed a complaint claiming that his employer dismissed him in retaliation for his complaints about lack of overtime pay.

CONCISE RULE OF LAW: Findings by an ALJ that reflect an evaluation of witness demeanor are entitled to more weight on review.

FACTS: Kopack (P) worked as a truck driver at a construction site at Inland Steel. There were complaints about his poor driving for several years, but no action other than a verbal reprimand was taken. In early 1978, Kopack (P) complained about certain overtime pay provisions. In June 1978, Kopack (P) was seen speeding and failing to stop at stop signs and was discharged. He immediately filed an unfair labor practice charge and after a two-day hearing, an ALJ found that the reason for the discharge was pretextual based on the testimony presented, including what he called "exaggerations" by the company. However, the NLRB (D) overturned the decision, finding that Kopack's (P) reckless driving was the cause of the discharge. Kopack (P) petitioned for review of this decision.

ISSUE: Are findings by an ALJ that reflect an evaluation of witness demeanor entitled to more weight on review?

HOLDING AND DECISION: (Pell, J.) Yes. Findings by an ALJ that reflect an evaluation of witness demeanor are entitled to more weight on review. However, where an ALJ makes a judgement based on testimony that does not involve a witness's demeanor, the Board (D) can draw its own inferences and exercise its own discretion. In the present case, the decision of the ALJ did not turn on the credibility and demeanor of the witnesses. The ALJ explained that the history of lenient treatment of Kopack (P) and the failure to give an explanation at the time of the discharge were the key factors in finding that poor driving was a pretext. Since these factors did not involve an evaluation of demeanor, the Board (D) was entitled to its own determination that they reflected other considerations. Given the undisputed evidence that Kopack (P) did drive dangerously on many occasions, it cannot be said that the Board's (D) finding rested on testimonial evidence that was discredited by the ALJ. Thus, the Board's (D) decision is affirmed.

EDITOR'S ANALYSIS: This case presents an interesting situation. The court has to take into account that both the ALJ's finding and the Board's (D) subsequent ruling are entitled to considerable deference. The Board (D) must first defer to the ALJ and then the court must defer to the Board (D).

QUICKNOTES

PRETEXT - Ostensible reason or motive assigned or assumed as a color or cover for the real reason or motive.

NOTES:

JACKSON v. VETERANS ADMINISTRATION

Employee (P) v. Employer (D)

768 F.2d 1325 (Fed. Cir. 1985).

NATURE OF CASE: Appeal of agency employment discharge.

FACT SUMMARY: Jackson (P) was discharged from the Veterans Administration (D) due to allegations of sexual harassment of a subordinate which were disputed.

CONCISE RULE OF LAW: A board must articulate sound reasons, based on the record of evidence, when its evaluation of testimony is contrary to that of the presiding official.

FACTS: Jackson (P) worked as a supervisor in the Veterans Administration (D). He was accused of sexual harassment, involving five separate incidents of misconduct and was dismissed. A presiding official conducted a hearing and reversed the removal based on a determination that none of the incidents were established by a preponderance of the evidence. The agency requested a review and the board (D) reversed, concluding that two of the incidents were supported by the evidence. In the first incident, a subordinate employee claimed that Jackson (P) had kissed her while she was on the telephone, and the second incident involved his request for a kiss so that another employee could leave early. Jackson (P) appealed the board's ruling to this court.

ISSUE: Must a board articulate sound reasons, based on the record of evidence, when its evaluation of testimony is contrary to that of the presiding official?

HOLDING AND DECISION: (Nies, J.) Yes. A board must articulate sound reasons, based on the record of evidence, when its evaluation of testimony is contrary to that of the presiding official. The issue is whether the board's evaluation of the weight of the evidence is reasonable and supported by substantial evidence, taking into consideration that the presiding official made a different evaluation after actually hearing the witnesses. In the present case, the presiding official decided that the first alleged incident was unproven because it came down to conflicting accounts that could not be corroborated by other witnesses. Given these circumstances, the board (D) should not have reversed the presiding official given that it was largely based on credibility determinations. However, with regard to the second alleged incident, the presiding official apparently ignored the account of a witness who corroborated the testimony and did not discredit it. Therefore, the board (D) was certainly entitled to weigh this evidence on its own and find that a preponderance of evidence showed Jackson's (P) guilt. Jackson's (P) claim for review is denied.

EDITOR'S ANALYSIS: The board must have "substantial evidence" to support its determination when there is a factual dispute. When there is a dispute as to the legal issues involved, courts may simply look to see whether the agency action at issue conforms to the applicable law. It is a more difficult matter when the dispute revolves around a matter that is not clearly legal or factual.

QUICKNOTES

PREPONDERANCE OF THE EVIDENCE - A standard of proof requiring the trier of fact to determine whether the fact sought to be established is more probable than not.

NOTES:

NATIONAL LABOR RELATIONS BOARD v. HEARST PUBLICATIONS, INC.
Labor board (P) v. News publisher (D)
322 U.S. 111 (1944).

NATURE OF CASE: Appeal of an NLRB bargaining order.

FACT SUMMARY: The NLRB (P) found that newsboys selling Hearst (D) newspapers were employees under the NLRA and, therefore, Hearst (D) was ordered to engage in collective bargaining with their representative.

CONCISE RULE OF LAW: A reviewing court must accept an agency's application of a broad statutory term if such application is supported in the record and has a reasonable basis in law.

FACTS: Several Hearst (D) newspapers were distributed in Los Angeles through vendors, called newsboys. The price at which the newsboys bought the papers from Hearst (D) and the price they could charge the public were set by Hearst (D). The location, conditions, and hours within which the papers could be sold were determined either expressly or implicitly by Hearst (D). The newsboys organized to bargain collectively, claiming they were "employees" under the NLRA. Hearst (D) refused to bargain, contending the newsboys were independent contractors and therefore not protected by the NLRA. The NLRB (P) concluded the newsboys were employees and ordered Hearst (D) to bargain. The court of appeals made an independent evaluation of the record and found the newsboys were independent contractors. The NLRB (P) appealed.

ISSUE: Must a reviewing court accept an agency's application of a broad statutory term if such application is supported in the record and has a reasonable basis in law?

HOLDING AND DECISION: (Rutledge, J.) Yes. A reviewing court must accept an agency's application of a broad statutory term if such application is supported in the record and has a reasonable basis in the law. Congress has vested the duty of administering the NLRA in the NLRB (P). The NLRB's (P) experience in dealing with labor matters makes it a logical choice to determine the application of broad statutory terms within the context of national labor policy. Therefore, the NLRB's (P) application of the term "employee" within the present context must be upheld if supported in the record and if reasonably based in law. The measure of control over the newsboy's activities exercised by Hearst (D) is sufficient evidence for the NLRB (P) to conclude the existence of an employer-employee relationship under recognized legal principles. Therefore, the court of appeals improperly substituted its own application of the term. Reversed.

EDITOR'S ANALYSIS: In Gary v. Powell, 314 U.S. 402 (1941), the Court laid the foundation for Hearst. It held that where a term's definition is delegated to an agency, the development of the definition will be upheld in respect of the delegation. After the Hearst decision, Congress amended the NLRA to exclude persons having a common law independent contractor status. In Hearst, the court of appeals holding of independent contractor status was based on common law interpretations, while the NLRB's determination of employee status was a modification of the common law idea of independent contractor status as equivalent to employee status under the NLRA.

[For more information on covert review of mixed questions of law and fact, see Casenote Law Outline on Administrative Law, Chapter 9, Judicial Control of the Administrative Processes, §IV, Level of Review Determined by the Nature of the Controverted Issues.]

QUICKNOTES

DELEGATION - The authorization of one person to act on another's behalf.

QUESTION OF LAW - An issue regarding the legal significance of a particular act or event, which is usually left to the judge to ascertain.

QUESTION OF FACT - An issue relating to a factual assertion that is disputed at trial and left to the jury to resolve.

INDEPENDENT CONTRACTOR - A party undertaking a particular assignment for another who retains control over the manner in which it is executed.

NOTES:

EVENING STAR NEWSPAPER COMPANY v. KEMP

Employer (P) v. Employee (D)

533 F.2d 1224 (D.C. Cir. 1976).

NATURE OF CASE: Appeal of order awarding benefits to widow of employee.

FACT SUMMARY: Kemp (D) was killed by his own gun while on the job for Evening Star (D) but not engaged with company business.

CONCISE RULE OF LAW: Decisions by Administrative Law Judges should be upheld on judicial review, unless they are irrational or unsupported by substantial evidence on the record.

FACTS: Kemp (D) was employed by Evening Star (P) as a truck driver who delivered newspapers. Between delivery runs early in the mornings, there was an hour of time where Kemp (D) was "on the clock" but allowed to do whatever he wanted. On August 10, 1971, Kemp (D) was working on his own car in a garage where the Evening Star (P) mechanics worked during this hour period. A friend began playing with a gun that Kemp (D) kept in his own car and accidentally killed Kemp (D). At a hearing before an ALJ to determine whether Kemp's widow (D) was entitled to compensation under a worker's compensation law, the ALJ found for the widow (D) because Kemp's death occurred in the course of his employment. The Department of Labor's Benefits Review Board affirmed and Evening Star (P) appealed.

ISSUE: Should decisions by Administrative Law Judges be upheld on judicial review, unless they are irrational or unsupported by substantial evidence on the record?

HOLDING AND DECISION: (Van Pelt, J.) Yes. Decisions by Administrative Law Judges should be upheld on judicial review, unless they are irrational or unsupported by substantial evidence on the record. The role of judicial review of agency adjudications is not to make independent decisions based on its own evaluation, but rather only to make sure that the decision was not arbitrary and capricious. In the present case, the ALJ expressly found that Kemp (D) was killed during an enforced lull, a condition required by the employment. His presence at the garage was clearly acquiesced in by Evening Star (P) and the ALJ found that the handgun that killed Kemp (D) was sometimes carried by him for protection while delivering newspapers. Given these findings, it cannot be said the activity that Kemp (D) was engaged in was so totally unreasonable to sever the connection between the employee and the employment. Thus, the ALJ's ruling was not unreasonable and unsupported by the evidence. Accordingly, it must be affirmed.

DISSENT: (Danaher, J.) Kemp (D) was not engaged at the time of the injury in an activity of benefit to Evening Star (P). Thus, his death did not arise out of the employment.

EDITOR'S ANALYSIS: The dissent pointed out the ALJ seemed to go out of its way to develop a record that would support compensation for the widow (D). The dissent noted that it felt that many of the facts puts on the record were hardly relevant. The majority, on the other hand, seemed to more concerned with deferring to the factual record and findings.

QUICKNOTES

JUDICIAL REVIEW - The authority of the courts to review decisions, actions or omissions committed by another agency or branch of government.

NOTES:

DURRAH v. WASHINGTON METROPOLITAN AREA TRANSIT AUTHORITY

Employee (P) v. Employer (D)

760 F.2d 322 (D.C. Cir. 1985).

NATURE OF CASE: Petition for review of denial of benefits claim.

FACT SUMMARY: Durrah (P) was a special police officer for the WMATA (D) and was injured when he left his guard post to buy a soda.

CONCISE RULE OF LAW: Employees need not be engaged directly in an activity to the benefit of the employer at the time of an injury to be entitled to workers compensation.

FACTS: Durrah (P) worked as a special police officer for the WMATA (D) and was posted at a guard post during the overnight shift at a large bus depot. At 4:00 a.m., Durrah (P) left his spot to buy a soda from a vending machine in the employees' lounge on the premises. Durrah (P) was supposed to obtain a substitute to cover his post when he took such a break but failed to do so on this occasion. On returning to his post, Durrah (P) slipped on a staircase and injured his knee. His claim for benefits was denied by an ALJ because he had left his post without permission. The Benefits Review Board affirmed the ALJ, also decision this basis. Durrah (P) petitioned for review.

ISSUE: Do employees need to be engaged directly in an activity to the benefit of the employer at the time of an injury to be entitled to worker's compensation?

HOLDING AND DECISION: (Ginsburg, J.) No. Employees need not be engaged directly in an activity to the benefit of the employer at the time of an injury to be entitled to worker's compensation. If the "obligations or conditions" of employment create a "zone of danger" out of which an injury arises, then it is covered by worker's compensation. In the present case, it is clear that even if Durrah (P) had found a replacement for his post before leaving to buy the soda, his injury still would have occurred in the same place and in the same manner. The activity of going to the employees' lounge for a break was anticipated and expected by the WMATA (D) and Durrah's (P) violation of a policy did not place him in the path of any additional risks. The injury clearly resulted from an activity that was incidental to the employment. Accordingly, the ALJ's ruling was unsupported by the law and reason behind workers compensation. Reversed and remanded.

EDITOR'S ANALYSIS: The court noted that the violation of policy fell far short of disconnecting Durrah (P) from the service of his employer. The court noted that Durrah (P) could have been disciplined in a separate proceeding. But eliminating his right to compensation was not properly at issue.

QUICKNOTES

JUDICIAL REVIEW - The authority of the courts to review decisions, actions or omissions committed by another agency or branch of government.

NOTES:

CITIZENS TO PRESERVE OVERTON PARK v. VOLPE
Memphis citizens group (P) v. Secretary of Transportation (D)
401 U.S. 402 (1971).

NATURE OF CASE: Suit to set aside administrative action.

FACT SUMMARY: A group of concerned citizens (P) sued the Secretary of Transportation (D), challenging his decision to construct a highway through a public park.

CONCISE RULE OF LAW: When reviewing administrative decisions which are not supported by formal factual findings, courts should determine the scope of the appropriate official's authority, whether that authority was abused, and whether all applicable procedural requisites have been observed.

FACTS: The Citizens to Preserve Overton Park (P) sued Secretary Volpe (D) of the Department of Transportation. He was accused of violating the Department of Transportation Act and the Federal Aid Highway Act by approving plans to construct a six-lane highway through Overton Park, a popular recreation site. The Citizens (P) assailed Volpe (D) for his failure to state the factual findings upon which he based his decision. The Citizens (P) also alleged Volpe (D) failed to explain why he believed, as required by statute, that no feasible alternative location was available and that all possible steps had been taken to minimize harm to the park. The Citizens (P) sought to have Volpe's (D) decision nullified, but the district court granted the Secretary's (D) motion for summary judgment, basing its ruling on the contents of affidavits which had been prepared specifically in response to the litigation. The court of appeals affirmed, but the Supreme Court granted a stay and agreed to review the decisions below. On appeal, the Citizens (P) sought either a de novo review of the Secretary's (D) decision or application of the substantial evidence test.

ISSUE: In reviewing administrative decisions which are unembellished by formal findings of fact, must the court confine its evaluation to the contents of affidavits submitted by the agency at trial?

HOLDING AND DECISION: (Marshall, J.) No. The reviewing court must determine the scope of the duties of the official involved in a decision, whether he abused the authority vested in him, and whether in arriving at his decision he observed all applicable procedural requisites. This case is not one in which the Court may appropriately undertake a de novo review of the Secretary's (D) decision since it presents neither a circumstance in which an adjudicatory proceeding was supported by inadequate fact-finding procedures, nor one in which new issues are raised in a proceeding to enforce nonadjudicatory agency action. Likewise, the substantial evidence test should not be applied to the Secretary's (D) action since his decision was neither the product of a public adjudicatory hearing nor an exercise of the rulemaking function. However, the applicable statutes clearly mandate that the Secretary (D) shall act only when all effective alternative sites for highway construction have been ruled out and, even then, only after taking all available steps to minimize harm to the chosen location. The Citizens (P) were entitled to a review of the Secretary's (D) deliberative processes, which took account of more evidence than that upon which the lower courts based their decisions. Therefore, it is necessary that this case be remanded for reconsideration, based on broader evidence of whether the Secretary (D) observed the required procedure of investigating alternative routes and insuring only minimal harm to Overton Park. In reviewing the Secretary's (D) decision, the district court may undertake the unusual procedure of requiring the administrative officials to reveal the thought processes used to arrive at their conclusions. Although the district court need not adopt this drastic course, it may resort to this procedure as a means of compensating for the lack of any factual findings upon which to predicate its decision. Reversed and remanded.

EDITOR'S ANALYSIS: The principal significance of Citizens to Preserve Overton Park v. Volpe rests in its concern with insuring that judicial review of administrative decisions will be meaningful. To that end, the Overton Park Court countenanced the extraordinary procedure of probing the deliberative processes of administrative officials. It seems clear that the provisions of the Administrative Procedure Act calling for judicial review of administrative determinations cannot be implemented in the absence of a record sufficient to accommodate review and, that when such a record is absent the courts must choose between ordering its compilation or undertaking their own review de novo.

[For more information on standards of review, see Casenote Law Outline on Administrative Law, Chapter 9, Judicial Control of the Administrative Processes, § II, "Standards of Review."]

QUICKNOTES

U.S.C. § 701 - Administrative actions are subject to judicial review.

JUDICIAL REVIEW - The authority of the courts to review decisions, actions or omissions committed by another agency or branch of government.

DE NOVO - The review of a lower court decision by an appellate court, which is hearing the case as if it had not been previously heard and as if no judgment had been rendered.

YEPES-PRADO v. U.S. IMMIGRATION AND NATURALIZATION SERVICE

Immigrant (P) v. Government agency (D)

10 F.3d 1363 (9th Cir. 1993).

NATURE OF CASE: Petition for review of deportation order.

FACT SUMMARY: Yepes-Prado (P) was ordered deported based on a drug conviction, but the Board of Immigration Appeals (D) failed to explain why it ignored or discounted factors in Yepes-Prado's (P) favor.

CONCISE RULE OF LAW: Agencies must offer reasoned explanations for their rulings, even if the ruling appears reasonable and plausible.

FACTS: Yepes-Prado (P) was admitted to the United States in 1974 as a lawful permanent resident. Over ten years later, he was convicted of possession of heroin with intent to distribute and sentenced to one year in jail. On the basis of this conviction, the INS (D) ordered Yepes-Prado (P) to show cause why he should not be deported. Yepes-Prado (P) conceded that he was eligible for deportation, but sought a discretionary waiver. An immigration judge found several equities weighed in his favor, but denied the waiver. The Board of Immigration Appeals (BIA) (D) found that he had "outstanding equities" but nonetheless affirmed the immigration judge's decision. Yepes-Prado (P) petitioned for review.

ISSUE: Must agencies offer reasoned explanations for their rulings, even if the ruling appears reasonable and plausible?

HOLDING AND DECISION: (Reinhardt, J.) Yes. Agencies must offer reasoned explanations for their rulings, even if the ruling appears reasonable and plausible. Discretionary relief from deportation is available to lawful permanent residents who meet a seven-year residency requirement. The factors that are relevant to this discretionary determination include family ties, hardship to the petitioner, service in the armed forces, employment history, value and service to the community, proof of rehabilitation if a criminal record exists, and evidence of the resident's good character. These are to be weighed against the underlying circumstances of the deportation, the seriousness of any criminal record, and the bad character of the resident. The BIA (D) must indicate how it weighed the factors and arrived at its conclusion. While they have considerable flexibility to make decisions, they cannot rule capriciously. This discretion is abused if conclusions are reached arbitrarily. In the present case, the immigration judge and the BIA (D) failed to offer an explanation of why the only adverse factor, Yepes-Prado's (P) drug conviction, outweighed all the other equities in his favor. Accordingly, the decision must be vacated.

EDITOR'S ANALYSIS: Apparently, the deportation decision at issue would have been upheld if the BIA (D) had simply given any reasonable explanation. The court equated providing no reason with being arbitrary. The problem was compounded in this case because there was a clear indication that many factors did favor a deportation waiver.

NOTES:

DAVILA-BARDALES v. IMMIGRATION AND NATURALIZATION SERVICE

Immigrant (P) v. Government agency (D)

27 F.3d 1 (1st Cir. 1994).

NATURE OF CASE: Petition to review deportation order.

FACT SUMMARY: Davila-Bardales (P), fifteen years old, admitted entering the United States illegally but was unrepresented while making the admission.

CONCISE RULE OF LAW: Agencies are prohibited from adopting inconsistent policies that result in conflicting lines of precedent governing identical situations.

FACTS: In July 1989, Davila-Bardales (P), then fifteen years old, entered the United States illegally. Deportation hearings were instituted by the INS (D) before an Immigration Judge. The INS (D) presented a form on which Davila-Bardales (P) admitted illegal entry into the country. The immigration judge ordered that Davila-Bardales (P) be deported, but he appealed on the ground that INS (D) regulations prohibit the use of admissions by a person under sixteen who is not represented or accompanied by a parent or guardian.

ISSUE: Are agencies prohibited from adopting inconsistent policies that result in conflicting lines of precedent governing identical situations?

HOLDING AND DECISION: (Selya, J.) Yes. Agencies are prohibited from adopting inconsistent policies that result in conflicting lines of precedent governing identical situations. The purpose of this doctrine is to prevent agencies from "significantly changing [its] policies without conscious awareness of, and consideration of the need for, change." In the present case, there is a long record of cases from the Board of Immigration Appeals showing that if the INS (D) seeks to use an admission form against a juvenile, the circumstances surrounding the form must be carefully examined. In Davila-Bardales' (P) case, the INS (D) is now insisting that the form is enough since it memorializes an interview that took place with a Border Patrol officer. While it is too much to expect that all decisions made by an agency will be identical, the position taken by the INS (D) and BIA here, that the admission form alone is enough to justify deportation, is completely at odds with its interpretation in other cases, that the circumstances behind an interview with an unrepresented juvenile are relevant. Therefore, the petition for review is granted and the case is remanded for proceedings consistent with this opinion.

EDITOR'S ANALYSIS: The INS (D) was distinguishing between admissions by juveniles regarding deportability during proceedings and admissions made at other times. That was their basis for introducing the alleged admission to the officer. But as the court noted, the BIA normally found such use suspect without more context.

QUICKNOTES

JUDICIAL REVIEW - The authority of the courts to review decisions, actions or omissions committed by another agency or branch of government.

NOTES:

Notes

CHAPTER 4
CHOICE OF PROCEDURES AND NON-LEGISLATIVE RULES

QUICK REFERENCE RULES OF LAW

1. **Choice of Adjudication Over Rulemaking.** Even when confronted with novel issues, agencies may make adjudications which are binding upon the parties to the controversy rather than announcing rules of prospective application only. (Securities and Exchange Commission v. Chenery Corp.)

   [For more information on agency ad hoc case-by-case adjudication, see Casenote Law Outline on Administrative Law, Chapter 4, § I, The First Step in Analyzing a Question About Internal Process.]

2. **Choice of Adjudication Over Rulemaking.** The NLRB is not precluded from announcing new principles in an adjudicative proceeding. (National Labor Relations Board v. Bell Aerospace Company)

3. **Concerns with Retroactive Application.** The rulemaking provisions of the Administrative Procedure Act may not be avoided by making rules in the course of adjudicatory proceedings. (National Labor Relations Board v. Wyman-Gordon)

   [For more information on policy formation and policymaking instruments, see Casenote Law Outline on Administrative Law, Chapter 7, § I, An Agency May Make General "Policy" or "Agency Law" by Adjudication or Rulemaking.]

4. **Concerns with Retroactive Application.** The retroactive application of a new agency rule depends upon a balancing of the danger of reaching a result contrary to law against the negative effect of the retroactive application. (Retail, Wholesale and Dept. Store Union v. National Labor Relations Board)

5. **Ambiguous Rules.** Agencies may not impose liability where a regulation is not sufficiently clear to provide fair notice to the affected party. (General Electric Company v. U.S. Environmental Protection Agency)

6. **Policy Statements.** Agency positions that are only statements about what a statute or regulation means are interpretative rules and exempt from notice and comment requirements. (Phillips Petroleum Co. v. Johnson)

7. **Policy Statements.** Interpretive rules are statements as to what an administrative officer thinks a statute or regulation means and are not subject to notice and comment requirements. (Metropolitan School Dist. v. Davilla)

8. **Policy Statements.** Agencies are not bound to adhere to their general statements of policy. (Brock v. Cathedral Bluffs Shale Oil Co.)

9. **Equitable Estoppel and Due Process.** Persons dealing with federal administrative agencies are charged with the knowledge of all pertinent federal regulations much as all persons are charged with knowledge of the law and, as such, when a person joins into a government contract (with a government agent) which is contrary to federal regulations, the knowledge so charged to him will prevent him from invoking the doctrine of estoppel when the government cites such regulations as a defense to an action on the contract. (Federal Crop Insurance Corp. v. Merrill)

[For more information on notice of rules, see Casenote Law Outline on Administrative Law, Chapter 7, § III, The Procedural Norm is "Notice and Comment" Rulemaking.]

10. **Equitable Estoppel and Due Process.** Regulations must provide persons and entities with fair warning of the meaning and requirements of a statute. (United States v. Pennsylvania Industrial Chemical)

11. **Equitable Estoppel and Due Process.** No money shall be drawn from the Treasury, but in consequence of appropriations made by law. (Office of Personnel Management v. Richmond)

[For more information on the reviewability of an administrative decision, see Casenote Law Outline on Administrative Law, Chapter 9, Judicial Control of the Administrative Processes, §V, Administrative Decision May Become Unreviewable.]

12. **Equitable Estoppel and Due Process.** Agencies deny due process when they apply different standards after causing persons to rely on lesser standards. (Appeal of Eno (New Hampshire Dept. of Employment Security))

13. **Judicial Deference.** In resolving a controversy which no agency has been authorized to adjudicate, the courts may consider the reports and opinions of an administrator whose duty it is to seek injunctive relief from violations of the laws involved in the controversy. (Skidmore v. Swift & Co.)

[For more information on the employment of nonlegislative rules, see Casenote Law Outline on Administrative Law, Chapter 7, Rulemaking Processes, §VIII, Certain Rules Have the Effect of Law.]

14. **Judicial Deference.** Courts must defer to reasonable agency interpretation of ambiguous statutes. (Wagner Seed Co., Inc. v. Bush)

15. **Judicial Deference.** Interpretive rules are only entitled to deference based on the validity and consistency of the agency's reasoning. (Atchison, Topeka and Santa Fe Railway Co. v. Pena)

SECURITIES AND EXCHANGE COMMISSION v. CHENERY CORP.

Government agency (D) v. Corporation (P)

332 U.S. 194 (1947).

NATURE OF CASE: Appeal from an administrative order.

FACT SUMMARY: The SEC (D) withheld approval of a corporate reorganization plan in which the Chenery Corporation (P) was a participant. A court refused to sustain the Commission's (D) order, but on remand, the SEC (D) again declined to permit operation of the proposed plan, although on the second occasion the SEC (D) cited different reasons for its order.

CONCISE RULE OF LAW: Even when confronted with novel issues, agencies may make adjudications which are binding upon the parties to the controversy rather than announcing rules of prospective application only.

FACTS: A reorganization plan for the Federal Water Service Company, a holding company registered under the Public Utility Company Act of 1935, was submitted to the Securities and Exchange Commission (SEC) (D) for approval. Officers (P), directors (P), and controlling shareholders (P) of Federal, including Chenery (P), purchased a substantial amount of Federal's preferred stock, and under the reorganization plan this stock was to be converted into common stock in a new corporation. For this reason, the plan was unacceptable to the SEC (D), which ruled that the directors (P), etc., were fiduciaries and therefore not entitled to deal in securities of the company. The SEC's (D) order was reversed by the court upon a finding that the decision lacked legal precedent. On remand, however, the SEC (D) reached the same result, this time predicating its order on the fact that it was the product of agency expertise. Chenery Corporation (P) again sought judicial review, contending that, inasmuch as the SEC (D) had acknowledged that no precedent existed for its order, it should proceed only by announcing a rule of prospective application and not by rendering an adjudication which would bind the parties to the present controversy.

ISSUE: Must agencies deal with novel issues by promulgating rules of prospective application only, or may they render adjudications which are binding upon the parties to an actual controversy as well?

HOLDING AND DECISION: (Murphy, J.) Yes. Agencies confronted with novel issues of law may announce rules of prospective application, but they may also render adjudications which are binding upon the parties to such controversies as are presented to the agency. Although the application of a ruling to a current controversy may present a retroactivity problem, the detriment of such an effect must be balanced against the agency's need to reach a satisfactory resolution of the case before it. Thus, in the present, where the SEC's (D) general experience and the facts of the case support a conclusion that the Chenery Corporation (P) should have been precluded from converting its preferred stock into common stock of a new corporation, any problem of retroactivity is outweighed by the necessity of prohibiting the proscribed conduct in the immediate case. Accordingly, the SEC (D) was not required in this case to proceed by prospective rule only, although such a procedure may ordinarily be preferable to ad hoc determinations.

EDITOR'S ANALYSIS: Although the courts apparently prefer that agencies proceed by general rulemaking rather than by ad hoc case-by-case adjudication, the latter procedure is clearly countenanced by the courts. And in rendering its decisions on an ad hoc basis, agencies are permitted a freer hand than are courts themselves. For instance, inconsistent decisions rendered by an agency may not be attacked on that basis, unless the inconsistency is so glaring as to constitute an abuse of agency discretion. And rules of res judicata have traditionally been relaxed in the agency context, although there is an apparent trend toward recognizing res judicata principles as essential elements of agency decision-making.

[For more information on agency ad hoc case-by-case adjudication, see Casenote Law Outline on Administrative Law, Chapter 4, § I, The First Step in Analyzing a Question About Internal Process.]

QUICKNOTES

AD HOC - For a specific purpose.

RES JUDICATA - The rule of law that a final judgment by a court precludes subsequent litigation between the parties regarding the same cause of action.

NOTES:

NATIONAL LABOR RELATIONS BOARD v. BELL AEROSPACE COMPANY

Government agency (D) v.
Aerospace products manufacturer (P)

416 U.S. 267 (1974).

NATURE OF CASE: Appeal from denial of enforcement of a agency order.

FACT SUMMARY: Bell (P) opposed a representation election on the grounds that its buyers were "managerial employees" and were thus not covered by the National Labor Relations Act or entitled to elect union representation.

CONCISE RULE OF LAW: The NLRB is not precluded from announcing new principles in an adjudicative proceeding.

FACTS: Bell Aerospace (P), which operated a plant engaging in research and development in the design and fabrication of aerospace products, opposed the petition of its employee buyers in the purchasing and procurement department for an election to decide whether a union would be certified as the buyers' bargaining representative. Bell (P) contended that the buyers were "managerial employees" and were not covered by the National Labor Relations Act (NLRA), and therefore, were not entitled to the NLRA's protections. The NLRB (D), after a representation hearing, issued an order holding that the buyers did constitute an appropriate unit for the purpose of collective bargaining and directed an election. An election was held and the union was certified by the NLRB (D) as the exclusive bargaining representative for Bell's (P) buyers. Bell (P), encouraged by an Eighth Circuit decision holding that "managerial employees" were not covered by the NLRA, moved the NLRB (D) for reconsideration of its order. The NLRB (D) denied the motion. Bell (P) then petitioned for review of the NLRB's (D) order, and the NLRB (D) cross-petitioned for enforcement. The Second Circuit Court of Appeals denied enforcement and the NLRB (D) appealed.

ISSUE: Is the NLRB precluded from announcing new principles in an adjudicative proceeding?

HOLDING AND DECISION: (Powell, J.) No. The NLRB (D) is not precluded from announcing new principles in an adjudicative proceeding and the choice between rulemaking and adjudication lies in the first instance within the NLRB's (D) discretion. Two questions are presented here. The first is whether the NLRB (D) properly determined that all "managerial employees" except those whose participation would create a conflict of interest with their job responsibilities are covered by the NLRA. The NLRB's (D) early decisions, the effect of the Taft-Hartley Act, the NLRB's (D) subsequent consistent construction of the NLRA for more than two decades, and the decisions of the courts of appeal all point unmistakably to the conclusion that "managerial employees" are not covered by the NLRA. The NLRB (D) is not now free to read a new and more restrictive meaning into the NLRA. The second question to be addressed is whether the NLRB (D) must proceed by rulemaking rather than by adjudication in deciding whether certain buyers are "managerial employees." Here, there is ample indication that adjudication is especially appropriate. The duties of buyers vary widely depending on the company or industry. It is doubtful whether any generalized standard could be framed that would have more than marginal utility. The NLRB (D) thus has reason to proceed with caution, developing its standards in a case-by-case manner with attention to the specific character of the buyer's authority and duties in each company. The NLRB's (D) judgment that adjudication best serves this purpose is entitled to great weight, and the NLRB (D) has discretion to decide that the adjudicative procedures in this case may also produce the relevant information necessary to mature and fair consideration of the issues. Affirmed in part and reversed and remanded in part.

EDITOR'S ANALYSIS: When the Taft-Hartley Act of 1947 was passed, both the U.S. Senate and the House of Representatives voiced concern over the NLRB's (D) broad reading of the term "employee" which then included those clearly within the managerial hierarchy. The Senate noted that unionization of supervisors had hurt productivity, increased the accident rate, upset the balance of power in collective bargaining, and tended to blur the lines between management and labor. The House echoed the concern for reduction of industrial output and noted that unionization of supervisors had deprived employers of the loyal representatives to which they were entitled.

[For more information on policymaking instruments, see Casenote Law Outline on Administrative Law, Chapter 4, § I, The First Step in Analyzing a Question About Internal Process.]

QUICKNOTES

MANAGERIAL EMPLOYEE - An employee whose duties involve the administration of the business' affairs or the supervising of the work of other employees.

SUPERVISORY EMPLOYEE - An employee authorized to implement his independent judgment in the management, direction and discipline of other employees.

TAFT-HARTLEY ACT - An amendment to the National Labor Relations Act, imposing limitations on unions and safeguarding the rights of employers.

NATIONAL LABOR RELATIONS BOARD v. WYMAN-GORDON COMPANY

Federal agency (P) v. Employer (D)

394 U.S. 759 (1969).

NATURE OF CASE: Appeal from decision invalidating agency order.

FACT SUMMARY: The National Labor Relations Board (NLRB) (P), after ordering an election among the production and maintenance employees at Wyman-Gordon Co. (W-G) (D), ordered W-G (D) to supply two unions with names and addresses of its employees, but W-G (D) refused to cooperate.

CONCISE RULE OF LAW: The rulemaking provisions of the Administrative Procedures Act may not be avoided by making rules in the course of adjudicatory proceedings.

FACTS: On petition of a union, the NLRB (P) ordered an election among the production and maintenance employees of W-G (D) to choose one of two labor unions as their exclusive bargaining representatives. In accordance with a rule it had announced in a previous adjudication, Excelsior Underware, Inc., 156 N.L.R.B. No. 111, the NLRB (P) ordered W-G (D) to furnish a list of names and addresses of its employees who could vote in the election so that the unions could use the list for election purposes. W-G (D) refused to comply, and the election was held without the list. Both unions were defeated. The NLRB (P) upheld the unions' objections to the election because W-G (D) had not furnished the list and the NLRB (P) ordered a new election. When W-G (D) again refused to supply an employee list, the NLRB (P) filed an action seeking to have its subpoena enforced or to have a mandatory injunction issued to compel W-G (D) to comply with its order. The district court held the NLRB's (P) order valid and directed W-G (D) to comply. On appeal, the First Circuit Court of Appeals reversed on the grounds that the NLRB's (P) order was invalid. The court concluded that the so-called Excelsior rule was defective, having not been based on a rule promulgated in accordance with APA requirements. The NLRB (P) appealed.

ISSUE: May the rulemaking provisions of the Administrative Procedure Act be avoided by making rules in the course of adjudicatory proceedings?

HOLDING AND DECISION: (Fortas, J.) No. The rulemaking provisions of the Administrative Procedure Act may not be avoided by making rules in the course of adjudicatory proceedings. The Administrative Procedure Act (APA) contains specific provisions governing agency rulemaking, which it defines as an agency statement of general or particular applicability and future effect. The APA requires publication in the Federal Register of notice of proposed rulemaking and of hearing; opportunity to be heard; a statement in the rule of its basis and purposes; and publication in the Federal Register of the rule as adopted. Here, the NLRB (P) does not deny that it ignored the rulemaking provisions of the APA, but still argues that Excelsior's command is a valid substantive regulation because the NLRB (P) promulgated it in the Excelsior proceeding, in which requirements for valid adjudication had been met. This argument misses the point. In Excelsior, the NLRB (P) did not even apply the rules it made to parties in that proceeding, the only entities that could be properly be subject to the order in that case. Instead, the NLRB (P) purported to make a rule, i.e., to exercise its quasi-legislative power. But, the defectiveness of the Excelsior rule notwithstanding, here W-G (D) was specifically directed by the NLRB (P) to submit the list of employee names and addresses for union use in connection with the election. This direction, which was part of the order directing that an election be held, is unquestionably valid. Reversed.

CONCURRENCE: (Black, J.) The Excelsior requirement that an employer supply the union with the names and addresses of its employees prior to an election is solid on its merits and can be enforced by subpoena. The prevailing opinion seems to hold that the Excelsior requirement cannot be considered the result of adjudication because the NLRB (P) did not apply it to the parties in the Excelsior case itself. But the Excelsior order was nevertheless an inseparable part of the adjudicatory process.

EDITOR'S ANALYSIS: In Mr. Justice Black's concurrence, he was somewhat critical of the majority opinion, although he agreed with its conclusion. He stated that he was convinced that the "Excelsior rule" was adopted by the NLRB (P) as a legitimate incident to the adjudication of a specific case before it, and for that reason, would hold that the NLRB (P) properly followed the procedures applicable to adjudication. Under these circumstances, so long as the matter involved could be dealt with in a way satisfying the definition of either "adjudication" or "rulemaking" under the Administrative Procedure Act, that Act should be read as conferring upon the NLRB (P) the authority to decide whether to proceed by rulemaking or by adjudication.

[For more information on policy formation and policymaking instruments, see Casenote Law Outline on Administrative Law, Chapter 7, § I, An Agency May Make General "Policy" or "Agency Law" by Adjudication or Rulemaking.]

QUICKNOTES

NLRA § 6 - Empowers Labor Board to enact rules necessary to carry out Act.

5 U.S.C. § 551 - Prescribes the manner of agency rulemaking.

ADJUDICATORY PROCEEDING - A hearing conducted by an administrative agency resulting in a final judgment regarding the rights of the parties involved.

**NATIONAL LABOR RELATIONS BOARD v.
BELL AEROSPACE COMPANY**
*Government agency (D) v.
Aerospace products manufacturer (P)*
416 U.S. 267 (1974).

NATURE OF CASE: Appeal from denial of enforcement of a agency order.

FACT SUMMARY: Bell (P) opposed a representation election on the grounds that its buyers were "managerial employees" and were thus not covered by the National Labor Relations Act or entitled to elect union representation.

CONCISE RULE OF LAW: The NLRB is not precluded from announcing new principles in an adjudicative proceeding.

FACTS: Bell Aerospace (P), which operated a plant engaging in research and development in the design and fabrication of aerospace products, opposed the petition of its employee buyers in the purchasing and procurement department for an election to decide whether a union would be certified as the buyers' bargaining representative. Bell (P) contended that the buyers were "managerial employees" and were not covered by the National Labor Relations Act (NLRA), and therefore, were not entitled to the NLRA's protections. The NLRB (D), after a representation hearing, issued an order holding that the buyers did constitute an appropriate unit for the purpose of collective bargaining and directed an election. An election was held and the union was certified by the NLRB (D) as the exclusive bargaining representative for Bell's (P) buyers. Bell (P), encouraged by an Eighth Circuit decision holding that "managerial employees" were not covered by the NLRA, moved the NLRB (D) for reconsideration of its order. The NLRB (D) denied the motion. Bell (P) then petitioned for review of the NLRB's (D) order, and the NLRB (D) cross-petitioned for enforcement. The Second Circuit Court of Appeals denied enforcement and the NLRB (D) appealed.

ISSUE: Is the NLRB precluded from announcing new principles in an adjudicative proceeding?

HOLDING AND DECISION: (Powell, J.) No. The NLRB (D) is not precluded from announcing new principles in an adjudicative proceeding and the choice between rulemaking and adjudication lies in the first instance within the NLRB's (D) discretion. Two questions are presented here. The first is whether the NLRB (D) properly determined that all "managerial employees" except those whose participation would create a conflict of interest with their job responsibilities are covered by the NLRA. The NLRB's (D) early decisions, the effect of the Taft-Hartley Act, the NLRB's (D) subsequent consistent construction of the NLRA for more than two decades, and the decisions of the courts of appeal all point unmistakably to the conclusion that "managerial employees" are not covered by the NLRA. The NLRB (D) is not now free to read a new and more restrictive meaning into the NLRA. The second question to be addressed is whether the NLRB (D) must proceed by rulemaking rather than by adjudication in deciding whether certain buyers are "managerial employees." Here, there is ample indication that adjudication is especially appropriate. The duties of buyers vary widely depending on the company or industry. It is doubtful whether any generalized standard could be framed that would have more than marginal utility. The NLRB (D) thus has reason to proceed with caution, developing its standards in a case-by-case manner with attention to the specific character of the buyer's authority and duties in each company. The NLRB's (D) judgment that adjudication best serves this purpose is entitled to great weight, and the NLRB (D) has discretion to decide that the adjudicative procedures in this case may also produce the relevant information necessary to mature and fair consideration of the issues. Affirmed in part and reversed and remanded in part.

EDITOR'S ANALYSIS: When the Taft-Hartley Act of 1947 was passed, both the U.S. Senate and the House of Representatives voiced concern over the NLRB's (D) broad reading of the term "employee" which then included those clearly within the managerial hierarchy. The Senate noted that unionization of supervisors had hurt productivity, increased the accident rate, upset the balance of power in collective bargaining, and tended to blur the lines between management and labor. The House echoed the concern for reduction of industrial output and noted that unionization of supervisors had deprived employers of the loyal representatives to which they were entitled.

[For more information on policymaking instruments, see Casenote Law Outline on Administrative Law, Chapter 4, § I, The First Step in Analyzing a Question About Internal Process.]

QUICKNOTES

MANAGERIAL EMPLOYEE - An employee whose duties involve the administration of the business' affairs or the supervising of the work of other employees.

SUPERVISORY EMPLOYEE - An employee authorized to implement his independent judgment in the management, direction and discipline of other employees.

TAFT-HARTLEY ACT - An amendment to the National Labor Relations Act, imposing limitations on unions and safeguarding the rights of employers.

RETAIL, WHOLESALE AND DEPARTMENT STORE UNION v. NATIONAL LABOR RELATIONS BOARD

Union (D) v. Government agency (P)

466 F.2d 380 (D.C. Cir. 1972).

NATURE OF CASE: Appeal from unfair labor practice decision.

FACT SUMMARY: Coca-Cola (D) complained that a new rule from the NLRB (P) about replacing striking workers should not be applied retroactively.

CONCISE RULE OF LAW: The retroactive application of a new agency rule depends upon a balancing of the danger of reaching a result contrary to law against the negative effect of the retroactive application.

FACTS: Coca-Cola (D) failed to hire workers who were permanently replaced during a strike. At the time, it was a well-settled rule with the NLRB (P) that when an employer replaced a striker, there was no obligation to hire back that employee. However, the NLRB (P) overturned this rule and held that former strikers were entitled to offers of reinstatement when the replacements vacated their positions. The NLRB (P) found that Coca-Cola (D) violated this new rule and imposed backpay liability on the company, although the underlying events occurred before the new rule was adopted. Coca-Cola (D) appealed on the basis of this retroactive application of the new rule.

ISSUE: Does the retroactive application of a new agency rule depend upon a balancing of the danger of reaching a result contrary to law against the negative effect of the retroactive application?

HOLDING AND DECISION: (McGowan, J.) Yes. The retroactive application of a new agency rule depends upon a balancing of the danger of reaching a result contrary to law against the negative effect of the retroactive application. The retroactive application of a new agency rule depends on factors such as whether the case is one of first impression. The Administrative Procedure Act authorizes agencies to conduct formal rule making so as to have rules that have prospective application. But many agencies fashion new rules and standards on a case-by-case basis through adjudications. Whether a new rule should be applied retroactively depends on the equities of the particular case, and courts may review this decision without deference to the agency. Among the key considerations are whether the case is one of first impression, whether the new rule is an abrupt departure from the old practice, the extent of reliance on the old rule, and the degree of burden the new rule imposes. The present case involving Coca-Cola (D) is not one of first impression, because the rule was changed in a prior case. Therefore, the reasons for applying it retroactively in the first impression case may not be present in the instant case. Looking at the equities in this case, it appears that Coca-Cola (D) tried to conform its conduct with the well-established and accepted old rule and the burden of imposing the new standard is considerable. Accordingly, it is highly unfair to punish Coca-Cola (D) for failing to conform to a standard subsequently adopted. Therefore, enforcement of the NLRB (P) order is denied.

EDITOR'S ANALYSIS: The court noted that Supreme Court precedent in this area did not establish any bright line guidelines. Agencies can choose not to apply a rule retroactively after it has been adopted in one case. On the other hand, reviewing courts may refuse to enforce retroactive agency orders.

QUICKNOTES

RETROACTIVE - Having an effect on something that occurred in the past.

NOTES:

GENERAL ELECTRIC COMPANY v.
U.S. ENVIRONMENTAL PROTECTION AGENCY
Alleged polluter (D) v. Government agency (P)
53 F.3d 1324 (D.C. Cir. 1995).

NATURE OF CASE: Appeal from fine for illegal polluting.

FACT SUMMARY: General Electric (D) was fined for disposing of toxic materials in a manner that the EPA (P) believed was impermissible under its interpretation of the regulations.

CONCISE RULE OF LAW: Agencies may not impose liability where a regulation is not sufficiently clear to provide fair notice to the affected party.

FACTS: General Electric (D) had a service shop in Georgia that decommissioned large electric transformers. Inside the transformers were PCBs, a dangerous pollutant, that had to be disposed of in compliance with EPA (P) regulations. Essentially, the regulations stated that the PCBs had to incinerate. General Electric (D) began a process that involved an intermediary step of recycling and distillation before incineration. The EPA (P) charged the company with violating the regulations and assessed a $25,000 fine. An ALJ and the Environmental Appeals Board upheld the fine and General Electric (D) petitioned for review.

ISSUE: May agencies impose liability where a regulation is not sufficiently clear to provide fair notice to the affected party?

HOLDING AND DECISION: (Tatel, J.) No. Agencies may not impose liability where a regulation is not sufficiently clear to provide fair notice to the affected party. Ordinarily, an agency's interpretation of its regulations is entitled to a high level of deference. However, it may be overturned if it is plainly wrong. Additionally, an order to comply with an interpretation carries more weight than a decision that a violation has occurred where an interpretation has not been expressly made before. Due process requires that parties receive fair notice before being deprived of property. This fair notice rule applies to both criminal and civil liability. An agency's pre-enforcement efforts to bring about compliance often provide adequate notice. If a regulated party could have identified the standards it was expected to have conformed to through regulations and other agency statements, then that is fair notice. In the instant case, the regulations at issue provide no notice whatsoever with regard to pre-disposal processes such as distillation. It certainly cannot be said that a reasonable person would know that distillation was to be considered a means of disposal. While the EPA (P) is entitled to conclude that it is, given the area of expertise, it does stray from a common understanding of the terms and would be unexpected without an express statement. Accordingly, General Electric (D) had no fair warning that the EPA (P) would make such an interpretation and the fine must be vacated.

EDITOR'S ANALYSIS: The court left the EPA (P) with room to apply its interpretation in future cases. But the court clearly found that the interpretation barring General Electric's (D) method to be unnatural given the language of the prior regulations. Thus, it had difficulty in finding that there was no fair prior warning and notice.

QUICKNOTES

NOTICE AND COMMENT - Informal rulemaking.

NOTICE - Communication of information to a person by an authorized person or an otherwise proper source.

DUE PROCESS - The constitutional mandate requiring the courts to protect and enforce individuals' rights and liberties consistent with prevailing principals of fairness and justice and prohibiting the federal and state governments from such activities that deprive its citizens of a life, liberty or property interest.

NOTES:

PHILLIPS PETROLEUM CO. v. JOHNSON
Oil Company (P) v. Department of Interior (D)
22 F.3d 616 (5th Cir. 1994).

NATURE OF CASE: Petition for review of lease royalty rate orders.

FACT SUMMARY: The Department of Interior (DOI) (D) developed new criteria for the royalty rate companies had to pay for leasing federal lands to extract natural gas.

CONCISE RULE OF LAW: Agency positions that are only statements about what a statute or regulation means are interpretative rules and exempt from notice and comment requirements.

FACTS: The DOI (D) is authorized by statute to determine the royalties that private companies must pay for extracting natural gas liquid products (NGLPs) from federal lands. Until March 1988, the royalty rate was dependent on several factors, including a sampling of different prices. The DOI (D) then developed new criteria for valuing NGLPs in a Procedure Paper and ordered companies to use this Procedure Paper to calculate royalties. Phillips (P) sought judicial review of the DOI's (D) orders on the ground that the DOI (D) promulgated a new rule without notice and comment. An appellate court agreed with Phillips (P) and the DOI (D) appealed.

ISSUE: Are agency positions that are only statements about what a statute or regulation means interpretative rules and exempt from notice and comment requirements?

HOLDING AND DECISION: (Smith, J.) Yes. Agency positions that are only statements about what a statute or regulation means are interpretative rules and exempt from notice and comment requirements. Section 553 of the APA provides that agencies must provide notice of a proposed rule and afford an opportunity for interested persons to present their views. The DOI (D) failed to follow these requirements with respect to the Procedure Paper, claiming that interpretative rules and general statements of policy were exempt from the notice and comment requirements. However, the label that an agency puts upon a rule is not conclusive. A rule is substantive or legislative when it creates law. In the present case, the Procedure Paper does not merely clarify or give an opinion on the meaning of a statute or regulation. Instead, it effects a change in the method used by DOI (D) in valuing NGLPs. Thus, it is not interpretative and should have been subject to the notice and comment requirement.

EDITOR'S ANALYSIS: The court also rejected the argument that the Procedure Paper was a general statement of policy. They noted that these are announcements to the public presaging an upcoming rule or course of action. The Procedure Paper was an immediate change in method, not a future goal.

QUICKNOTES

APA § 553 - Provides that agencies must provide notice of a proposed rule and allow interested parties to present their views.

NOTES:

METROPOLITAN SCHOOL DISTRICT v. DAVILA

Local school district (P) v. Department of Education (D)

969 F.2d 485 (7th Cir. 1992).

NATURE OF CASE: Appeal from summary judgment in action challenging agency regulation.

FACT SUMMARY: A Michigan school district (P) claimed that a Department of Education (D) regulation should have been subject to notice and comment requirements.

CONCISE RULE OF LAW: Interpretive rules are statements as to what an administrative officer thinks a statute or regulation means and are not subject to notice and comment requirements.

FACTS: Part B of the Individuals with Disabilities Act provides federal funding to states to support the education of disabled children. In order to qualify for the funds, a state must establish a policy of assuring a free education to all disabled children. The Office of Special Education and Rehabilitative Services (OSERS) administers the Act. Davila (D), an administrator for OSERS, sent a letter regarding the policy for states providing educational services to disabled children who are expelled. This position was not made subject to notice and comment requirements. The Metropolitan School District (P) sued the Department (D) on behalf of all districts, asserting that the position in Davila's (D) letter imposed a large financial burden and should have been subject to notice and public comment. Both parties moved for summary judgment. The district court granted Metropolitan's (P) motion and the Department (D) appealed.

ISSUE: Are interpretive rules statements as to what an administrative officer thinks a statute or regulation means and not subject to notice and comment requirements?

HOLDING AND DECISION: (Bauer, C.J.) Yes. Interpretive rules are statements as to what an administrative officer thinks a statute or regulation means and are not subject to notice and comment requirements. The APA does not require that administrative agencies follow notice and comment procedures in all situations. Interpretive rules and general statements of policy are exempt from this process. The starting point in determining whether a rule is interpretive is the agency's characterization of the rule. An interpretive rule simply states what the agency thinks the underlying statute means and reminds affected parties of existing duties. On the other hand, substantive or legislative rules create new duties, have the force and effect of law, and have effects independent of the statute. Interpretative rules, although entitled to deference, do not bind reviewing courts. In the present case, the letter from Davila (D) purports to be interpretative and satisfies the general test. It relies upon the language of the statute and legislative history. Accordingly, it was not subject to notice and comment. Reversed and remanded.

EDITOR'S ANALYSIS: The distinction between interpretative and legislative rules is a very blurry one, as even many courts have remarked. For a time, some courts used a "substantial impact" test to make the distinction. But this test has fallen out of favor.

QUICKNOTES

INTERPRETIVE RULES - A rule issued by an administrative agency for the purpose of explaining or interpreting a statute.

LEGISLATIVE RULE - The promulgation of a rule by an administrative agency, acting within the scope of its power pursuant to statute, enacting a law governing a particular activity.

SUMMARY JUDGMENT - Judgment rendered by a court in response to a motion by one of the parties, claiming that the lack of a question of material fact in respect to an issue warrants disposition of the issue without consideration by the jury.

NOTES:

BROCK v. CATHEDRAL BLUFFS SHALE OIL CO.

Department of Labor (P) v. General contractor (D)

796 F.2d 533 (D.C. Cir. 1986).

NATURE OF CASE: Petition for review of agency decision regarding work safety violation.

FACT SUMMARY: The Department of Labor (P) sought to impose a civil penalty against Occidental (D) for a violation by one of its independent contractors.

CONCISE RULE OF LAW: Agencies are not bound to adhere to their general statements of policy.

FACTS: Occidental (D), one of the co-owners of the Cathedral Bluff Shale Oil project, hired Gilbert Corporation to construct three vertical underground shafts at the site. A federal mine inspector found a violation of safety standards at the shaft and cited both Occidental (D) and Gilbert. Occidental (D) contested its citation and an ALJ dismissed it based on the opinion that the citation was not a proper application of the Department of Labor's (P) independent contractor enforcement policy. The Department (P) had initiated a rule making independent contractors responsible for safety violations, although an appendix to the rule allowed that there might be circumstances where both the operator and independent contractor would be cited for the same violation.

ISSUE: Are agencies bound to adhere to their general statements of policy?

HOLDING AND DECISION: (Scalia, J.) No. Agencies are not bound to adhere to their general statements of policy. However, agencies must comply with their own regulations. There is no easy distinction between a substantive rule and a statement of policy. Usually, a policy statement is issued by an agency to advise the public prospectively of the manner in which an agency proposes to exercise its discretionary power. A pronouncement is not a binding regulation merely because it has a substantive impact if there is still discretion for the administrator. In the present case, the Department (P) characterizes the enforcement guidelines as a statement of policy. This is entitled to some deference, but more important is the language of the rule at issue. Here, the language of the guidelines is replete with indications that the Department (P) would retain discretion to cite operators as well as independent contractors. Therefore, the applicable rule here is not a binding norm and is a general statement of policy. Accordingly, the decision dismissing Occidental's (D) citation is reversed and remanded for further action consistent with this opinion.

EDITOR'S ANALYSIS: Nonlegislative rules are exempt from notice and comment even if they have a substantive impact on the public. Some commentators believe that an agency's characterization of its action should be given much deference. The majority of courts use it only as one factor in their analysis.

QUICKNOTES

INDEPENDENT CONTRACTOR - A party undertaking a particular assignment for another who retains control over the manner in which it is executed.

INTERPRETIVE RULES - A rule issued by an administrative agency for the purpose of explaining or interpreting a statute.

NOTES:

FEDERAL CROP INSURANCE CORPORATION v. MERRILL
Government agency (D) v. Farmer (P)
332 U.S. 380 (1947).

NATURE OF CASE: Action to recover under federal crop insurance contract.

FACT SUMMARY: Merrill (P) suffered extensive damage to his federally insured wheat crop, but the government refused to pay his claim because the agent who entered Merrill (P) into the insurance contract had disregarded certain federal regulations in the process.

CONCISE RULE OF LAW: Persons dealing with federal administrative agencies are charged with the knowledge of all pertinent federal regulations much as all persons are charged with knowledge of the law and, as such, when a person joins into a government contract (with a government agent) which is contrary to federal regulations, the knowledge so charged to him will prevent him from invoking the doctrine of estoppel when the government cites such regulations as a defense to an action on the contract.

FACTS: Congress passed the Federal Crop Insurance Act to permit growers to insure against crop failure beginning in 1945. Pursuant to this act, the Federal Crop Insurance Corporation (D) was formed to administer the program. One of the regulations which the Corporation quickly formulated was one prohibiting the issuance of insurance on land which had been "reseeded." Merrill (P), a wheat grower, sought and obtained insurance on his wheat crop. The crop had been "reseeded" but, since neither Merrill (P) nor the Corporation's (D) agent knew of the reseeding regulation, the insurance was issued anyway. By July, Merrill's (P) entire crop had failed because of drought. He filed a claim for insurance but it was denied because of the reseeding regulation. Merrill (P) thereupon filed this action to recover on the claim, contending that the government should be estopped from asserting the regulation since its own agent disregarded it (albeit innocently) in entering the contract in the first place. This appeal followed.

ISSUE: Should the government be estopped from asserting an agency regulation because its agent disregarded it in entering into a contested contract?

HOLDING AND DECISION: (Frankfurter, J.) No. Persons dealing with federal administrative agencies are charged with the knowledge of all pertinent federal regulations much as all persons are charged with knowledge of the law and, as such, when a person joins into a government contract (with a government agent) which is contrary to federal regulations, the knowledge so charged to him will prevent him from invoking the doctrine of estoppel when the government cites such regulations as a defense to an action on the contract. It is true that, had the Corporation (D) been a private insurance company, the doctrine of estoppel would have prevented it from avoiding the action of one of its agents. But the government is not a private party and those who deal with it must assume the burden of discovering all appropriate rules and regulations. To permit one agent of the government to bind it to all illegal agreement would be to undermine the whole system of government by law.

EDITOR'S ANALYSIS: Though the trend in the lower courts is clearly away from it, this case still represents authority on the role of estoppel in government contract cases. Note, however, that the Ninth Circuit particularly has taken the lead in applying estoppel to government activities. In Brandt v. Hickel, 427 F.2d 53 (1970), for example, the court held the Bureau of Land Management estopped from ignoring a 30-day extension it had made to a bidder for a government contract. Unfortunately, however, the court has not yet rejected the doctrine of Merrill. Though writers almost universally condemn it, it is still true that private parties may be charged with knowledge of the Federal Register and Code of Federal Regulations. Note that this ruling inevitably raises the cost of applying for government contracts, grants, insurance, etc., because it makes the hiring of legal counsel a practical necessity.

[For more information on notice of rules, see Casenote Law Outline on Administrative Law, Chapter 7, § III, The Procedural Norm is "Notice and Comment" Rulemaking.]

QUICKNOTES

ESTOPPEL - An equitable doctrine precluding a party from asserting a right to the detriment of another who justifiably relied on the conduct.

NOTES:

UNITED STATES v. PENNSYLVANIA INDUSTRIAL CHEMICAL CORPORATION

Government (P) v. Alleged polluter (D)

411 U.S. 655 (1973).

NATURE OF CASE: Appeal from criminal conviction for illegal polluting.

FACT SUMMARY: PICCO (D) discharged refuse into waters in the belief that it was permissible because the deposits did not affect navigation.

CONCISE RULE OF LAW: Regulations must provide persons and entities with fair warning of the meaning and requirements of a statute.

FACTS: In August 1970, PICCO (D) discharged industrial refuse materials into the Monongahela River. These deposits did not affect the navigability of the river. The United States (P) filed a criminal complaint against PICCO (D) for violating §13 of the Rivers and Harbors Act of 1899 that prohibits any discharges without a permit. At trial, PICCO (D) wanted to introduce evidence that it hadn't attempted to obtain a §13 permit because the Army Corps of Engineers had consistently construed §13 as limited to discharges and deposits that would impede or obstruct navigation. PICCO (D) was convicted but a court of appeals ruled that the trial court should have allowed the evidence about the Corps' interpretation. The court of appeals set aside PICCO's (D) conviction and remanded. The United States (P) appealed.

ISSUE: Must regulations provide persons and entities with fair warning of the meaning and requirements of a statute?

HOLDING AND DECISION: (Brennan, J.) Yes. Regulations must provide persons and entities with fair warning of the meaning and requirements of a statute. There is no dispute that §13 of the Act applies to all deposits and discharges based on its express language. However, it is also undisputed that prior to 1970 the Army Corps of Engineers consistently construed §13 as limited to water deposits that affected navigation. Since PICCO (D) relied in good faith on this interpretation, it was affirmatively misled by the responsible administrative agency. The designed purpose of administrative rules is to guide persons as to the meanings and requirements of statutes. Accordingly, PICCO (D) was deprived of fair warning as to what conduct the United States (P) would hold as illegal. The conviction must be overturned, the decision of the court of appeals is affirmed.

EDITOR'S ANALYSIS: The court also noted that there was some dispute as to the extent of §13 in the courts. In 1966, it appeared that only serious injury to the waterways was at issue. But since then, §13 was read as imposing a flat ban on all unauthorized deposits.

QUICKNOTES

RIVERS AND HARBOR ACT §13 - Prohibits discharges that impede or obstruct navigation into navigable waters.

NOTES:

OFFICE OF PERSONNEL MANAGEMENT v. RICHMOND
Human resources office (D) v. Navy welder (P)
496 U.S. 414, (1990).

NATURE OF CASE: Appeal from an award of damages for loss of disability annuity.

FACT SUMMARY: Richmond (P) retired from his job as a welder after the Office of Personnel Management (OPM) (D) approved his application for a disability annuity due to his impaired eyesight.

CONCISE RULE OF LAW: No money shall be drawn from the Treasury, but in consequence of appropriations made by law.

FACTS: As a welder for the Navy, Richmond's (P) impaired eyesight qualified him for a disability annuity under 5 U.S.C. §8337(d). The statute, however, provided that disability payments would end if the retiree earned an amount fairly comparable to the current rate of pay of the position occupied at the time of retirement. The original measuring period for restoration of earning capacity was two years, but after 1982, the measuring period was changed to one year. Upon retirement, Richmond (P) took a part-time job. Concerned about losing his eligibility if he made too much money, Richmond (P) twice consulted the Navy's Civilian Personnel Department and was given advice based on the former two-year eligibility rule. Richmond (P) then worked overtime in the erroneous belief his eligibility would not be affected, and OPM (D) suspended his disability annuity for six months. The court of appeals ruled that estoppel was properly applied against the federal government and ordered the suspended payments restored to Richmond (P). This appeal by OPM (D) followed.

ISSUE: Will estoppel against the government lie where payment is requested from the Treasury without appropriations made by law?

HOLDING AND DECISION: (Kennedy, J.) No. No money shall be drawn from the Treasury, but in consequence of appropriations made by law (Appropriation Clause of the Constitution, Art. I, §9, cl. 7.) Judicial use of the equitable doctrine of estoppel cannot grant a money remedy that Congress has not authorized. The general purpose of the clause is to prevent fraud and corruption. But the direct purpose relevant to this case is to assure that public funds will be spent according to the letter of the difficult judgments reached by Congress as to the common good, and not according to the individual favor of government agents or the individual pleas of litigants. Estoppel claims based on real or imagined claims of misinformation by disgruntled citizens would impose an unpredictable drain on the public. An assertion of estoppel against the government by a claimant seeking public funds has never been upheld, for courts cannot estop the Constitution. Reversed.

EDITOR'S ANALYSIS: Because of dicta in the Court's more recent cases, the courts of appeals had begun to apply equitable estoppel against the government. In Richmond (P), the Court declared it was not deciding whether an estoppel claim could ever succeed against the government. However, it also declared that it has reversed every finding of estoppel that it has reviewed.

[For more information on the reviewability of an administrative decision, see Casenote Law Outline on Administrative Law, Chapter 9, Judicial Control of the Administrative Processes, §V, Administrative Decision May Become Unreviewable.]

QUICKNOTES

ESTOPPEL - An equitable doctrine precluding a party from asserting a right to the detriment of another who justifiably relied on the conduct.

ANNUITY - The payment or right to receive payment of a fixed sum periodically, for a specified time period.

APPROPRIATION - The act of making something one's own or making use of something to serve one own's interest.

NOTES:

APPEAL OF ENO (NEW HAMPSHIRE DEPARTMENT OF EMPLOYMENT SECURITY)

Applicant for benefits (P) v. State agency (D)

N.H. Sup. Ct., 126 N.H. 650 (N.H. 1985).

NATURE OF CASE: Appeal from denial of unemployment benefits.

FACT SUMMARY: Eno (P) was denied unemployment benefits because the Department (D) claimed that she had made insufficient efforts to find a job.

CONCISE RULE OF LAW: Agencies deny due process when they apply different standards after causing persons to rely on lesser standards.

FACTS: Eno (P) was laid off from her job in February. In March, she applied for unemployment benefits from the New Hampshire Department of Employment Security (D). She was given a pamphlet which stated the conditions of eligibility including a provision for seeking employment. When she appeared to make weekly applications, 0Eno (P) was asked if she was seeking employment and answered affirmatively. There was no further explanation or inquiry. Eno (P) had been answering want ads by telephone and sending out resumes, but did not make personal visits to possible employers. The Department (D) later determined that she was ineligible for benefits since she had made insufficient efforts to obtain other employment. Eno (P) appealed.

ISSUE: Do agencies deny due process when they apply different standards after causing persons to rely on lesser standards?

HOLDING AND DECISION: (Souter, J.) Yes. Agencies deny due process when they apply different standards after causing persons to rely on lesser standards. A claim of entitlement to unemployment compensation is a claim to a property interest that is subject to due process guarantees. Thus, the Department (D) may not deny a claim by a procedure that is fundamentally unfair. In the present case, it appears that Eno (P) did not comply with the statutory standard for eligibility because she did not make personal visits to potential employers. However, the Department's (D) contacts with Eno (P) indicated that different standards were applicable. When asked whether she was seeking employment, she answered truthfully that she had. Since these answers were accepted without further inquiry, it left Eno (P) with the natural impression that she had satisfied the eligibility conditions. It also signaled to Eno (P) that she should continue on that course. If she had been told that it was insufficient, she could have made a greater effort the following week. Since Eno (P) acted in reliance on the Department's (D) apparent standards, it was unfair to deny her benefits based on more exacting conditions. Reversed.

EDITOR'S ANALYSIS: The court also noted that the Department (D) revised its pamphlets after this case. The pamphlet now states that personal visits to employers are expected. The court sympathized with the Department's (D) indication that it was understaffed at the time Eno (P) was seeking benefits, but found that it didn't justify the denial of benefits.

QUICKNOTES

DUE PROCESS - The constitutional mandate requiring the courts to protect and enforce individuals' rights and liberties consistent with prevailing principals of fairness and justice and prohibiting the federal and state governments from such activities that deprive its citizens of a life, liberty or property interest.

NOTES:

SKIDMORE v. SWIFT & CO.
Employees (P) v. Employer (D)
323 U.S. 134 (1944).

NATURE OF CASE: Suit to recover overtime wages allegedly due.

FACT SUMMARY: Skidmore (P) and other employees of Swift & Co. (D) sued to recover overtime pay for time spent waiting for fires to occur.

CONCISE RULE OF LAW: In resolving a controversy which no agency has been authorized to adjudicate, the courts may consider the reports and opinions of an administrator whose duty it is to seek injunctive relief from violations of the laws involved in the controversy.

FACTS: Skidmore (P) and six other employees (P) of Swift & Co. (D) sued to recover overtime pay for time spent on company (D) premises waiting to respond to fire alarms. The only duties imposed upon the employees (P) were those of remaining within hearing distance of the alarms and responding to alarms and actual fires. The employees (P) were permitted to occupy reasonably comfortable quarters which included recreational facilities, and were allowed to engage in any activities, including eating and sleeping. They (P) received no pay for the time spent waiting and listening, but were compensated for each occasion on which they (P) actually responded to a fire or an alarm. By their suit, they (P) sought compensation for time spent waiting as well. The company (D) argued that the hours thus spent did not constitute "working time" within the meaning of the Fair Labor Standards Act. The lower court denied the employees' (P) claim, relying upon an administrative bulletin which expressed the opinion that time spent waiting did not constitute time worked.

ISSUE: May courts, in determining controversies not committed to the jurisdiction of any agency, take account of reports, recommendations and opinions of administrators?

HOLDING AND DECISION: (Jackson, J.) Yes. In determining controversies such as the present one, which no agency has been given the authority to resolve, the court may take account of opinions and recommendations of administrators. Congress has, in fact, appointed a special Administrator whose duty it is to inform himself of matters pertaining to industries subject to the Fair Labor Standards Act. The Administrator is also empowered to bring injunctive relief against violators of the Act. He possesses considerable knowledge and expertise, much of which is reflected in the interpretive bulletins and informal rulings which he issues. His expressions, while not binding on the court, are entitled to an amount of respect commensurate with their thoughtfulness, thoroughness, and internal consistency. In the present case, the court below seems to have accorded proper weight to the opinions of the Administrator that all on-the-job time is compensable except those periods spent eating and sleeping. However, that court's interpretations were colored by its mistaken legal conclusion that waiting time will never be "working time." The case must, therefore, be remanded for reconsideration of the evidence and the Administrator's opinions, this time viewed in light of the conclusion that time spent waiting may also be determined to be "working time."

EDITOR'S ANALYSIS: Skidmore v. Swift & Co. is significant for its expression of the proposition that courts may rely upon interpretive rules promulgated by agencies. Rules of this type do not have the force of law, and the courts are, in fact, free to ignore them. However, interpretive rules typically are accorded some deference, and are more likely to be relied upon when the problems with which the court must grapple are uncomfortably complex. In evaluating the authority of interpretive rules, courts are likely to be influenced by: (1) the formality and public participation involved in their promulgation; (2) the sophistication and expertise of the agency involved; (3) the consistency with which the interpretive rules have been maintained; (4) whether Congress has reenacted the applicable enabling statute with knowledge of the interpretive rules promulgated pursuant to it; and (5) the period of time which elapsed between passage of the enabling statute and the adoption of the interpretive rules. Note that the Skidmore court expressly adverted to several of these factors.

[For more information on the employment of nonlegislative rules, see Casenote Law Outline on Administrative Law, Chapter 7, Rulemaking Processes, §VIII, Certain Rules Have the Effect of Law.]

QUICKNOTES

INJUNCTIVE RELIEF - A court order issued as a remedy, requiring a person to do, or prohibiting that person from doing, a specific act.

JURISDICTION - The authority of a court to hear and declare judgment in respect to a particular matter.

RULEMAKING - The promulgation of a rule by an administrative agency, acting within the scope of its power pursuant to statute, enacting a rule governing a particular activity.

NOTES:

WAGNER SEED COMPANY, INC. v. BUSH

Seed company (P) v. Government agency (D)

946 F.2d 918 (D.C. Cir. 1991).

NATURE OF CASE: Appeal from agency denial of reimbursement for pollution clean-up costs.

FACT SUMMARY: Wagner (P) sought reimbursement for its clean-up costs under the new Superfund legislation, although the law was passed after the clean-up was complete.

CONCISE RULE OF LAW: Courts must defer to reasonable agency interpretation of ambiguous statutes.

FACTS: In December 1985, the Environmental Protection Agency (D) issued a clean-up order requiring Wagner Seed (P) to immediately remove hazardous substances that were released when a fire destroyed its warehouse. Wagner (P) had substantially complied by October 1986 when Congress passed the so-called Superfund amendments, which entitled persons and companies who complied with EPA (D) orders to reimbursement for reasonable clean-up costs. In January 1988, the EPA (D) certified that Wagner (P) had complied with the order and Wagner (P) petitioned for reimbursement. However, the EPA (D) interpreted the Superfund legislation as applying only prospectively from the date the statute was adopted. Thus, Wagner's (P) claim was rejected and they filed suit. The district court dismissed and Wagner appealed.

ISSUE: Must courts defer to reasonable agency interpretation of ambiguous statutes?

HOLDING AND DECISION: (Ginsburg, J.) Yes. Courts must defer to reasonable agency interpretation of ambiguous statutes. If a law is silent or ambiguous with respect to a specific issue, considering the traditional tools of statutory construction, the administering agency is entitled to make a reasonable policy choice and the courts must defer to this interpretation. Although courts may give greater deference to administrative rules that result from deep analysis and formal rulemaking, deference is still owed to interpretations that don't come with all the procedural trappings. In the present case, looking at the statute in question it seems that there is no plain and unambiguous answer as to whether Congress intended reimbursement to apply retrospectively. It also appears that the EPA (D) gave due consideration to the issue before deciding that it should only apply prospectively. The EPA (D) interpretation is certainly reasonable in that it remains consistent with the objective of the law. Accordingly, that interpretation must be upheld. Affirmed.

EDITOR'S ANALYSIS: The EPA (D) decided that it was a better allocation of resources to restrict reimbursement to those who hadn't completed their clean-up before the Superfund law. It is unclear if Wagner (P) would have been better off if they hadn't promptly followed the clean-up order. Still, the majority seems perfectly correct in deciding that the EPA (D) was at least reasonable.

QUICKNOTES

SUPERFUND - Amendment to the Comprehensive Environmental Response, Compensation and Liability Act that made funds available to reimburse parties who cleaned up hazardous substances.

NOTES:

ATCHISON, TOPEKA AND SANTA FE RAILWAY COMPANY v. PENA

Railroad company (P) v. Federal Railroad Administration (D)

44 F.3d 437 (7th Cir. 1994).

NATURE OF CASE: Petition for review of agency re-interpretation of the Hours of Service Act of 1907.

FACT SUMMARY: The FRA (D) changed its interpretation of a statute only in order to comply with an unfavorable decision by a court of appeals.

CONCISE RULE OF LAW: Interpretive rules are only entitled to deference based on the validity and consistency of the agency's reasoning.

FACTS: The Hours of Service Act imposes a limit on the maximum hours of service that a train crew can continuously operate trains while on duty. In order to comply with this law, railroads must sometimes stop trains before their destinations and transport the crews in other trains or cars. The time that the crews spend in transit is considered neither on duty nor off duty, but "limbo time." However, the Act does not specify how the time that crews wait for this special transportation should be characterized. The FRA (D) had treated this time as limbo time and had never construed the Act to require that this waiting time be considered time on duty. But in 1992, the Ninth Circuit Court of Appeals rejected this interpretation. As a result, the FRA (D) notified the railroads (P) by letter that while it didn't agree with the Ninth Circuit, it would now adopt the new rule and enforce it. Atchison (P) and other railroad companies (P) challenged this re-interpretation.

ISSUE: Are interpretive rules only entitled to deference based on the validity and consistency of the agency's reasoning?

HOLDING AND DECISION: (Bauer, J.) Yes. Interpretive rules are only entitled to deference based on the validity and consistency of the agency's reasoning. Generally, the interpretation of an ambiguous statute by an agency that is authorized to promulgate rules is to be upheld if it is reasonable. However, agencies that are not charged with rule-making powers are not entitled to the same deference. In such cases, the agency's application of statutory provisions are only interpretive. They not only are exempt from the notice and comment procedures, but are also not to be rubber-stamped by the courts. The deference that interpretive rules are paid depends on the thoroughness, validity and consistency of the agency's reasoning. In the present case, the FRA's (D) re-interpretation does not meet these goals. By its own admission, it is not the position that the FRA (D) takes itself on the issue. It is inconsistent with years of agency enforcement and was not made contemporaneously with the legislation or its relevant amendments. It was adopted for no other reason than because the Ninth Circuit disagreed with the prior interpretation. Accordingly, it is entitled to no deference. As to the statute itself, the court believes that the waiting time should be considered limbo time in light of the purposes of the Act. Petition for review granted.

CONCURRENCE: (Easterbrook, J.) A better form of analysis for the deference issue would be to separate the delegation, respect and persuasion elements from each other. In this case, there is no delegation element so the FRA (D) is relying on its persuasive reasoning.

EDITOR'S ANALYSIS: The court's opinion only briefly touched upon its reasoning for determining that the FRA's (D) old interpretation was correct. This decision sets up a conflict between different circuits on this issue. The standard of deference that is owed when an agency that has the authority to make regulations with the force of law, but instead makes interpretive rules, remains an open question in the courts.

QUICKNOTES

INTERPRETIVE RULE - A rule issued by an administrative agency for the purpose of explaining or interpreting a statute.

NOTES:

CHAPTER 5
REVIEWABILITY

QUICK REFERENCE RULES OF LAW

1. **Litigation of Standing.** A general allegation of visits "in the vicinity" of reclassified land is not sufficient to show "injury in fact" as a result of the reclassification. (Lujan v. National Wildlife Federation)

   [For more information on standing to secure judicial review, see Casenote Law Outline on Administrative Law, Chapter 10, Process of Judicial Review, §II, A Party Must Have Standing to Appeal.]

2. **Litigation of Standing.** Standing is established when a plaintiff shows that he has suffered an actual and redressable injury that is fairly traceable to the challenged action of the defendant. (Lujan v. Defenders of Wildlife)

   [For more information on standing, see Casenote Law Outline on Administrative Law, Chapter 10, § II, A Party Must Have Standing to Appeal.]

3. **Cause of Action.** Where a class of plaintiffs itself is not the subject of the contested regulatory action, the essential inquiry under the "zone of interest" test is whether Congress intended for that particular class of plaintiffs to be relied upon to challenge agency disregard of the law. (Clarke v. Securities Industry Association)

   [For more information on standing and the "zone of interests" test, see Casenote Law Outline on Administrative Law, Chapter 10, Process of Judicial Review, §II, A Party Must Have Standing to Appeal.]

4. **Cause of Action.** Plaintiffs have no standing to challenge the suspension of a statute, unless they are within that statute's zone of interest. (Air Courier Conference of America v. American Postal Workers Union, AFL-CIO)

   [For more information on standing, see Casenote Law Outline on Administrative Law, Chapter 10, § II, A Party Must Have Standing to Appeal.]

5. **Exclusions From Judiciary Review Under the APA: Statutory Preclusion**. Only upon a showing of clear and convincing evidence of a contrary legislative intent should the courts restrict access to judicial review of final agency actions. (Abbot Laboratories v. Gardner (I))

6. **Exclusions From Judiciary Review Under the APA: Statutory Preclusion**. Consumers do not have standing to challenge regulations promulgated under the Agricultural Marketing Agreement Act of 1937. (Block v. Community Nutrition Institute)

   [For more information on no general standing to sue, see Casenote Law Outline on Administrative Law, Chapter 10, Process of Judicial Review, § I, Litigant Must Appeal to Court with Jurisdiction.]

7. **Exclusions From Judiciary Review Under the APA: Statutory Preclusion**. Initial judicial review of an agency order is determined by the statute's language, structure, purpose and legislative history. (Thunder Basin Coal Company v. Reich)

8. **Exclusions From Judiciary Review Under the APA: Committed to Agency Discretion.** A decision by the FDA to refrain from enforcement proceedings is not subject to judicial review. (Heckler v. Chaney)

   [For more information on review of agency discretion, see Casenote Law Outline on Administrative Law, Chapter 6, § II, Agencies Have Almost Unbridled Authority to Decide.]

9. **Exclusions From Judiciary Review Under the APA: Committed to Agency Discretion.** Under § 102(e) of the National Security Act, employee termination decisions made by the Director of the CIA are not judicially reviewable. (Webster v. Doe)

[For more information on judicial reviewability, see Casenote Law Outline on Administrative Law, Chapter 9, § V, Administrative Decision May Become Unreviewable.]

10. **Timing: Exhaustion.** Exhaustion of administrative remedies is not required when the litigant's interests in immediate judicial review outweigh the government's interests in efficiency or administrative autonomy. (McCarthy v. Madigan)

[For more information on exhaustion of administrative remedies, see Casenote Law Outline on Administrative Law, Chapter 10, Processes of Judicial Review, §V , The Courts Will Only Hear Appeals When the Plaintiff Has Exhausted All Administrative Remedies.]

11. **Timing: Exhaustion.** A litigant seeking judicial review of a final agency action under the Administrative Procedure Act need not exhaust available administrative remedies, unless such exhaustion is expressly required by statute or agency rule. (Darby v. Cisneros)

12. **Timing: Exhaustion**. Courts are reluctant to apply injunctive and declaratory judgment remedies to administrative determinations, unless they arise in the context of a controversy which is "ripe" for judicial resolution. (Abbott Laboratories v. Gardner (II))

LUJAN v. NATIONAL WILDLIFE FEDERATION

Government official (D) v. Environmental group (P)

497 U.S. 871 (1990).

NATURE OF CASE: Appeal of preliminary injunction against federal reclassification of wildlife lands.

FACT SUMMARY: Two members of the National Wildlife Federation (NWF) (P) claimed an injury due to the reclassification of wildlife lands by Lujan (D), the Secretary of the Interior, because the two members had visited "in the vicinity" of the reclassified lands.

CONCISE RULE OF LAW: A general allegation of visits "in the vicinity" of reclassified land is not sufficient to show "injury in fact" as a result of the reclassification.

FACTS: Lujan (D), the Secretary of the Interior, reclassified vast tracts of federal land in a way that the NWF (P) claimed opened those lands to various kinds of detrimental development, including mining. To establish standing and demonstrate an "injury in fact," the NWF (P) relied primarily upon affidavits from two members who asserted that they visited places "in the vicinity" of areas that two of Lujan's (D) land decisions had affected. The NWF (P) claimed that Lujan's (D) reclassification of the wildlife lands violated NEPA and the APA, along with certain other land management statutes, by failing to follow various procedures and failing to pay proper attention to the environment. The NWF (P) appeared to be seeking improvement overall of the programs established by the Department of the Interior and the Bureau of Land Management. Lujan (D) filed a motion for summary judgment challenging NWF's (P) standing. The district court found for Lujan (D) and dismissed the action. The D.C. Circuit reversed, with the result that for two years a preliminary injunction prohibited Lujan (D) from making changes in the use classifications of millions of acres of public lands. The Supreme Court then reviewed the matter.

ISSUE: Is a general allegation of visits "in the vicinity" of reclassified land sufficient to show "injury in fact" as a result of the reclassification?

HOLDING AND DECISION: (Scalia, J.) No. A general allegation of visits "in the vicinity" of reclassified land is not sufficient to show "injury in fact" as a result of the reclassification. While there is some room for debate as to how "specific" the "specific facts" required for summary judgment under Rule 56(e) must be in a particular case, the Rule is not satisfied by averments which state only that some NWF (P) members use unspecified portions of an immense tract of territory, on some portions of which mining activity has occurred or probably will occur by virtue of the governmental action. Further, the overall programmatic improvements sought by NWF (P) are normally made by actions of the Interior Department or Congress, not through court decree. The NWF (P) cannot demand a general judicial review of the Department of the Interior's and the Bureau of Land Management's day-to-day operations.

DISSENT: (Blackmun, J.) The affidavits were sufficiently specific.

EDITOR'S ANALYSIS: The Court distinguished its decision in United States v. Students Challenging Regulatory Agency Procedures (SCRAP), 412 U.S. 669 (1973), on the ground that SCRAP involved a Rule 12(b) motion to dismiss on the pleadings, not a Rule 56 motion for summary judgment. The Court stated that a Rule 12(b) motion presumes that general allegations embrace those specific facts that are necessary to support the claim, unlike a Rule 56 motion for summary judgment. However, the Court's decision in SCRAP represented a very expansive interpretation of what constitutes standing. Since SCRAP, the Court's decisions as to standing and the "injury in fact" requirement have been much less expansive, as demonstrated in the instant case.

[For more information on standing to secure judicial review, see Casenote Law Outline on Administrative Law, Chapter 10, Process of Judicial Review, §II, A Party Must Have Standing to Appeal.]

QUICKNOTES

JUDICIAL REVIEW - The authority of the courts to review decisions, actions or omissions committed by another agency or branch of government.

STANDING - Whether a party possesses the right to commence suit against another party by having a personal stake in the resolution of the controversy.

PRELIMINARY INJUNCTION - A judicial mandate issued to require or restrain a party from certain conduct; used to preserve a trial's subject matter or to prevent threatened injury.

NOTES:

LUJAN v. DEFENDERS OF WILDLIFE

Secretary of Interior (D) v. Environmental protection group ((P)

504 U.S. 555 (1992).

NATURE OF CASE: Appeal from denial of defense motion for summary judgment in action for injunctive relief.

FACT SUMMARY: In Defenders' (P) action against Lujan (D), the appellate court, agreeing with the district court, denied Lujan's (D) motion for summary judgment that challenged, on specificity grounds, the standing of this action.

CONCISE RULE OF LAW: Standing is established when a plaintiff shows that he has suffered an actual and redressable injury that is fairly traceable to the challenged action of the defendant.

FACTS: Section 7 (a)(2) of the Endangered Species Act (ESA) of 1973 requires federal agencies to consult with the Secretary of the Interior to "insure that any action authorized, funded, or carried out by such agency . . . is not likely to jeopardize the continued existence of an endangered" or threatened species or to adversely modify its habitat. In lieu of the ESA, the Secretary, Lujan (D), issued a regulation which limited the consultation requirement to agency action "in the United States or upon the high seas." As a result, Defenders of Wildlife (Defenders) (P) challenged this regulation in federal district court, averring, that the regulation threatened the habitat of various endangered species abroad and, caused injury to its cognizable interests. In rebuttal, Lujan (D) moved for summary judgment based on standing, on the grounds that Defenders' (P) complaint failed to adequately specify the connection between the regulation and its alleged injuries. The district court and the appellate court on appeal, however, denied this motion. Lujan (D) appealed.

ISSUE: Is standing established when a plaintiff shows that he has suffered an actual and redressable injury that is fairly traceable to the challenged action of the defendant?

HOLDING AND DECISION: (Scalia, J.) Yes. Standing is established when a plaintiff shows that he has suffered an actual and redressable injury that is fairly traceable to the challenged action of the defendant. This rule represents the end result of common law principles requiring, at a bare minimum, that a plaintiff establish the actuality, redressability, and traceability of an injury in order to have standing. In this vein, various stages of the litigative process require varying degrees of specificity for a plaintiff to establish standing; however, at the summary judgment stage, he must set forth, by his evidence, specific facts which for the purposes of the summary judgment motion will be taken true. Even still, when this plaintiff asserts an injury arising from the government's allegedly unlawful action or inaction as affecting someone else, he must cross an even larger threshold to satisfy the necessary standing elements since, in this instance, causality and redressability issues become somewhat strained. In the instant case, since Defenders (P) failed to adequately demonstrate that any of its members suffered injury to a cognizable interest or, assuming injury, that relief would satisfactorily cushion this interest, Lucan's (D) motion to summarily dismiss Defenders (P) injunctive action was wrongly denied. Reversed.

CONCURRENCE: (Kennedy, J.) Although the Court reached the correct result, the possibility that in different circumstances an ecosystem, animal, or vocational nexus theory might support a claim to standing should not be foreclosed.

CONCURRENCE: (Stevens, J.) A person who has visited a critical habitat of an endangered species, has a professional interest in preserving the species and its habitat, and intends to revisit them in the future, has standing to challenge agency action that threatens their destruction. An injury to an individual's interest in studying or enjoying a species and its natural habitat occurs when someone takes action that harms that species and habitat. Injury to the Defenders of Wildlife (P) will occur as soon as the animals at issue here are destroyed.

DISSENT: (Blackmun, J.) A reasonable finder of fact could conclude from the averred evidence that Defenders (P) suffered a cognizable injury and that this injury was redressable.

EDITOR'S ANALYSIS: In Japan Whaling Association v. American Cetacean Society, 478 U.S. 221 (1986), the Society brought suit against the Secretary of Commerce to compel him to certify that Japan's whaling practices "diminish the effectiveness" of the International Convention for the Regulation of Whaling because Japan's annual harvest exceeded quotas established under the Convention. Such a certification would have required the President to impose economic sanctions against the offending nation. The Court raised the standing issue only in a footnote in the Solicitor General's Supreme Court brief, whereby it noted, in effect, that since the Society's right of action was expressly created by the APA, which states that "final agency action for which there is no other adequate remedy in court [is] subject to judicial review" (§ 704) at the behest of "[a] person . . . adversely affected or aggrieved by agency action," (§ 702) no separate indication of congressional intent to make agency action reviewable under the APA is necessary.

[For more information on standing, see Casenote Law Outline on Administrative Law, Chapter 10, § II, A Party Must Have Standing to Appeal.]

QUICKNOTES

ENDANGERED SPECIES ACT § 7 - Provides that federal agencies insure that their actions do not threaten endangered species.

CLARKE v. SECURITIES INDUSTRY ASSOCIATION

Government official (D) v. Trade association (P)

479 U.S. 388 (1987).

NATURE OF CASE: Review of order reversing administrative decision regarding financial services.

FACT SUMMARY: Clarke (D) argued that the Securities Industry Association (P) did not have standing to challenge his decision allowing national banks to offer discount brokerage services.

CONCISE RULE OF LAW: Where a class of plaintiffs itself is not the subject of the contested regulatory action, the essential inquiry under the "zone of interest" test is whether Congress intended for that particular class of plaintiffs to be relied upon to challenge agency disregard of the law.

FACTS: Clarke (D), the Comptroller of Currency, issued a regulation permitting national banks to open offices selling discount brokerage services to the public. The Securities Industry Association (SIA) (P), an organization made up of securities dealers, challenged the ruling as contrary to law, particularly the McFadden Act, which placed limitations on the activities in which bank branches could engage. The Court of Appeals invalidated the decision. The Supreme Court granted review, and first addressed the Comptroller's (D) argument that the SIA (P) lacked standing.

ISSUE: Where a class of plaintiffs itself is not the subject of the contested regulatory action, is the essential inquiry under the "zone of interest" test whether Congress intended for that particular class of plaintiffs to be relied upon to challenge agency disregard of the law?

HOLDING AND DECISION: (White, J.) Yes. Where a class of plaintiffs itself is not the subject of the contested regulatory action, the essential inquiry under the "zone of interest" test is whether Congress intended for that particular class of plaintiffs to be relied upon to challenge agency disregard of the law. Whether a party has standing to challenge an administrative decision is largely governed by the "zone of interests" test. Under this test, if a party is within the zone of interests protected by any statute relevant to the agency action, standing will exist. If a party's interests are so marginally related to or inconsistent with the statute, standing will be held not to exist. Here, the SIA (P) has standing to challenge a Comptroller of Currency (D) decision allowing national banks to offer discount brokerage services. The McFadden Act was largely concerned with excessive accumulation of power by national banks through branching, and the SIA (P) and its constituent members would seem to be within the zone of interests here. [The Court went on to address the merits, and reversed.]

CONCURRENCE: (Stevens, J.) One of the purposes of the McFadden Act was to protect banks' competitors, such as the SIA (P). Standing was such an obvious matter here that the Court's analysis was unnecessary.

EDITOR'S ANALYSIS: When all is said and done, standing is a matter of congressional intent. The zone of interests test is merely the Court's formulation of a manner of ascertaining such intent. If a party falls within the zone, but is still not within Congress' contemplation of who should be a plaintiff, the test could not be applied by the reviewing court to grant standing.

[For more information on standing and the "zone of interests" test, see Casenote Law Outline on Administrative Law, Chapter 10, Process of Judicial Review, §II, A Party Must Have Standing to Appeal.]

QUICKNOTES

STANDING - Whether a party possesses the right to commence suit against another party by having a personal stake in the resolution of the controversy.

ADMINISTRATIVE HEARING - A hearing conducted before an administrative agency.

JUDICIAL REVIEW - The authority of the courts to review decisions, actions or omissions committed by another agency or branch of government.

ZONE OF INTERESTS - The range or category of interests that a constitutional guarantee or statute is intended to protect.

NOTES:

AIR COURIER CONFERENCE OF AMERICA v. AMERICAN POSTAL WORKERS UNION, AFL-CIO

Agency (D) v. Union (P)

498 U.S. 517 (1991).

NATURE OF CASE: Appeal from refusal to dismiss action to reinstate suspended statutes.

FACT SUMMARY: In the APWU's (P) suit against Air Courier (D), challenging the Postal Service's suspension of the Private Express Statutes, the court of appeals, agreeing with the district court, found that the APWU (P) had standing to bring the suit.

CONCISE RULE OF LAW: Plaintiffs have no standing to challenge the suspension of a statute, unless they are within that statute's zone of interest.

FACTS: The American Postal Workers Union (APWU) (P) challenged the Postal Service's suspension of the Private Express Statutes, which prohibited private express carriers from competing with the Postal Service, by arguing that the suspension jeopardized postal worker job security. The court of appeals, agreeing with the district court, found that the APWU (P) had standing to bring the challenge since the revenue-protective purposes of the statutes plausibly related to the APWU's (P) interest in preventing the reduction of employment opportunities. Air Courier (D), a private express carrier, appealed.

ISSUE: Do plaintiffs have standing to challenge the suspension of a statute if they are outside that statute's zone of interest?

HOLDING AND DECISION: (Rehnquist, C.J.) No. Plaintiffs have no standing to challenge the suspension of a statute, unless they are within that statute's zone of interest. In respect to examining the legitimacy of the APWU's (P) standing to challenge the suspension of the Private Express Statutes, the express language and legislative purpose of these statutes shed light. First, their express language appears to be concerned not with opportunities for postal workers but with the receipt of necessary revenues for the Postal Service. Second, the legislative purpose behind the statutes is not to ensure employment for postal workers but to ensure that postal service is provided to the citizenry at large. Hence, postal unions are not within the Private Express Statutes' zone of interest. In the instant case, since APWU (P) is not within the Private Express Statutes' zone of interest, it lacks standing to challenge the Statutes' suspension by the Postal Service. Reversed.

EDITOR'S ANALYSIS: Justice White was one of the justices to join the majority above. He also authored Clarke v. Securities Industry Ass'n, 479 U.S. 388 (1987), where he expansively read the zone-of-interests test. However, the remaining majority justices above did not join his reading of this test in Clarke. This raises the possibility that the Court may be retooling the doctrine, perhaps because of a changed understanding of the purposes to be served by deploying the injury-in-fact and zone-of-interests tests.

[For more information on standing, see Casenote Law Outline on Administrative Law, Chapter 10, § II, A Party Must Have Standing to Appeal.]

NOTES:

ABBOTT LABORATORIES v. GARDNER (I)
Pharmaceutical manufacturers (P) v.
Commissioner of Food and Drugs (D)
387. U.S. 136 (1967).

NATURE OF CASE: Suit challenging regulations promulgated by the Commissioner of Foods and Drugs (D).

FACT SUMMARY: Manufacturers of prescription drugs (P) brought suit against the Commissioner of Food and Drugs (D), challenging regulations requiring the manufacturers to include both their "established name" and the proprietary name of the drugs on all labels and in all advertisements.

CONCISE RULE OF LAW: Only upon a showing of clear and convincing evidence of a contrary legislative intent should the courts restrict access to judicial review of final agency actions.

FACTS: In 1962 Congress amended the federal Food, Drug and Cosmetic Act to require manufacturers of prescription drugs to print the "established name" corresponding to any proprietary name of the drug prominently on its labels. A similar rule was passed with respect to advertisements for such drugs. Thirty seven (37) individual drug manufacturers (P) and the Pharmaceutical Manufacturers Association (P) to which they belong brought suit challenging the regulations on the basis that the Commissioner (D) exceeded his authority in promulgating the rule.

ISSUE: Should the courts restrict access to judicial review of final agency actions only upon a showing of clear and convincing evidence of a contrary legislative intent?

HOLDING AND DECISION: (Harlan, J.) Yes. Only upon a showing of clear and convincing evidence of a contrary legislative intent should the courts restrict access to judicial review of final agency actions. The issue here is whether Congress intended to forbid pre-enforcement review of this type of regulation promulgated by the Commissioner (D). Cases have held that judicial review of a final agency action by an aggrieved person will not be cut off unless it appears that that was Congress' intent. The Administrative Procedure Act (APA) also provides for review of agency actions for which review is provided by statute or for which there is no other adequate legal remedy. The statutory scheme of the Act does not preclude judicial review of such actions as those taken in the present case, nor has the government demonstrated such an intent.

EDITOR'S ANALYSIS: The Court notes that the intent to preclude judicial review must be gleaned from the statutory scheme as a whole. Furthermore, where a statute expressly provides that certain actions are reviewable, it should not be presumed that all other actions are not reviewable by the courts.

NOTES:

BLOCK v. COMMUNITY NUTRITION INSTITUTE

Federal agency (D) v. Milk producer (P)

467 U.S. 340 (1984).

NATURE OF CASE: Appeal of a reversal of a dismissal of an action challenging certain milk pricing regulations.

FACT SUMMARY: The Community Nutrition Institute (P) challenged the Department of Agriculture (D) minimum milk price regulations.

CONCISE RULE OF LAW: Consumers do not have standing to challenge regulations promulgated under the Agricultural Marketing Agreement Act of 1937.

FACTS: In 1937 Congress enacted the Agricultural Marketing Agreement Act, which provided, among other things, for extensive rulemaking authority in the Department of Agriculture (D) to prevent dairy price collapses. Pursuant to this authority, the Department (D) promulgated rules fixing minimum prices on various classes of milk products. These rules were challenged by individual consumers, several milk handlers, and a consumer organization, the Community Nutrition Institute (P). The district court dismissed for lack of standing and failure to exhaust administrative remedies. The court of appeals reversed as to the consumers, holding that the statutory scheme did not expressly prohibit consumer challenges.

ISSUE: Do consumers have standing to challenge regulations promulgated under the Agricultural Marketing Agreement Act of 1937?

HOLDING AND DECISION: (O'Connor, J.) No. Consumers do not have standing to challenge regulations promulgated under the Agricultural Marketing Agreement Act of 1937. The Administrative Procedure Act gives rise to a presumption of such standing, but it is only a presumption. Where such standing is contrary to the legislative scheme or expressly prohibited, it will not be found. Contrary to the holding of the court of appeals, an explicit prohibition on such standing need not be found. Here, Congress envisioned a complex administrative procedure, and to allow consumer suits would bypass this procedure. Reversed.

EDITOR'S ANALYSIS: Prior to this decision some courts tended to hold, as the court of appeals did here, that congressional desire to prevent citizen standing in challenges to regulations had to be explicit. This was described as "clear and convincing evidence." The Supreme Court, in this opinion, quite clearly rejected this standard.

[For more information on general standing to sue, see Casenote Law Outline on Administrative Law, Chapter 10, Process of Judicial Review, § I, Litigant Must Appeal to Court with Jurisdiction.]

QUICKNOTES

STANDING - Whether a party possesses the right to commence suit against another party by having a personal stake in the resolution of the controversy.

ADMINISTRATIVE REMEDIES - Relief that is sought before an administrative body as opposed to a court.

NOTES:

THUNDER BASIN COAL COMPANY v. REICH

Coal mine operator (P) v. Government agency (D)

510 U.S. 200 (1994).

NATURE OF CASE: Petition for pre-enforcement injunctive relief from agency order.

FACT SUMMARY: Thunder Basin (P) sought pre-enforcement relief from an order by the Mine Safety and Health Administration (MSHA) (D).

CONCISE RULE OF LAW: Initial judicial review of an agency order is determined by the statute's language, structure, purpose and legislative history.

FACTS: Congress adopted the Mine Act to require regular inspections of the nation's mines. Under the law, the miner's are entitled to designate representatives that accompany the government inspectors. After this designation, the mine operator must post information regarding these designees at the mine. Nonunion employees working for Thunder Basin (P) selected two union non-employees as their representatives. However, Thunder Basin (P) refused to post the information as required by the Mine Act. The MSHA (D) responded with a letter instructing that they comply with the law. But Thunder Basin (P) did not wait for any consequences and filed suit seeking pre-enforcement injunctive relief, contending that the designation of non-employees violated their right to exclude union organizers from their property. The court of appeals decided that Thunder Basin (P) was not entitled to this relief.

ISSUE: Is the availability of initial judicial review of an agency order determined by the statute's language, structure, purpose and legislative history?

HOLDING AND DECISION: (Blackmun, J.) Yes. Initial judicial review of an agency order is determined by the statute's language, structure, purpose and legislative history. The Mine Act establishes a detailed structure for reviewing violations of safety standards. The mine operator can challenge a citation before an administrative commission or the citation becomes final. Operators may challenge adverse commission decisions in the appropriate court of appeals. While, the Act is completely silent with respect to pre-enforcement claims, the structure of the Act, however, demonstrates that Congress intended to preclude such challenges. There is no distinction made between pre- and post-enforcement challenges in the review process outlined in the Act. The legislative history of the Act supports this position as well. Therefore, Thunder Basin (P) is not entitled to challenge the decision of MSHA (D) until there has been actual enforcement and/or penalty. Affirmed.

CONCURRENCE: (Scalia, J.) Legislative history is a not proper basis for deciding what a statute means.

EDITOR'S ANALYSIS: The court also rejected the position of Thunder Basin (P) that they would suffer irreparable harm if not allowed to challenge the order before enforcement. Justice Scalia disagreed with this holding, but stated that pre-enforcement judicial review is constitutional even if there was significant harm. Another factor in this case was that Thunder-Basin (P) would have been allowed to challenge a fine for non-compliance if they had let the matter go that far.

QUICKNOTES

JUDICIAL REVIEW - The authority of the courts to review decisions, actions or omissions committed by another agency or branch of government.

INJUNCTIVE RELIEF - A court order issued as a remedy, requiring a person to do, or prohibiting that person from doing, a specific act.

NOTES:

HECKLER v. CHANEY

FDA director (D) v. Prison inmate (P)

470 U.S. 821 (1985).

NATURE OF CASE: Appeal of reversal of dismissal of action to compel FDA (D) enforcement proceedings.

FACT SUMMARY: Chaney (P) brought an action to compel the FDA (D) to stop the use of lethal drugs in executions.

CONCISE RULE OF LAW: A decision by the FDA (D) to refrain from enforcement proceedings is not subject to judicial review.

FACTS: The Food, Drug and Cosmetic Act mandated that the FDA (D) take steps to prevent unauthorized or dangerous uses of approved drugs. Chaney (P), contending that use of approved drugs for execution by injection constituted an unauthorized and dangerous use of drugs, petitioned the FDA (D) to take steps to prevent such use. The FDA (D) declined. Chaney (P) brought an action to compel the FDA (D) to take such steps. The district court granted the FDA (D) summary judgment and dismissed, holding that such agency actions were unreviewable. The appellate court reversed, holding that such actions were reviewable, and further held the decision by the FDA (D) to be improper.

ISSUE: Is a decision by the FDA (D) to refrain from enforcement proceedings subject to judicial review?

HOLDING AND DECISION: (Rehnquist, J.) No. A decision by the FDA (D) to refrain from enforcement proceedings is not subject to judicial review. Traditionally, agency decisions to decline enforcement proceedings have been unreviewable. This is largely due to a respect for the greater knowledgeability that an agency will be presumed to have over a court. Another reason is that agency lack of enforcement generally does not involve coercive intrusion upon personal liberty, the protection of which is the main concern of the courts. As the Act in question gives no hint of an exception of this rule, the decision of the court of appeals must be reversed.

CONCURRENCE: (Brennen, J.) While Congress intended to afford administrative agencies broad discretion in making enforcement decisions, Congress did not intend administrative agencies to ignore clear jurisdictional, regulatory, statutory or constitutional requirements.

CONCURRENCE: (Marshall, J.) Refusals to enforce should be reviewable in the absence of clear and convincing legislative intent to the contrary.

EDITOR'S ANALYSIS: Judicial unreviewability of agency inaction is often likened to prosecutorial discretion. In both instances, societal, not individual, interests are at stake. Justice Marshall takes issue with the analogy, contending that societal interests in criminal prosecutions are much more intangible than agency decisions.

[For more information on review of agency discretion, see Casenote Law Outline on Administrative Law, Chapter 6, § II, Agencies Have Almost Unbridled Authority to Decide.]

QUICKNOTES

5 U.S.C. § 701 - Judicial review does not apply where statistics preclude it.

5 U.S.C. § 706 - Authorizes judicial review of all orders establishing federal motor vehicle safety standards.

FICA § 306 - Provides that FDA is not required to report minor violation if public warning is adequate.

NOTES:

WEBSTER v. DOE

CIA director (D) v. CIA employee (P)

486 U.S. 592 (1988).

NATURE OF CASE: Appeal from vacation of denial of claim for reinstatement.

FACT SUMMARY: When the CIA (D) terminated Doe's (P) employment on learning that he was homosexual, Doe (P) filed an action alleging statutory and constitutional violations by Webster (D), the CIA (D) director.

CONCISE RULE OF LAW: Under § 102(c) of the National Security Act, employee termination decisions made by the Director of the CIA are not judicially reviewable.

FACTS: After working for the Central Intelligence Agency (D) for nine years, being promoted to a position as a covert electronics technician, and being consistently rated as an excellent or outstanding employee, John Doe's (P) employment was terminated after he revealed to the CIA (D) that he was a homosexual. Webster (D), director of the CIA (D), concluded that Doe's (P) homosexuality presented a security threat. Doe (P) submitted to a polygraph test concerning his homosexuality and possible security violations, denied having sexual relations with any foreign nationals, and maintained that he had not disclosed classified information to any of his sexual partners. The test results indicated he had answered all questions truthfully. When Doe (P) refused the CIA's (D) request that he resign, Webster (D) "deemed it necessary and advisable in the interests of the United States to terminate his employment." Doe (P) then filed an action, asserting a variety of statutory and constitutional claims against Webster (D), who moved for dismissal on the ground that § 102(c) of the NSA precluded judicial review of his termination decisions under §§ 701, 702, and 706 of the Administrative Procedure Act (APA). The district court granted Doe's (P) motion for partial summary judgment, and found that Doe (P) had been unlawfully discharged. The court of appeals vacated the district court's judgment and remanded the case for further proceedings, deciding first that judicial review of the CIA's (D) decision was not precluded under APA § 701(a)(1) or (a)(2) and, second, that the CIA (D) regulations cited by Doe (P) did not limit Webster's (D) discretion in making termination decisions.

ISSUE: Under § 102(c) of the National Security Act, are employee termination decisions made by the Director of the CIA judicially reviewable?

HOLDING AND DECISION: (Rehnquist, C.J.) No. Under § 102(c) of the National Security Act, employee termination decisions made by the Director of the CIA are not judicially reviewable. Section 701(a) of the APA limits application of the entire APA to situations in which judicial review is not precluded by statute; subsection (a)(1) is concerned with whether Congress expressed an intent to prohibit judicial review, while subsection (a)(2) applies "in those rare instances where 'statutes are drawn in such broad terms that in a given case there is no law to apply.'" The standard set forth in § 102(c) of the NSA defers to the director and appears to foreclose the application of any meaningful judicial standard of review. Thus, the language and structure of § 102(c) indicate that Congress meant to commit individual employee discharges to the director's discretion and that § 701(a)(2) accordingly precludes judicial review of these decisions under the APA. However, nothing in § 102(c) demonstrates that Congress meant to preclude consideration of colorable constitutional claims arising out of the actions of the director pursuant to that section. Reversed [as to judicial review of terminations under § 102(c)]; remanded [for consideration of Doe's (P) constitutional claims].

DISSENT: (Scalia, J.) Congress can prescribe, at least within broad limits, that for certain jobs the dismissal decision will be unreviewable — that is, will be "committed to agency discretion by law." Further, it is entirely beyond doubt that if Congress intended to exclude judicial review of the President's decision (through the Director of Central Intelligence) to dismiss an officer of the CIA (D), that disposition would be constitutionally permissible. Not the Constitution, our laws, or common sense gives an individual a right to come into court to litigate the reasons for his dismissal as an intelligence agent.

EDITOR'S ANALYSIS: On remand, Doe v. Webster, 769 F. Supp. 1 (D.D.C. 1991), the district court concluded that CIA (D) regulations gave Doe (P) a postprobation property interest in his position and that his discharge without a statement of reasons why his homosexuality posed a security threat and an opportunity to respond to those reasons violated due process. Contrary to the opinion expressed by both Justices O'Connor and Scalia that judicial review of constitutional claims is also precluded in this context, the majority's rejection of all arguments made on this point by Webster (D) sends a clear message that a legislative attempt to preclude review of constitutional claims would be unacceptable. Further, even where national security is concerned, methods exist to balance the need of the individual asserting constitutional claims against the extraordinary needs of the CIA (D) for confidentiality.

[For more information on judicial reviewability, see Casenote Law Outline on Administrative Law, Chapter 9, § V, Administrative Decision May Become Unreviewable.]

QUICKNOTES

NATIONAL SECURITY ACT § 102 - Precludes judicial review of CIA director's employment decisions.

5 U.S.C. § 701 - Judicial review does not apply where statistics preclude it.

McCARTHY v. MADIGAN

Inmate (P) v. Prison employees (D)

503 U.S. 140 (1992).

NATURE OF CASE: Appeal from dismissal of action for damages for constitutional rights violations.

FACT SUMMARY: McCarthy (P), an inmate, contended that he should not have to resort to an internal grievance procedure before initiating suit against prison employees (D) for money damages.

CONCISE RULE OF LAW: Exhaustion of administrative remedies is not required when the litigant's interests in immediate judicial review outweigh the government's interests in efficiency or administrative autonomy.

FACTS: McCarthy (P), an inmate in a federal prison, filed a complaint against four prison employees (D) for violating his constitutional rights under the Eighth Amendment. He sought money damages only. He chose not to pursue the grievance procedure set up by the Federal Bureau of Prisons, which requires an inmate to first seek informal resolution of his claim. If this fails, the inmate must file a written complaint within fifteen days, then appeal within thirty days to the Regional Director, and file a final appeal within an additional thirty days. The district court dismissed the complaint on the ground that McCarthy (P) had failed to exhaust prison administrative remedies, and McCarthy (P) appealed.

ISSUE: Is exhaustion of administrative remedies required when the litigant's interests in immediate judicial review outweigh the government's interests in efficiency or administrative autonomy?

HOLDING AND DECISION: (Blackmun, J.) No. Exhaustion of administrative remedies is not required when the litigant's interests in immediate judicial review outweigh the government's interests in efficiency or administrative autonomy. The general rule is that exhaustion is required because it protects administrative agency authority and promotes judicial efficiency. However, the Court has recognized three sets of circumstances in which individual interests weigh against requiring exhaustion: 1) when exhaustion principles would unduly prejudice subsequent court action; 2) when an administrative agency is unable to grant effective relief; and 3) when an agency is shown to be biased. In this case, the prison grievance procedure imposes rapid filing deadlines that could penalize an inmate who is unable to comply with them. Furthermore, it does not authorize an award of monetary damages — the only relief requested by McCarthy (P). Therefore, given the type of claim raised by McCarthy (P) and the particular characteristics of the Bureau's grievance procedure, McCarthy's (P) individual interests outweigh institutional interests favoring exhaustion. McCarthy (P) is not required to exhaust the grievance procedure. Reversed.

EDITOR'S ANALYSIS: In addition to those articulated in this case, courts have fashioned a number of exceptions to the doctrine of exhaustion. For example, exhaustion is not required when the administrative agency's decision is a forgone conclusion, according to Orion Corp. v. State, 693 P.2d 1369 (Wash. 1985). Nor is it required in instances where the agency's action would have a chilling effect on the plaintiff's First Amendment rights. See Wolff v. Selective Serv. Local Bd., 372 F.2nd 817 (2d Cir. 1967).

[For more information on exhaustion of administrative remedies, see Casenote Law Outline on Administrative Law, Chapter 10, Processes of Judicial Review, § V, The Courts Will Only Hear Appeals When the Plaintiff Has Exhausted All Administrative Remedies.]

NOTES:

DARBY v. CISNEROS

Real estate developer (P) v. HUD (D)
509 U.S. 137 (1993).

NATURE OF CASE: Appeal from dismissal of action to enjoin administrative sanctions.

FACT SUMMARY: Darby (P) and Garvin (P) argued that they should not be required to exhaust available administrative remedies prior to seeking judicial review after being barred from participating in HUD (D) programs.

CONCISE RULE OF LAW: A litigant seeking judicial review of a final agency action under the Administrative Procedure Act need not exhaust available administrative remedies, unless such exhaustion is expressly required by statute or agency rule.

FACTS: Darby (P), a South Carolina real estate developer, and Garvin (P), a mortgage banker,developed a plan to obtain single-family mortgage insurance from HUD for multi-unit projects. The plan circumvented HUD (D) rules that prevented rental properties from receiving single-family mortgage insurance if the mortgagor had financial interests in seven or more similar rental properties in the same project. Darby (P) ultimately obtained financing for three separate multi-unit projects using this plan, but defaulted in 1988, making HUD (D) responsible for $6.6 million in insurance claims. Although HUD (D) had previously audited Garvin's (P) financing plan and concluded there was no wrongdoing, upon default, HUD (D) prohibited Darby (P) and Garvin (P) from participating in any South Carolina HUD (D) program for one year. Darby (P) and Garvin (P) sought administrative review of the decision. The Administrative Law Judge (ALJ) conducted hearings and found that good cause existed to bar petitioners for 18 months. Instead of seeking further administrative review of the ALJ's decision, as permitted under HUD (D) regulations, Darby (P) and Garvin (P) filed suit in district court seeking injunctive relief. HUD (D) moved to dismiss the complaint for failure to seek review. The district court denied the motion and HUD (D) appealed. The Court of Appeals reversed, and the Supreme Court granted certiorari.

ISSUE: Must a litigant seeking judicial review of a final agency action under the APA exhaust all available administrative remedies?

HOLDING AND DECISION: (Blackmun, J.) No. A litigant seeking judicial review of a final agency action under the Administrative Procedure Act need not exhaust available administrative remedies, unless such exhaustion is expressly required by statute or agency rule. APA § 10(a) grants individuals who are adversely affected by an administrative agency's action the general right to seek judicial review. However, APA § 10 establishes that such review is only available when the aggrieved party has exhausted all administrative remedies expressly prescribed by statute or agency rule. When both §§ 10 (a) and (c) are satisfied, the agency action is final and therefore subject to review. As such, courts are not free to impose an additional exhaustion requirement where agency action has become final under APA § 10(c). Reversed and remanded.

EDITOR'S ANALYSIS: Notice that the APA provides a two-prong test. The agency decision must be final and the aggrieved party must have exhausted all administrative remedies if mandated to do so by statute or regulation. While finality is concerned with whether the decisionmaker has reached a definitive position that inflicts an actual, concrete injury, exhaustion refers to the procedures by which an injured party may seek review of an adverse decision.

QUICKNOTES

APA, § 10 (a) - Provides for a general right of judicial review.

APA, § 10 (c) - Judicial review is available for final agency actions.

NOTES:

ABBOTT LABORATORIES v. GARDNER (II)
Pharmaceutical manufacturers (P) v. Commissioner of Food and Drugs (D)
387. U.S. 136 (1967).

NATURE OF CASE: Suit challenging regulations promulgated by the Commissioner of Foods and Drugs (D).

FACT SUMMARY: Manufacturers of prescription drugs (P) brought suit against the Commissioner of Food and Drugs (D), challenging regulations requiring the manufacturers to include both their "established name" and the proprietary name of the drugs on all labels and in all advertisements.

CONCISE RULE OF LAW: Courts are reluctant to apply injunctive and declaratory judgment remedies to administrative determinations, unless they arise in the context of a controversy which is "ripe" for judicial resolution.

FACTS: In 1962 Congress amended the federal Food, Drug and Cosmetic Act to require manufacturers of prescription drugs to print the "established name" corresponding to any proprietary name of the drug prominently on its labels. A similar rule was passed with respect to advertisements for such drugs. Thirty seven (37) individual drug manufacturers (P) and the Pharmaceutical Manufacturers Association (P) to which they belong brought suit challenging the regulations on the basis that the Commissioner (D) exceeded his authority in promulgating the rule.

ISSUE: Are courts reluctant to apply injunctive and declaratory judgment remedies to administrative determinations, unless they arise in the context of a controversy which is "ripe" for judicial resolution?

HOLDING AND DECISION: (Harlan, J.) Yes. Courts are reluctant to apply injunctive and declaratory judgment remedies to administrative determinations, unless they arise in the context of a controversy which is "ripe" for judicial resolution. The ripeness doctrine serves to prevent the courts from adjudicating matters as to which there has not yet been a final agency decision and for which the parties may feel the effects of the court's decision. This also precludes courts from involving themselves in disputes as to administrative policies. This requires the court to consider two questions: (1) whether the matter is fit for a judicial decision; and (2) the hardship to the parties of failure to render such a decision. Here the issues presented are appropriate for judicial resolution. There are no further administrative proceedings to be held regarding the issue, and both parties have moved for summary judgment. Also, the regulations at issue constitute "final agency action." Moreover, the impact of the regulations upon the drug manufacturers (P) is sufficiently direct and immediate so that judicial review is proper. The regulations have a direct and immediate effect on the daily operations of all drug companies. The manufacturers (P) must either invest heavily in printing new labels and advertisements or risk criminal and civil penalties.

DISSENT: (Fortas, J.) A suit for injunctive or declaratory relief does not lie in the absence of a clear indication that the type of review provided by the law is inadequate, the controversies are "ripe" for adjudication, and no public interest outweighs the private interests which the litigation seeks to advance.

EDITOR'S ANALYSIS: The Court declined review of another case, Toilet Goods Association v. Gardner, 387 U.S. 158 (1967), on the basis that the matter was not "ripe" for review. There the challenged regulation authorized the Commissioner (D) to "immediately suspend" the FDA's approval of products containing color additives if the manufacturer did not provide access to FDA administrators to all aspects of the manufacturing process. The Court declined review on the following grounds: (1) the matter presented a "purely legal" issue; (2) the statute was permissive in that it only gave notice that such inspections may be required; and (3) the impact of the regulation would not be felt in the companies' daily operations.

CHAPTER 6
AGENCY STRUCTURE

QUICK REFERENCE RULES OF LAW

1. **Delegation of Legislative Power: Third Phase.** Establishment of the U.S. Sentencing Commission is constitutional. (Mistretta v. United States)

   [For more information on the nondelegation doctrine, see Casenote Law Outline on Administrative Law, Chapter 3, Empowerment Process, §II, The Non-Delegation Clause.]

2. **Delegation of Legislative Power: Statutory Interpretation.** OSHA (D) must demonstrate a significant risk of harm as a predicate to issuing a new or revised standard. (Industrial Union Dept. v. American Petroleum Institute)

   [For more information on cost-benefit analyses, see Casenote Law Outline on Administrative Law, Chapter 7,Rulemaking Processes, § IV, Cost-Benefit Analysis May Be Required.]

3. **Delegation of Judicial Power: Article 3, § I.** The adjudication of common law counterclaims by the CFTC is not unconstitutional. (Commodity Futures Trading Commission v. Schor)

   [For more information on agency adjudication, see Casenote Law Outline on Administrative Law, Chapter 3, Empowerment Processes, § I, Agencies Can Adjudicate Some Controversies.]

4. **The Legislative Veto: Presentment and Bicameralism.** Where the action of either house of Congress is legislative in nature, such action is subject to the presentment and bicameral requirements of Article I of the Constitution. (Immigration and Naturalization Services v. Chadha)

   [For more information on the legislative veto, see Casenote Law Outline on Administrative Law, Chapter 3, Empowerment Process, §II, The Non-Delegation Clause.]

5. **Post-Veto Developments: Congressional Review of Agency Rulemaking.** Legislative agents may make non-binding recommendations to agencies of the executive branch. (Lear Siegler, Inc. v. Lehman)

6. **Appointment of "Officers of the United States."** Officers of the United States must be appointed in a manner consistent with Article II, § 2 of the Constitution. (Buckey v. Valeo)

   [For more information on congressional appointment powers, see Casenote Law Outline on Administrative Law, Chapter 3, Empowerment Process, § III, President Has Authority to Appoint Agency Administrators.]

7. **Appointment of "Inferior Officers."** The independent counsel provision of the Ethics in Government Act is not unconstitutional. (Morrison v. Olson)

   [For more information on legislative powers, see Casenote Law Outline on Administrative Law, Chapter 3, § III, President Has Authority to Appoint Agency Administrators.]

8. **Limitations on Presidential Removal.** The President cannot remove officials whose agency functions are quasi-legislative and quasi-judicial in nature, and not merely extensions of the Executive Branch of government. (Humphrey's Executor v. United States)

[For more information on restrictions on the Presidential removal authority, see Casenote Law Outline on Administrative Law, Chapter 3, Empowerment Process, § III, President Has Authority to Appoint Agency Administrators.]

9. **Limitations on Presidential Removal.** Congress may impose a "good cause" restriction on the President's power to remove an executive official. (Morrison v. Olson)

10. **Legislative Removal.** Congress cannot retain power to remove executive branch officers except by impeachment. (Bowsher v. Synar)

[For more information on the removal of agency administrators, see Casenote Law Outline on Administrative Law, Chapter 3, Empowerment Process, § III, President Has Authority to Appoint Agency Administrators.]

MISTRETTA v. UNITED STATES

Sentenced criminal (D) v. Federal government (P)

488 U.S. 361 (1989).

NATURE OF CASE: Review of challenge to federal law establishing the U.S. Sentencing Commission.

FACT SUMMARY: Mistretta (D) contended that the establishment of the U.S. Sentencing Commission was unconstitutional as a violation of separation of powers.

CONCISE RULE OF LAW: Establishment of the U.S. Sentencing Commission is constitutional.

FACTS: Congress enacted a law establishing the U.S. Sentencing Commission. The Commission, which was empowered to promulgate binding sentencing guidelines in criminal cases, was to be made up of seven members, three of whom had to be federal judges. Members were to be appointed by the President, with the ratification of the Senate. Members could be removed for "good cause." The Commission was established as part of the judicial branch of the federal government. Mistretta (D), in appealing the sentence he received under the guidelines promulgated by the Commission, challenged the law establishing it as an unconstitutional violation of separation of powers. The court of appeals rejected this challenge, and the Supreme Court granted review.

ISSUE: Is establishment of the U.S. Sentencing Commission constitutional?

HOLDING AND DECISION: (Blackmun, J.) Yes. Establishment of the U.S. Sentencing Commission is constitutional. This Court has never held that the three branches of government must be hermetically sealed. Rather, the concern with separation of powers is that one branch not be allowed to aggrandize itself at the expense of another. Mistretta (D) makes the alternative arguments that the law either unacceptably empowers or weakens the judiciary. Neither argument stands up. Merely placing a nonjudicial body within the judiciary does not inappropriately augment the judiciary's power; only if the body more appropriately belongs in another branch will this be so. Here, it cannot be denied that sentencing is an appropriate judicial function, so the excessive empowerment argument fails. Neither does the law weaken the judiciary. Even though the Commission's three judges can be removed from the Commission by the President, they remain Article III judges, appointed for life and not removeable from their judgeships by the president. Consequently, the placement of judges on the Commission does not weaken the judiciary. In view of these considerations, the constitutional attack on the Commission must fail. Affirmed.

EDITOR'S ANALYSIS: Federal judges may be removed only by impeachment. The law at issue here permitted removal for "good cause," something not encompassed within the Constitution's definition of impeachment. Nonetheless, the law was not seen as inconsistent with the Constitution. A Commission member removed for good cause remains a judge and so is in no worse a position than before his Commission appointment.

[For more information on the nondelegation doctrine, see Casenote Law Outline on Administrative Law, Chapter 3, Empowerment Process, § II, The Non-Delegation Clause.]

QUICKNOTES

DELEGATION - The authorization of one person to act on another's behalf.

IMPEACHMENT - The discrediting of a witness by offering evidence to show that the witness lacks credibility.

SEPARATION OF POWERS - The system of checks and balances preventing one branch of government from infringing upon exercising the powers of another branch of government.

NOTES:

INDUSTRIAL UNION DEPARTMENT, AFL-CIO v. AMERICAN PETROLEUM INSTITUTE
Parties not identified.
448 U.S. 607 (1980).

NATURE OF CASE: Appeal from invalidation of OSHA standard.

FACT SUMMARY: OSHA (D) set a very low 1 ppm exposure standard for occupational benzene exposure.

CONCISE RULE OF LAW: OSHA (D) must demonstrate a significant risk of harm as a predicate to issuing a new or revised standard.

FACTS: OSHA (D) set a 1 pm exposure standard for occupational benzene exposure. The majority of evidence presented showed that cancer was only shown to be caused by exposure above 10 ppm. Showings of cancer occurrences in exposures under 10 ppm could not be conclusively linked to the benzene exposure. OSHA (D) set the level at 1 ppm because it presented an increased risk of causing cancer. The court of appeals found that the level set by OSHA (D) was not supported by the evidence and thus was not valid.

ISSUE: Must OSHA (D) demonstrate a significant risk of harm as a predicate for issuing a new or revised standard?

HOLDING AND DECISION: (Stevens, J.) Yes. OSHA (D) must demonstrate a significant risk of harm as a predicate for issuing a new or revised standard. The burden of proof in an administrative hearing is on the agency promulgating the rule. Unless Congress has shifted the burden, an agency must prove the validity of its decisions. In this case Congress did not shift the burden of proof away from the agency. OSHA (D) failed to demonstrate that there was a significant risk caused by levels under 1 ppm. OSHA (D) only demonstrated that cancer was likely to occur from exposures between 1 ppm and 10 ppm; this did not meet its burden of proof. Affirmed.

CONCURRENCE: (Rehnquist, J.) Congress here improperly delegated authority to the executive branch; Congress must establish the general policy and standards supporting the law and allow agencies to refine such standards.

DISSENT: (Marshall, J.) The majority undertakes its own factual inquiry based on the record. The record demonstrated substantial evidence that exposure to benzene caused cancer, and thus OSHA's (D) regulation should be upheld.

EDITOR'S ANALYSIS: The Court here is walking a fine line between determining whether an agency's decision is justified based on the facts or whether the agency is operating in its policy-making capacity to make a determination when the facts are insufficient. Note that this was a closely divided decision that contained four dissents and had no majority opinion. Therefore it is of little use in predicting how courts will view subsequent cost-benefit analyses.

[For more information on cost-benefit analyses, see Casenote Law Outline on Administrative Law, Chapter 7, § IV, Cost-Benefit Analysis May Also Be Required.]

QUICKNOTES

OCCUPATIONAL SAFETY AND HEALTH ACT OF 1970 - Enacted for the purpose of ensuring safe and healthy working conditions.

29 USC § 655 - The Secretary of Labor, in promulgating standards for dealing with toxic materials shall make sure the standard is safe for workers based on the best avaiable evidence.

NOTES:

COMMODITY FUTURES TRADING COMMISSION v. SCHOR

Government agency (D) v. Investor (P)

478 U.S. 833 (1986).

NATURE OF CASE: Review of dismissal of counterclaims appended to a complaint seeking reparations filed with the CFTC.

FACT SUMMARY: Schor (P), seeking reparations from a commodities broker before the CFTC (D), contended that the CFTC (D) had no jurisdiction to entertain common law counterclaims.

CONCISE RULE OF LAW: The adjudication of common law counterclaims by the CFTC (D) is not unconstitutional.

FACTS: Schor (P), dissatisfied with the performance of certain commodity futures investments he had made, filed an action seeking reparations with the Commodity Futures Trading Commission (CFTC) (D) against Conti (D), a commodities broker. Conti (D) counterclaimed for payment of certain fees. The CFTC (D) Administrative Law Judge ruled in Conti's (D) favor in both the complaint and the counterclaim. Schor (P) then appealed, contending that the CFTC (D) had no jurisdiction to entertain common law counterclaims. The court of appeals dismissed the counterclaim, holding that the CFTC (D) lacked jurisdiction to entertain it. Conti (D) obtained review in the Supreme Court.

ISSUE: Is the adjudication of common law counterclaims by the CFTC (D) unconstitutional?

HOLDING AND DECISION: (O'Connor, J.) No. The adjudication of common law counterclaims by the CFTC (D) is not unconstitutional. First, the CFTC (D) itself considers such jurisdiction to be valid, and the views of an administrative agency towards matters germane to it are given no small weight. More importantly, CFTC (D) jurisdiction over counterclaims in actions before it does not violate the purposes underlying Article III. Article III is meant to ensure a free and independent judiciary. It was not meant to, nor does it, confer plenary jurisdiction over all matters in Article III courts. In deciding whether the delegation of quasi-judicial power to a non-Article III court is constitutional, the main question must be whether the delegation tends to encroach on the essential attributes of judicial power. Here, this does not appear to be the case. For one, only a particularized area of law is implicated here; the CFTC (D) has not been given broad power to adjudicate common law cases. Further, decisions of the CFTC (D) ALJs are subject to de novo review. Finally, the level of review, "weight of the evidence," is not excessively deferential. In short, the enabling statute has not expanded the power of the legislature or executive at the expense of the judiciary and, therefore, was valid. Reversed.

EDITOR'S ANALYSIS: Four years prior to the present action, the Court had invalidated the statutory bankruptcy system based on the same considerations discussed here. Congress had entrusted the bankruptcy system to non-Article III judges and had given them very broad powers. The Court in this action distinguished that case, Northern Pipeline Construction Co. v. Marathon Pipe Line Co., 458 U.S. 50 (1982), by noting that the jurisdiction of the CFTC here was much narrower.

[For more information on agency adjudication, see Casenote Law Outline on Administrative Law, Chapter 3, § I, Agencies Can Adjudicate Some Controversies.]

QUICKNOTES

U.S. CONSTITUTION, ARTICLE III - Guarantees an independent an impartial adjudication by federal judiciary.

DE NOVO - The review of a lower court decision by an appellate court, which is hearing the case as if it had not been previously heard and as if no judgment had been rendered.

NOTES:

IMMIGRATION AND NATURALIZATION SERVICE v. CHADHA

INS (P) v. Deported immigrant (D)

462 U.S. 919 (1983).

NATURE OF CASE: Challenge to constitutionality of resolution procedure for overturning deportation suspension.

FACT SUMMARY: Chadha (D) challenged the constitutionality of an Immigration and Nationality Act (INA) provision allowing either the House of Representatives (P) or the Senate, acting individually, to overturn the Attorney General's suspension of deportation proceedings by passing a resolution stating in substance that the deportation suspension is not favored.

CONCISE RULE OF LAW: Where the action of either house of Congress is legislative in nature, such action is subject to the presentment and bicameral requirements of Article I of the Constitution.

FACTS: Chadha (D), an East Indian born in Kenya, remained in the United States after his visa expired. He was ordered deported, but the Attorney General suspended the deportation. Pursuant to an INA provision allowing either House of Congress to overturn a deportation suspension by adopting a resolution to that effect, the House of Representatives (P) adopted a resolution overturning Chadha's (D) suspension, and he was ordered deported. There was no public hearing, report, or meaningful statement of reasons on the committee's recommendation favoring the resolution. Chadha (D) challenged the constitutionality of the House of Representatives' (P) action under the INA provision.

ISSUE: Where the action of either house of Congress is legislative in nature, is such action subject to the presentment and bicameral requirements of Article I of the Constitution?

HOLDING AND DECISION: (Burger, C.J.) Yes. Where the action of either house of Congress is legislative in nature, such action is subject to the presentment and bicameral requirements of Article I of the Constitution. The clear and unambiguous dictates of Article I of the Constitution require that, before any legislation is to take effect, it must have been passed with the concurrence of the prescribed majority of both houses of Congress, and must be presented to the President for approval. Presentment of legislation to the President establishes a salutary check on the legislature, and assures that a "national" perspective is grafted on the legislative process. The bicameral requirement assures that the legislative power will be exercised only after full study and debate in separate settings. The powers delegated to each branch of government are identifiable, and when any branch acts, it presumptively exercises the power delegated to it. The legislative character of the House's (P) action in the present case is apparent, since it is conceded that, absent the INA provision, Chadha's (D) deportation could only have been accomplished by legislation requiring deportation. The House's (P) action does not fall into one of the constitutionally prescribed exceptions to the bicameral requirement, and involves determinations of policy which should only be implemented by adhering to the presentment and bicameral requirements of Article I. The action taken by the House (P) pursuant to the INA provision was in violation of Article I of the Constitution.

DISSENT: (White, J.) If possible, this decision should have been decided on the narrower grounds of separation of powers and sounds a death knell for nearly 200 other statutes where Congress has reserved a legislative veto. The decision is inconsistent with the accepted practice of delegating lawmaking power to independent executive agencies and private persons and ignores the fact that the operation of the INA provision at question satisfies the bicameral and presentment requirements of Article I.

EDITOR'S ANALYSIS: It is not clear to what extent the "legislative veto" is dead. It is clear, however, that Congress can accomplish many of the legislative veto's objectives through the use of traditional weapons in its legislative and political arsenal. Among others, Congress can tailor statutes more carefully, can provide that an agency's legislative power will expire after a given period of time, and perhaps most importantly, can control an agency's budget. Each of these alternatives has obvious drawbacks and can serve to greatly undermine an agency's effectiveness.

[For more information on the legislative veto, see Casenote Law Outline on Administrative Law, Chapter 3, Empowerment Process, §II, The Non-Delegation Clause.]

QUICKNOTES

LEGISLATIVE VETO - A resolution passed by one or both legislature houses that is intended to block an administrative regulation or action.

SEPARATION OF POWERS - The system of checks and balances preventing one branch of government from infringing upon exercising the powers of another branch of government.

PRESENTMENT - The act of bringing a Congressional decision before the President for his approval or veto.

BICAMERALISM - The necessity of approval by a majority of both houses of Congress in ratifying legislation or approving other legislative action.

LEAR SIEGLER, INC. v. LEHMAN

Bidder for government contract (P) v. Department of Navy (D)

842 F.2d 1102 (9th Cir. 1988).

NATURE OF CASE: Appeal from decision upholding judicial enforcement of a stay on the awarding of a contract.

FACT SUMMARY: The Navy (D) refused to obey a stay on the awarding of a contract following a protest by Lear Siegler (P) to the Comptroller General.

CONCISE RULE OF LAW: Legislative agents may make non-binding recommendations to agencies of the executive branch.

FACTS: Congress passed the Competition in Contracting Act of 1984. The Act authorized the Comptroller General, who heads the legislature's General Accounting Office, to investigate protests lodged by losing bidders regarding competitive procedures. The law provided for an automatic 90-day stay on the award of a contract while the investigation proceeded. The agency involved is not bound by the recommendations produced by the Comptroller General after the investigation. Lear Siegler (P) protested the bidding procedure in a case involving a Navy contract. The Navy (D) refused to obey the stay provision, objecting that it was an unconstitutional restriction on executive branch powers. Siegler (P) sought judicial enforcement and the district court affirmed the constitutionality of the provision. The Navy (D) appealed.

ISSUE: May legislative agents make non-binding recommendations to agencies of the executive branch?

HOLDING AND DECISION: (Fletcher, J.) Yes. Legislative agents may make non-binding recommendations to agencies of the executive branch. Generally, Congress may not vest itself, or its own agents to discharge executive branch tasks and powers. Furthermore, it may not take action that has the purpose and effect of altering the legal rights and duties of parties without going through the standard procedure for enacting legislation. Thus, the court struck down as unconsitutional the legislative veto of the Immigration and Nationality Act, whereby Congress directly controlled the execution of the laws. In the present case, the stay provisions do not establish any control for the Comptroller over the disposition of a particular issue. The recommendations to the agency are non-binding, so the stay cannot be used to coerce the agency to make a particular decision. Instead, the stay only forces a temporary dialogue between the agency and the legislature. Therefore, the stay provision is not an unconstitutional incursion by the legislature into the executive powers. Affirmed.

EDITOR'S ANALYSIS: The case of INS v. Chadha, 462 U.S. 919 (1983), is where the court first struck down the legislative veto. Congress tried a few different strategies to get around the problem. Fast-track procedures were instituted in order to correct agency mistakes, as viewed by Congress.

QUICKNOTES

LEGISLATIVE VETO - A resolution passed by one or both legislature houses that is intended to block an administrative regulation or action.

NOTES:

BUCKLEY v. VALEO
Member of Federal Election Commission (P) v. Opposing member (D)
424 U.S. 1 (1976).

NATURE OF CASE: Appeal of challenge to portions of the Federal Election Campaign Act of 1971.

FACT SUMMARY: Members of the Federal Election Commission were to be appointed by a method deviating from Article II, § 2 of the Constitution.

CONCISE RULE OF LAW: Officers of the United States must be appointed in a manner consistent with Article II, § 2 of the Constitution.

FACTS: The Federal Election Campaign Act of 1971 created the Federal Election Campaign Commission, which was given broad sanctioning and investigative power with respect to elections. The Commission consisted of six voting members appointed by the President Pro Tem of the Senate, the Speaker of the House, and the President, each selecting two. The Secretary of the Senate and the Clerk of the House were nonvoting members. The Act was challenged on constitutional grounds. The court of appeals upheld the section dealing with the Commission.

ISSUE: Must officers of the United States be appointed in a manner consistent with Article II, § 2 of the Constitution?

HOLDING AND DECISION: [Per curiam.] Yes. Officers of the United States must be appointed in a manner consistent with Article II, § 2 of the Constitution. The Constitution provides that no member of Congress will be appointed an officer of the United States during his term. This demonstrates that the Framers intended that strict separation be maintained between executive officers and legislative officials. Further, the Constitution mandates that all such executive officials shall be nominated by the President and confirmed by the Senate. The Commission in question exercises important executive functions, and, therefore, its members are officers of the United States. This being the case, they must be appointed per the constitutional requirements of Article II. Reversed.

EDITOR'S ANALYSIS: In theory, the Court created a fairly simple standard to follow in this area. Congress may appoint officials who perform purely legislative acts but not officers who perform executive or judicial acts. Of course, the principle is much easier in theory than in practice, and uncertainty will always exist as to which sort of officials do not have to be appointed pursuant to Article II.

[For more information on congressional appointment powers, see Casenote Law Outline on Administrative Law, Chapter 3, Empowerment Processes, § III, President Has Authority to Appoint Agency Administrators.]

QUICKNOTES

U.S. CONSTITUTION, ARTICLE II, § 2 - Provides that the President shall nominate, with The Senate's advice and consent, executive officials.

FEDERAL ELECTION CAMPAIGN ACT - Created a commission to investigate and administrate federal elections.

NOTES:

MORRISON v. OLSON

Assistant attorney general (D) v. Independent prosecutor (P)

487 U.S. 654 (1988).

NATURE OF CASE: Appeal from order quashing subpoenas issued at behest of a special prosecutor.

FACT SUMMARY: The independent counsel provisions of the Ethics in Government Act were challenged as unconstitutional.

CONCISE RULE OF LAW: The independent counsel provision of the Ethics in Government Act is not unconstitutional.

FACTS: In passing the Ethics in Government Act, Congress created the office of Special Prosecutor to investigate misdeeds by government officials. The Act provided that the Attorney General must investigate allegations and report to a special judicial division, which was enabled to appoint an independent counsel which in turn would have full prosecutorial authority. The counsel could be removed only by impeachment or by the Attorney General for good cause. The Act also provided for congressional oversight. Olson (P), under investigation by Prosecutor Morrison (D), filed an action seeking to quash certain grand jury subpoenas issued at the behest of Morrison (D). The district court denied such relief, but the court of appeals reversed, holding the independent counsel portions of the Act unconstitutional. The Supreme Court accepted review.

ISSUE: Are the independent counsel provisions of the Ethics in Government Act unconstitutional?

HOLDING AND DECISION: (Rehnquist, C.J.) No. The independent counsel provisions of the Ethics in Government Act are not unconstitutional. Due to the limited scope of the counsel's office, the counsel is an inferior officer, not a principal officer that must be appointed by the President. Also, there is no constitutional prohibition on interbranch appointments, so a judicial body appointing an executive officer does not in itself violate the Constitution. This Court is of the opinion that the supervisory powers of the special division are of a ministerial nature and do not trespass on the authority of the Executive. Apart from impeachment, it is only the Attorney General who can remove the Special Prosecutor. Finally, this Court is of the opinion that the office of the Special Prosecutor does not violate the principle of separation of powers. While the Prosecutor does report to Congress, he is much more answerable to the Attorney General, who, significantly, retains the power to remove the Prosecutor. The Court believes that this does not unduly interfere with the powers of the President in enforcing the laws. For these reasons, the Court considers the office of the Special Prosecutor to be constitutional. Reversed.

DISSENT: (Scalia, J.) The function of the independent counsel is clearly an executive function. However, in the light of the position's broad powers and the fact that the independent counsel cannot be removed at the will of the executive branch, it cannot be considered an inferior position. Thus, the Court is incorrect in using the inferior status to uphold the appointment. The independent counsel infringes on the President's power, which the Congress cannot limit by legislation.

EDITOR'S ANALYSIS: The Appointments Clause of Article II mandates appointment of noninferior officers the President, with consent of the Senate. The Special Prosecutor is not so appointed. The Court looked to the breadth of the Prosecutor's office and decided that although the Prosecutor has wide-ranging powers, the ad hoc nature of the office mandated a conclusion that the office was inferior.

[For more information on legislative powers, see Casenote Law Outline on Administrative Law, Chapter 3, Empowerment Processes, § III, President Has Authority to Appoint Agency Administrators.]

QUICKNOTES

ETHICS IN GOVERNMENT ACT - Allows for the appointment of a special prosecutor to investigate high ranking government officials.

APPOINTMENT'S CLAUSE, ARTICLE II, U.S. CONSTITUTION - President shall nominate principal officials with the Senator's advice and consent.

NOTES:

HUMPHREY'S EXECUTOR v. UNITED STATES

Executor of estate (P) v. Federal government (D)

295 U.S. 602 (1935).

NATURE OF CASE: Action to recover back pay for wrongful discharge.

FACT SUMMARY: Humphrey (P) contended that the President could not remove him as a commissioner of the Federal Trade Commission merely because of a difference in philosophy.

CONCISE RULE OF LAW: The President cannot remove officials whose agency functions are quasi-legislative and quasi-judicial in nature, and not merely extensions of the Executive Branch of government.

FACTS: President Roosevelt felt that his predecessors had appointed commissioners to the Federal Trade Commission whose philosophies were contradictory to the legislative intent in creating that body. As a result he attempted to remove Humphrey (P) as a commissioner, based on this conflict of philosophy, and not on any wrongdoing on Humphrey's (P) part. Humphrey (P) challenged his removal and unconstitutional as beyond the President's power. The government (D) defended, contending the President's power to remove administrators could not be constitutionally limited. The Court of Claims certified Humphrey's (P) suit for back pay to the Supreme Court.

ISSUE: Can the President remove administrative officials whose agencies perform quasi-legislative and quasi-judicial functions and are not merely extensions of the executive branch?

HOLDING AND DECISION: (Sutherland, J.) No. Although the President may remove administrators whose functions are merely executive in nature, those whose statutory authority and duty is to act in a legislature or judicial mode cannot be so removed unless by congressional consent. The Federal Trade Commission was created not as a department of the executive branch but as a means of carrying into effect legislative and judicial powers. Thus it is an agency of the legislative and judicial departments of government. Therefore, in order to prevent the executive department from obtaining indirect control over an agency outside its purview, the President is denied removal power except for enumerated reasons in the Federal Trade Commission Act. Therefore Humphrey's (P) removal was invalid.

EDITOR'S ANALYSIS: This case specifically clarifies and limits the holding of an earlier case, Myers v. United States, 272 U.S. 52 (1926), which held that the President could unilaterally remove an administrator whose function was purely executive in nature. The rationale stated in Myers was that the President must be able to command loyalty and confidence from those performing executive functions. The Court in this case limits Myers to executive agencies, and states the President's removal power depends upon the character of the office involved.

[For more information on restrictions on the Presidential removal authority, see Casenote Law Outline on Administrative Law, Chapter 3, Empowerment Process, § III, President Has Authority to Appoint Agency Administrators.]

QUICKNOTES

EXECUTIVE BRANCH - The branch of government responsible for the administration of the laws.

WRONGFUL DISCHARGE - Unlawful termination of an individual's employment.

NOTES:

BOWSHER v. SYNAR

Congress (D) v. Comptroller General (P)

478 U.S. 714 (1986).

NATURE OF CASE: Appeal from order invalidating the Balanced Budget Act.

FACT SUMMARY: Synar (P) contended that the Balanced Budget Act violated separation of powers by providing strict requirements for appointment of an executive branch office.

CONCISE RULE OF LAW: Congress cannot retain power to remove executive branch officers except by impeachment.

FACTS: Congress enacted the Balanced Budget Act which invested in the Comptroller General the power to make broad budgetary decisions as a member of the executive branch. The Comptroller was appointed by the President from a list provided by Congress. Removal was obtained by a joint resolution of Congress. Synar (P) sued, contending the statute unconstitutionally violated the separation of powers doctrine. The district court invalidated the statute. The court of appeals affirmed, and the Supreme Court granted certiorari.

ISSUE: Can Congress retain power to remove executive branch officers?

HOLDING AND DECISION: (Burger, C.J.) No. Congress cannot retain power to remove executive branch officers except by impeachment. Any other removal power over executive officers imposes undue power over that branch and is inconsistent with separation of powers. Such would make the executive officer subservient to Congress and, in effect, allow Congress to execute the laws. As a result, the statute was unconstitutional. Affirmed.

CONCURRENCE: (Stevens, J.) The Comptroller has long been considered subservient to Congress.

DISSENT: (White, J.) The application of separation of powers in this manner interferes with the mutual workings of the legislative and executive branches.

DISSENT: (Blackmun, J.) The removal power does not equate with execution of the law.

EDITOR'S ANALYSIS: The Comptroller performs many functions which identify the office more closely with Congress than with the executive branch. The office settles all claims against the government and determines all accounts owed or owing. Despite this, the office was created under the executive branch.

[For more information on the removal of agency administrators, see Casenote Law Outline on Administrative Law, Chapter 3, Empowerment Process, § III, President Has Authority to Appoint Agency Administrators.]

QUICKNOTES

IMPEACHMENT - The discrediting of a witness by offering evidence to show that the witness lacks credibility.

SEPARATION OF POWERS - The system of checks and balances preventing one branch of government from infringing upon exercising the powers of another branch of government.

LEGISLATIVE BRANCH - The branch of government charged with the promulgation of laws.

EXECUTIVE BRANCH - The branch of government responsible for the administration of the laws.

NOTES:

Notes

CHAPTER 7
INSPECTIONS, REPORTS & SUBPOENAS

QUICK REFERENCE RULES OF LAW

1. **Legal Authority to Inspect.** Administrative searches are reasonable searches, but still require a warrant. (Camara v. Municipal Court)

2. **Legal Authority to Inspect.** An administrative inspection, based upon specific evidence of a violation, must bear a relation to that violation. (Trinity Industries, Inc. v. OSHRC)

3. **Legal Authority to Inspect.** A warrant application for an administrative search is valid if the plan is based on specific, neutral criteria and it adequately establishes that the particular company was selected pursuant to the neutral criteria. (In Re Trinity Industries, Inc.)

4. **Remedies for Illegal Inspections.** The exclusionary rule that bars illegally seized evidence from being used in a criminal prosecution does not apply against use in a civil proceeding. (United States v. Janis)

5. **Remedies for Illegal Inspections.** The exclusionary rule for illegally seized evidence does not apply in civil deportation hearings. (INS v. Lopez-Mendoza)

6. **Recordkeeping and Reporting Requirements: Fourth Amendment.** Government agencies may not use their subpoena powers for improper purposes. (Freese v. Federal Deposit Insurance Corp.)

7. **Recordkeeping and Reporting Requirements: Fourth Amendment.** Subpoenas are not too broad as long as the information sought is reasonably relevant. (Adams v. Federal Trade Commission)

8. **Recordkeeping and Reporting Requirements: Fifth Amendment.** The custodian of corporate records cannot resist a subpoena on the grounds that such production would violate his Fifth Amendment rights against self-incrimination. (Braswell v. U.S)

9. **Recordkeeping and Reporting Requirements: Fifth Amendment.** The required records doctrine with respect to self-incrimination does not apply to general records needed to determine tax liability. (Smith v. Richert)

10. **Parallel Proceedings.** Parallel investigations and proceedings by agencies are allowed as long as they do not prejudice substantial rights of the investigated party. (Securities and Exchange Commission v. Dresser Industries, Inc.)

11. **Parallel Proceedings.** Agencies do not have to choose between criminal and civil proceedings or delay civil proceedings pending the outcome of a criminal trial. (United States v. Kordel)

12. **Parallel Proceedings.** An IRS summons must be enforced if it is issued in good faith before a recommendation for criminal prosecution. (United States v. LaSalle National Bank)

CAMARA v. MUNICIPAL COURT

Apartment owner (D) v. Court (P)

387 U.S. 523 (1967).

NATURE OF CASE: Appeal from conviction for not permitting a building inspection.

FACT SUMMARY: Camara (D) refused to let city building inspectors enter his apartment.

CONCISE RULE OF LAW: Administrative searches are reasonable searches, but still require a warrant.

FACTS: San Francisco building inspectors sought to inspect Camara's (D) apartment pursuant to a general city ordinance. Camara (D) refused to allow the inspectors to enter his apartment without a warrant and was convicted of violating the municipal code. Camara (D) appealed, claiming that the proposed search violated the Fourth Amendment.

ISSUE: Are administrative searches reasonable searches requiring a warrant?

HOLDING AND DECISION: (White, J.) Yes. Administrative searches are reasonable searches, but still require a warrant. The Fourth Amendment was designed to safeguard the privacy and security of individuals against arbitrary invasions by governmental officials. Except in certain cases, a search of private property without proper consent is an unreasonable search, unless a warrant has authorized the search. Probable cause is the standard by which a decision to search is considered reasonable and constitutional. Administrative searches that cover an entire area to enforce community building standards have a long history of acceptance, are necessary to protect the public, and involve a limited invasion of privacy. Thus, an area inspection is reasonable as long as a warrant is issued prior to the inspection. A warrant does not need to consider a specific condition or knowledge about a particular dwelling. Without a warrant, a person is unable to verify the need for, or the appropriate limits of, the inspection. Accordingly, the city building inspectors should have obtained a warrant first, and Camara (D) should not have been charged with a crime for refusing to allow the inspection.

EDITOR'S ANALYSIS: The court acknowledged that some administrative searches might be justified by emergency situations. Obviously, this case did not provide that justification, since the inspectors tried on three different occasions to inspect Camara's (D) apartment. Subsequently, the court made an exception to the warrant requirement for administrative searches of industries that had a long history of close government regulation.

QUICKNOTES

FOURTH AMENDMENT - Provides that persons be secure as to their person and private belongings against unreasonable searches and seizures.

NOTES:

TRINITY INDUSTRIES, INC. v. OSHRC
Manufacturer (D) v. Government agency (P)
16 F.3d 1455 (6th Cir. 1994).

NATURE OF CASE: Appeal from administrative penalties for safety violations.

FACT SUMMARY: Trinity (D) complained that OSHA's (P) inspection was broader than the scope of the complaint that prompted the inspection.

CONCISE RULE OF LAW: An administrative inspection, based upon specific evidence of a violation, must bear a relation to that violation.

FACTS: Trinity (D) manufactures tanks and pressure vessels at its plant in Ohio. In 1988, an employee filed a complaint with OSHA (P) alleging multiple safety violations at the plant. Trinity (D) refused to permit an inspection, so OSHA (P) obtained an administrative inspection warrant. OSHA (P) ended up reviewing and inspecting Trinity records and sites that exceeded the allegations of the original complaint. Trinity (D) was charged with multiple violations and fined $33,000. Trinity (D) contested some of the citations based on that part of the inspection that went beyond the reach of the complaint, which enabled the warrant to be issued.

ISSUE: Must an administrative inspection, based upon specific evidence of a violation, bear a relation to that violation?

HOLDING AND DECISION: (Martin, J.) Yes. An administrative inspection, based upon specific evidence of a violation, must bear a relation to that violation. Warrants are required for administrative inspections. Probable cause justifying the issuance of a warrant for administrative purposes may be based on either specific evidence of an existing violation or on a showing that a specific business has been chosen for a search on the basis of a general administrative plan derived from neutral sources. Inspections done pursuant to a general administrative plan may properly extend to the entire workplace. However, warrants issued because of specific complaints have an increased danger of abuse of discretion and intrusiveness. Therefore, a complaint inspection must bear an appropriate relationship to the violation alleged in the complaint. In the present case, OSHA (P) used an employee complaint to trigger a full-scope inspection of Trinity (D) without the required showing of probable cause. However, OSHA (P) was entitled to review all the inspection records of Trinity (D), even if a comprehensive plant inspection was unauthorized. Reversed and remanded.

EDITOR'S ANALYSIS: The court noted that OSHA (P) should have reviewed Trinity's (D) records first. Then, if the review of the injury and illness records led to further suspicions, OSHA (P) could have applied for a second warrant. This second warrant could have included a full and comprehensive inspection of the physical facility.

NOTES:

IN RE TRINITY INDUSTRIES, INC.

Manufacturers (D) v. Government agency (P)

876 F.2d 1485 (11th Cir. 1989).

NATURE OF CASE: Appeal of order to permit inspection.

FACT SUMMARY: Two industrial manufacturers, Trinity (D) and Mosher (D), claimed that warrant applications for OSHA inspections of their plants were defective.

CONCISE RULE OF LAW: A warrant application for an administrative search is valid if the plan is based on specific, neutral criteria and it adequately establishes that the particular company was selected pursuant to the neutral criteria.

FACTS: OSHA regulations for safety and health inspections establish a ranking system for inspecting companies in high-hazard industries. The agency ranks employers based on lost workday injury rates, and companies that are below average are subject to placement on the inspection list. Companies that recently underwent inspections are taken off the list and higher priority is given to larger companies. Pursuant to this administrative search plan, OSHA obtained warrants for inspecting Trinity (D) and Mosher (D), two manufacturers. The companies refused to permit the inspections. Under threat of contempt, Mosher (D) permitted the inspection, but the court was forced to fine Trinity (D), who then appealed the court's order.

ISSUE: Is a warrant application for an administrative search valid if the plan is based on specific, neutral criteria and it adequately estabiishes that the particular company was selected pursuant to the neutral criteria?

HOLDING AND DECISION: (Cox, J.) Yes. A warrant application for an administrative search is valid if the plan is based on specific, neutral criteria and it adequately establishes that the particular company was selected pursuant to the neutral criteria. To satisfy the Fourth Amendment, a warrant for an administrative search must be obtained prior to the inspection. Probable cause for this warrant can justified by a general administrative plan for the enforcement of the law as long as the criteria for picking the individuals who will be inspected is neutral. In making this determination, the court must apply a two-priority test: 1) whether the plan pursuant to which the warrant is to be issued is based on neutral criteria; and 2) whether the warrant application clearly and adequately established that the company was selected for inspection pursuant to the neutral criteria. In the present case, the OSHA administrative plan is rational and neutral. It is intended and designed to protect the greatest number of employees who are exposed to the greatest risks. Although the plan may result in more frequent inspections of select portions of all industries, it seems eminently reasonable that OSHA has decided to allocate its resources in this manner. The warrant at issue in the present case contained a detailed description of the procedure used in selecting companies and a sworn affidavit that Trinity (D) and Mosher (D) were selected according to the procedure. This was sufficient for the magistrate to issue the warrant. Therefore, the district court was not in error in holding the companies in contempt for failing to allow the inspections. Affirmed.

EDITOR'S ANALYSIS: The probable cause standard for an administrative warrant is obviously somewhat less than for a criminal-type search. Still, illegal searches do happen. Agencies and officials can be liable for civil penalties for violating the Fourth Amendment.

QUICKNOTES

PROBABLE CAUSE - A reasonable basis for believing that a crime has been committed.

FOURTH AMENDMENT - Provides that persons be secure as to their person and private belongings against unreasonable searches and seizures.

NOTES:

UNITED STATES v. JANIS

IRS (P) v. Alleged bookie (D)

428 U.S. 433 (1976).

NATURE OF CASE: Appeal from motion to exclude evidence from back taxes proceeding.

FACT SUMMARY: Bookmaking records were seized in an illegal search but the IRS (P) sought to use the records against Janis (D) to prove that back taxes were owed.

CONCISE RULE OF LAW: The exclusionary rule that bars illegally seized evidence from being used in a criminal prosecution does not apply against use in a civil proceeding.

FACTS: Los Angeles police officers searched an apartment, seized records of illegal bookmaking and arrested the occupants. The records were then turned over to the Internal Revenue Service (P), which made an assessment for back taxes against Janis (D). Subsequently, a judge determined that the search was illegal based on defects in the warrant. Janis (D) argued that the IRS (P) claim should be dismissed because of the illegal search.

ISSUE: Does the exclusionary rule that bars illegally seized evidence from being used in a criminal prosecution apply against use in a civil proceeding?

HOLDING AND DECISION: (Blackmun, J.) No. The exclusionary rule that bars illegally seized evidence from being used in a criminal prosecution does not apply against use in a civil proceeding. In 1914, the Supreme Court ruled that the Fourth Amendment barred use of evidence from an illegal search at a federal criminal trial. The primary purpose of this exclusionary rule is to deter future unlawful police conduct. It is a judicially created remedy designed to safeguard Fourth Amendment rights. Thus, application of the rule is limited to those circumstances where the remedial objectives are served. The additional marginal deterrence provided by also forbidding use of the evidence in a separate civil proceeding does not outweigh the cost to society of the exclusion. Therefore, this Court declines to extend application of the exclusionary rule to civil proceedings.

DISSENT: (Stewart, J.) This decision undercuts the deterrent effect by allowing police to crack down on gambling by illegally seizing evidence and turning it over to the IRS (P).

EDITOR'S ANALYSIS: It should be noted that this decision does not allow agency officials to illegally seize evidence and use it in civil proceedings. It applies only to an illegal search by a police officer for use in a criminal trial. Still, the dissent does rightly point out that there is a potential for abuse.

QUICKNOTES

EXCLUSIONARY RULE - A rule precluding the introduction at trial of evidence unlawfully obtained in violation of the federal constitutional safeguards against unreasonable searches and seizures.

NOTES:

IMMIGRATION AND NATURALIZATION SERVICE v. LOPEZ-MENDOZA

Government agency (P) v. Illegal alien (D)
468 U.S. 1032 (1984).

NATURE OF CASE: Appeal from evidence ruling in a deportation hearing.

FACT SUMMARY: Lopez-Mendoza (D), an illegal alien, sought to have an admission barred from evidence because it was the product of an illegal arrest.

CONCISE RULE OF LAW: The exclusionary rule for illegally seized evidence does not apply in civil deportation hearings.

FACTS: Lopez-Mendoza (D) was arrested unlawfully and admitted that he was an illegal alien. At the deportation hearing conducted by the INS (P), Lopez-Mendoza (D) argued that the admission should be excluded because it was the product of the illegal arrest.

ISSUE: Does the exclusionary rule for illegally seized evidence apply in civil deportation hearings?

HOLDING AND DECISION: (O'Connor, J.) No. The exclusionary rule for illegal seized evidence does not apply in civil deportation hearings. The exclusionary rule barring the use of evidence from an illegal search applies only where its deterrent effect is greater than the costs imposed on society. In a civil deportation hearing, there are several factors that reduce the likely deterrent value. The INS (P) will still be able to deport with other evidence of alienage. Given that virtually all INS (P) agent arrests lead to voluntary deportations, the arresting officers are unlikely to change their conduct to avoid exclusion in a subsequent deportation hearing. The INS (P) also has its own comprehensive scheme for deterring Fourth Amendment violations by its officers. On the other hand, the social costs of applying the exclusionary rule are unusual and significant. It would require courts to look past an ongoing violation of the law - the continued presence of an illegal alien in the country. It would also necessitate changing the nature of deportation hearings, which are already strained by the numbers of illegal aliens and time constraints. Finally, applying the rule might preclude the INS (P) from conducting mass arrests of illegal aliens, even if they are usually in full compliance with the Fourth Amendment. Accordingly, the exclusionary rule should not be applied in civil deportation hearings and Lopez-Mendoza (D) may not exclude his admission.

EDITOR'S ANALYSIS: The court further noted that its conclusion could have been different if there was a record that INS (D) Fourth Amendment violations were widespread. It is interesting that one of the reasons for not applying the rule is that the INS (D) officers wouldn't change their conduct anyway. It seems unlikely that police officers would be allowed to make this argument against application of the exclusionary rule.

QUICKNOTES

EXCLUSIONARY RULE - A rule precluding the introduction at trial of evidence unlawfully obtained in violation of the federal constitutional safeguards against unreasonable searches and seizures.

FOURTH AMENDMENT - Provides that persons be secure as to their person and private belongings against unreasonable searches and seizures.

NOTES:

FREESE v. FEDERAL DEPOSIT INSURANCE CORP.

Former bank officer (P) v. Government agency (D)

837 F. Supp. 22 (D.N.H. 1993).

NATURE OF CASE: Motion to quash subpoena seeking personal financial records.

FACT SUMMARY: The FDIC (D) sought to examine the personal records of former bank officers (P) to see if they had any potential claims against them.

CONCISE RULE OF LAW: Government agencies may not use their subpoena powers for improper purposes.

FACTS: In 1991, the FDIC (D) was appointed receiver and liquidating agent for the New Hampshire Savings Bank. The following year, the FDIC (D) wanted to investigate whether there were any valid claims against the former officers (P) of the bank. In connection with this investigation, the FDIC (D) issued administrative subpoenas to the officers and directors seeking extensive personal financial information for the previous five years. Among the purposes for seeking the information claimed by the FDIC (D) were to see if there was enough money to satisfy any potential claims and to determine whether a suit would be cost effective. The officers (P) claimed that the subpoenas were issued in violation of the Fourth Amendment and challenged their legality.

ISSUE: May government agencies use their subpoena powers for improper purposes?

HOLDING AND DECISION: (Loughlin, J.) No. Government agencies may not use their subpoena powers for improper purposes. Agency subpoenas are enforceable if for a proper purpose and adequately determined in the subpoena, the information sought is relevant to that purpose, and the statutory procedures have been followed. A determination of whether a civil suit is cost effective against a potential defendant is not a proper purpose to issue a subpoena. It is impermissible to peruse a person's financial records to check their ability to satisfy a judgment. The potential liability of a person, however, could form the basis of a valid subpoena. In the present case, the FDIC (D) has not asserted any suspicion of wrongdoing on the part of the former officers (P). With no basis for potential liability, the FDIC (D) is "fishing" in the hope that some wrongdoing will surface. This is a violation of fundamental constitutional rights.

EDITOR'S ANALYSIS: The decision fell short of requiring that the agency make a showing of probable cause before a subpoena can be issued. However, the court came down hard on the FDIC (D) in this case. They acknowledged that the records in question were sealed and never given to the agency, but noted that the former officers (P) had nonetheless been forced to incur legal expenses and anxiety.

ADAMS v. FEDERAL TRADE COMMISSION

Dairy company (D) v. Government agency (P)

296 F.2d 861 (8th Cir. 1961).

NATURE OF CASE: Appeal of decision to deny enforcement of administrative subpoenas.

FACT SUMMARY: The FTC (P) issued a series of subpoenas covering an extensive amount of information pursuant to an investigation into whether Adams (D) had engaged in fixing prices.

CONCISE RULE OF LAW: Subpoenas are not too broad as long as the information sought is reasonably relevant.

FACTS: The FTC (P) issued a complaint against Adams Dairy Company (D) alleging that the company was involved in a conspiracy to fix prices. A hearing examiner issued several administrative subpoenas for various documents of Adams (D). Among those documents sought were product sales records from 1940 to 1959, the names of all companies that Adams did business with since its incorporation and all writings to these companies, and all types of corporate records. The FTC (P) was forced to seek judicial enforcement when Adams (D) refused to comply. The district court decided to deny enforcement of many of the aspects of the subpoenas based on the fact that they were too broad in scope. The FTC (P) appealed.

ISSUE: Can subpoenas be too broad if the information sought is reasonably relevant?

HOLDING AND DECISION: (Matthes, J.) No. Subpoenas are not too broad as long as the information sought is reasonably relevant. The critical issue in the validity of an administrative subpoena is the relevance of the requested information to the charges and allegations that the agency is making. In the present case, the FTC (P) is alleging a sweeping conspiracy involving many companies over a long period of time. Accordingly, the agency has wide latitude in seeking documents that pertain to the alleged conspiracy. Therefore, the district court's denial of enforcement of many of the subpoenas on the ground that they were too burdensome and broad is overruled. Where the district court found that the documents sought were not relevant because they dated back past 1954, denial in part of the scope of those administrative subpoenas was appropriate. Reversed in part, affirmed in part.

EDITOR'S ANALYSIS: The court had to look at each of the subpoena specifications individually to determine their relevance. This decision does indicate that claims of burden will not go far in quashing administrative subpoenas. This decision might also lead agencies to expand the scope of their allegations so that they have access to a fuller document record.

BRASWELL v. UNITED STATES

Business proprietor (D) v. Government (P)

487 U.S. 99 (1988).

NATURE OF CASE: Appeal from denial of motion to quash.

FACT SUMMARY: Braswell (D) contended he was not bound, as the custodian of corporate records, to comply with a subpoena for such records because the act of production would incriminate him in violation of his Fifth Amendment rights.

CONCISE RULE OF LAW: The custodian of corporate records cannot resist a subpoena on the grounds that such production would violate his Fifth Amendment rights against self-incrimination.

FACTS: Braswell (D) conducted business as a sole proprietor. He subsequently incorporated the business by forming two separate corporations. He, as president of each, was served with a subpoena by a federal grand jury ordering him to produce company records. He moved to quash the subpoena on the grounds that the act of production constituted testimony which could be used against him. Thus, he argued, the subpoena violated his right against self-incrimination. The district court refused to quash the subpoena. The Court of Appeals affirmed, and the Supreme Court granted review.

ISSUE: Can the custodian of corporate records avoid a subpoena for such records on the grounds that production would constitute self-incrimination?

HOLDING AND DECISION: (Rehnquist, C.J.) No. The custodian of corporate records cannot resist a subpoena on the grounds that production of the records would constitute self-incrimination. Corporations are treated differently under the self-incrimination analysis. The collective entity rule, which applies to corporate defendants, dictates that custodians of corporate records hold them in a representative capacity, not a personal capacity. Thus, production is a fulfillment of corporate duties and is not a personal testimonial act. Thus, no Fifth Amendment violation would occur when compelling a corporate act. Affirmed.

DISSENT: (Kennedy, J.) The self-incrimination right is sacrificed by an individual when he becomes a corporate officer under this decision. Clearly, this cannot be correct.

EDITOR'S ANALYSIS: The Court recognized that a different result in this case would simply hinder any prosecution of "white collar crime." All an individual would have to do to avoid turning over incriminating documents would be to make sure they were created in a corporate capacity. If in this case the business had remained a sole proprietorship, the subpoena might have been quashed because the custodian would hold the documents in a personal capacity.

QUICKNOTES

FIFTH AMENDMENT - Provides that no person shall be compelled to serve as a witness against himself, or be subject to trial for the same offense twice, or be deprived of life, liberty, or property without due process of law.

SUBPOENA - A mandate issued by court to compel a witness to appear at trial.

NOTES:

SMITH v. RICHERT

Alleged tax delinquent (D) v.
Indiana Department of Revenue (P)
35 F.3d 300 (7th Cir. 1994).

NATURE OF CASE: Appeal from conviction for failing to permit an examination of records.

FACT SUMMARY: Smith (D) did not file income tax returns and refused to comply with a subpoena commanding production of income records.

CONCISE RULE OF LAW: The required records doctrine with respect to self-incrimination does not apply to general records needed to determine tax liability.

FACTS: Smith (D) did not file Indiana tax returns for several years and the state's Department of Revenue (P) served him with a subpoena demanding the production of records necessary to determine his tax liability. An Indiana statute provided that any person subject to tax was required to keep records for purposes of determining their taxes. Smith (D) refused to comply with the subpoena on the ground that it violated his right against self-incrimination. He was convicted for failing to permit the examination of records required by the state. The conviction was affirmed. The court ruled that the records sought by the subpoena were required records and, thus, not self-incriminating. Smith (D) appealed.

ISSUE: Does the required records doctrine with respect to self-incrimination apply to general records needed to determine tax liability?

HOLDING AND DECISION: (Posner, C.J.) No. The required records doctrine with respect to self-incrimination does not apply to general records needed to determine tax liability. The Fifth Amendment protects the rights of individuals not to testify against themselves. The required records doctrine developed as an exception in the cases where a document was required to be kept as part of a regulated industry. Its only applicability now is when the act of production itself is testimonial and would be protected by the Fifth Amendment. In such instances, a person cannot resist the subpoena because compliance only shows acknowledgment that the regulatory program applies. However, this required records doctrine should only be used where an industry is closely regulated by the government. A statute that requires taxpayers to maintain general records is far too broad; taxpayers do not voluntarily enter into any implicit agreement to maintain documents for the government. Furthermore, production by Smith (D) of certain tax forms in this case would be testimonial and incriminating in that it would foreclose a defense that he omitted income because he had no record of it. Therefore, the district court should not have affirmed the conviction on the basis that the documents sought by the subpoena were required records. Reversed and remanded.

EDITOR'S ANALYSIS: The court pointed out that Indiana (P) could have agreed not to disclose at a prosecuting trial for wilful non-payment of taxes that Smith (D) had provided the documents that established his tax liability. This immunity-like use of the information would have protected Smith's (D) Fifth Amendment rights, while still allowing the subpoena to go forward. The required records doctrine has been used much since 1984, when the Supreme Court ruled that the compelled surrender of a self-incriminating document was not barred by the Fifth Amendment.

QUICKNOTES

FIFTH AMENDMENT - Provides that no person shall be compelled to serve as a witness against himself, or be subject to trial for the same offense twice, or be deprived of life, liberty, or property without due process of law.

SUBPOENA - A mandate issued by court to compel a witness to appear at trial.

NOTES:

SECURITIES AND EXCHANGE COMMISSION v. DRESSER INDUSTRIES, INC.

Government agency (P) v. Alleged records falsifier (D)

628 F.2d 1368 (D.C. Cir. 1980).

NATURE OF CASE: Appeal from decision to enforce administrative subpoena.

FACT SUMMARY: Dresser (D) claimed that an SEC (P) subpoena for records should not be enforced because the Department of Justice had a grand jury seeking the same information for a criminal prosecution.

CONCISE RULE OF LAW: Parallel investigations and proceedings by agencies are allowed as long as they do not prejudice substantial rights of the investigated party.

FACTS: In 1973, the Securities and Exchange Commission (P) began an investigation into whether Dresser (D) falsified its financial records in order to hide bribes to foreign officials. At about the same time, the Department of Justice began instituting its own criminal investigation with regard to illegal foreign payments. The SEC (P) gave Justice information that Dresser (D) had voluntarily provided to the SEC (P) and Justice brought the matter to a grand jury. Both the SEC (P) and the grand jury then issued subpoenas for more information from Dresser (D). The district court upheld enforcement of the subpoenas and Dresser (D) appealed the ruling with respect to the SEC (P) subpoena.

ISSUE: Are parallel investigations and proceedings by agencies allowed as long as they do not prejudice substantial rights of the investigated party?

HOLDING AND DECISION: (Wright, C.J.) Yes. Parallel investigations and proceedings by agencies are allowed as long as they do not prejudice substantial rights of the investigated party. The Constitution does not require a stay of civil proceedings pending the outcome of criminal proceedings. However, courts have the discretion to stay civil proceedings or postpone civil discovery when it appears in the interests of justice to do so. There are instances when noncriminal proceedings, if not deferred, might undermine the defendant's Fifth Amendment privileges. Thus, if a delay of the civil case would not injure the public interest, a court may be justified in delaying it. In the present case, there do not appear to be strong reasons for staying the SEC (P) investigation, since there has been no criminal indictment of Dresser (D) and the SEC (P) subpoena does not require Dresser (D) to reveal the basis of its defense. Furthermore, the SEC (P) must be able to respond quickly to violations of the securities laws and seek prompt redress if necessary. It cannot always wait for the completion of criminal proceedings if it is to further the public interest. Therefore, the SEC (P) subpoena should be enforced and its proceedings allowed to continue.

EDITOR'S ANALYSIS: The court noted that the Department of Justice similarly shouldn't be expected to wait for the completion of an SEC investigation. It pointed out that statute of limitations issues could arise if it did so. Another option available to the courts is a protective order with regard to discovery.

QUICKNOTES

STAY - An order by a court requiring a party to refrain from a specific activity until the happening of an event or upon further action by the court.

SUBPOENA - A mandate issued by court to compel a witness to appear at trial.

PROTECTIVE ORDER - Court order protecting a party against potential abusive treatment through use of the legal process.

NOTES:

UNITED STATES v. KORDEL

Government (P) v. Corporate officers (D)

397 U.S. 1 (1970).

NATURE OF CASE: Appeal from reversal of convictions for violations of the Federal Food, Drug and Cosmetics Act.

FACT SUMMARY: Kordel (D), a corporate officer, was convicted of criminal offenses after being required to respond to civil interrogatories from the Food and Drug Administration.

CONCISE RULE OF LAW: Agencies do not have to choose between criminal and civil proceedings or delay civil proceedings pending the outcome of a criminal trial.

FACTS: In June 1960, the Food and Drug Administration filed a suit against two products manufactured by Detroit Vital Foods, alleging that they violated the Food, Drug and Cosmetic Act. The company was served with interrogatories from the FDA. The government (P) then notified that it would begin a criminal prosecution. Vital Foods asked the district court to stay the FDA civil proceedings or delay the interrogatories until after the criminal trial was finished. However, Vital Foods did not raise the issue of self-incrimination and the court denied their request. Kordel (D), a corporate officer, and other officers answered the interrogatories and subsequently were convicted of violating the Act. The court of appeals reversed their convictions on the ground that the government's (P) use of the interrogatory responses in a nearly contemporaneous civil proceeding to obtain evidence was a violation of the right against self-incrimination. The government (P) appealed.

ISSUE: Do agencies have to choose between criminal and civil proceedings or delay civil proceedings pending the outcome of a criminal trial?

HOLDING AND DECISION: (Stewart, J.) No. Agencies do not have to choose between criminal and civil proceedings or delay civil proceedings pending the outcome of a criminal trial. In the present case, the court of appeals found that the interrogatory responses were involuntary after the district court's order. However, the privilege of self-incrimination is a personal right. The individuals at Vital Foods who could have invoked their privilege even though the corporation itself had no such right. Although it is possible that there would have been no one at Vital Foods could have answered without subjecting himself to the risk of self-incrimination, and in such a case, a protective order might have been warranted. However, the record before us does not present this question. Additionally, it cannot be said that the government's conduct was so unfair as to require reversal. It would stultify the enforcement of federal law to require an agency to choose between giving up criminal prosecutions or deferring civil proceedings pending the outcome of criminal trial. Often the decision of whether to proceed criminally against those responsible depends on having a full civil record. Therefore, Kordel (D) and the other officers' convictions are reinstated. Reversed.

EDITOR'S ANALYSIS: The Court seemed concerned with the public interest in having the FDA remove offending products as soon as possible without having to worry about implications to later criminal proceedings. The Court went out of its way to suggest that the attorneys for Vital Foods could have explored other options after the District Court insisted that the interrogatories be answered. The Court did note that a company could elude answering discovery by assigning the responsibility to someone who would invoke the Fifth Amendment.

QUICKNOTES

FIFTH AMENDMENT - Provides that no person shall be compelled to serve as a witness against himself, or be subject to trial for the same offense twice, or be deprived of life, liberty, or property without due process of law.

STAY - An order by a court requiring a party to refrain from a specific activity until the happening of an event or upon further action by the court.

PROTECTIVE ORDER - Court order protecting a party against potential abusive treatment through use of the legal process.

NOTES:

UNITED STATES v. LASALLE NATIONAL BANK

Internal Revenue Service (P) v. Taxpayer's bank (D)

437 U.S. 298 (1978).

NATURE OF CASE: Appeal from denial of enforcement of administrative subpoena.

FACT SUMMARY: LaSalle (D) refused to comply with a subpoena for a customer's bank records from the IRS (P).

CONCISE RULE OF LAW: An IRS summons must be enforced if it is issued in good faith before a recommendation for criminal prosecution.

FACTS: The IRS (P) assigned Olivero, a special agent, to investigate the tax liability of Gattuso. Olivero issued summons for Gattuso's records at two banks, including LaSalle National Bank (D). The banks (D) refused to comply and the IRS (P) sought enforcement in district court. Olivero and other IRS (P) officials testified that there had been no decision or recommendation as to whether criminal charges were justified at the time of the summons. But Gattuso insisted that the investigation was purely criminal and the district court agreed that Olivero's motivation seemed to be for criminal proceedings. The court refused to enforce the administrative subpoenas and the court of appeals affirmed. The IRS (P) appealed.

ISSUE: Must an IRS summons be enforced if it is issued in good faith before a recommendation for criminal prosecution?

HOLDING AND DECISION: (Blackmun, J.) Yes. An IRS summons must be enforced if it is issued in good faith before a recommendation for criminal prosecution. The legislative history of the Internal Revenue Code shows that Congress intended to design a system with interrelated civil and criminal elements. Thus, tax fraud investigations were not categorized and any limitation on an IRS (P) summons should reflect this. The criminal and civil aspects of tax fraud cases only diverge when a recommendation for prosecution is sent from the IRS (P) to the Department of Justice. It would be an improper use of the summons power for the IRS (P) to gather evidence solely for a criminal investigation. Otherwise, the IRS (P) may issue summons as long as it is done in good faith for a legitimate purpose. The determination of whether an improper purpose was behind a summons is not dependent on the motivation of one agent, but depends on institutional good faith. There are layers of review built into the IRS (P) administration that temper against the motivations of one agent. In the present case, LaSalle (D) has not demonstrated anything that goes against good faith other than that agent Olivero may have already possessed the information sought in the summons. Therefore, the summons should have been enforced. Reversed.

DISSENT: (Stewart, J.) The institutional good faith of the IRS (P) will be just as, if not more, difficult to decide as the purpose of an individual agent.

EDITOR'S ANALYSIS: The court stated that the good faith standard does not permit the IRS (P) to become an information-gathering agency for other agencies, regardless of the status of the criminal case involved. This decision reflects a trend in the cases where most parallel proceedings are allowed. The court noted that bad faith will rarely be found in cases of this type.

QUICKNOTES

SUBPOENA - A mandate issued by court to compel a witness to appear at trial.

NOTES:

CHAPTER 8
PUBLIC ACCESS TO AGENCY PROCESSES

QUICK REFERENCE RULES OF LAW

1. **The Freedom of Information Act (FOIA): The FOIA Request.** Only documents classified as agency records are subject to disclosure under the FOIA. (The Bureau of National Affairs, Inc. v. United States Dept. of Justice)

   [For more information on agency records, see Casenote Law Outline on Administrative Law, Chapter 11, Openness and Public Control of Processes, § I, Freedom of Information Act.]

2. **The Freedom of Information Act (FOIA): The FOIA Request.** The FOIA confers jurisdiction on the district courts to enjoin an agency from withholding agency records and to order the production of any agency records improperly withheld. (United States Dept. of Justice v. Tax Analysts)

   [For more information on FOIA, see Casenote Law Outline on Administrative Law, Chapter 11, Openness and Public Control of Processes, § I, Freedom of Information Act.]

3. **The Freedom of Information Act (FOIA): FOIA Exemptions.** The Freedom of Information Act may be invoked for the benefit of a person who has provided commercial or financial information if it can be shown that public disclosure is likely to cause substantial harm to his competitive position. (National Park and Conservation Assoc. v. Morton)

   [For more information on FOIA exceptions, see Casenote Law Outline on Administrative Law, Chapter 11, Openness and Public Control of Processes, § I, Freedom of Information Act.]

4. **The Freedom of Information Act (FOIA): FOIA Exemptions.** Financial or commercial information voluntarily provided to the government is confidential and exempt from disclosure if it would usually not be released to the public by the person who provided it. (Critical Mass Energy Project v. Nuclear Regulatory Commission)

   [For more information on FOIA exemptions, see Casenote Law Outline on Administrative Law, Chapter 11, Openness and Public Control of Processes, § I, Freedom of Information Act.]

5. **The Freedom of Information Act (FOIA): Reverse FOIA Suits.** The FOIA does not give rise to a private right to prevent disclosure of documents pursuant to unrelated regulations. (Chrysler Corp. v. Brown)

   [For more information on FOIA exemptions, see Casenote Law Outline on Administrative Law, Chapter 11, Openness and Public Control of Processes, § I, Freedom of Information Act.]

6. **The Federal Advisory Committee Act.** FACA was not meant to apply to the American Bar Association's review of judicial nominees. (Public Citizen v. U.S. Department of Justice)

7. **The Federal Advisory Committee Act.** State employees without federal duties may not be considered officers of the federal government for purposes of FACA. (Northwest Forest Resource Council v. Espy)

8. **The Government in the Sunshine Act.** The Sunshine Act applies only to discussions that effectively predetermine official actions. (Federal Communications Commission v. ITT World Communications, Inc.)

   [For more information on the Sunshine Act, see Casenote Law Outline on Administrative Law, Chapter 11,Openness and Public Control of Processes, § III, The Sunshine Act.]

BUREAU OF NATIONAL AFFAIRS, INC. v. UNITED STATES DEPARTMENT OF JUSTICE
Agency (P) v. Agency (D)
742 F.2d 1484 (D.C. Cir. 1984).

NATURE OF CASE: Appeal from a denial of disclosure of requested documents under the FOIA.

FACT SUMMARY: The Bureau of National Affairs (BNA) (P) sought disclosure of appointment records and calendars of an assistant Attorney General under the FOIA.

CONCISE RULE OF LAW: Only documents classified as agency records are subject to disclosure under the FOIA.

FACTS: BNA (P) sued to compel disclosure of daily agendas and appointment calendars of an assistant Attorney General. The daily agendas were prepared so that the individual's staff would know where to reach him, and were distributed to the staff daily. The appointment calendars were created for his personal convenience. The Department of Justice (D) contended the documents were not "agency records" and thus not subject to disclosure. The district court refused to compel production and the BNA (P) appealed.

ISSUE: Are only documents classified as agency records subject to disclosure under the FOIA?

HOLDING AND DECISION: (Mikva, J.) Yes. Only documents classified as agency records are subject to disclosure under the FOIA. The daily agendas were agency records as they were generated on agency time primarily for the use of agency personnel in the discharge of their duties. However the calendars were kept for the personal convenience of the individual, and thus were not agency records. Reversed in part and affirmed in part.

EDITOR'S ANALYSIS: The court in this case recognizes an absence of legislative and judicial guidance in defining the scope of "agency records." Some guidelines have been suggested such as how the records were generated, by whom, for what purpose, and under whose direction. Also whether the agency possesses the documentation is a factor.

[For more information on agency records, see Casenote Law Outline on Administrative Law, Chapter 11, Openness and Public Control of Processes, § I, Freedom of Information Act.]

NOTES:

UNITED STATES DEPARTMENT OF JUSTICE v. TAX ANALYSTS

Government agency (D) v. Publisher (P)

492 U.S. 136 (1989).

NATURE OF CASE: Appeal from order to comply with FOIA records request.

FACT SUMMARY: In July 1979, Tax Analysts (P) filed a Freedom of Information Act (FOIA) request asking the Department of Justice (D) to make available all district court tax opinions and final orders received by the Tax Division earlier that month, but the Department (D) denied the request.

CONCISE RULE OF LAW: The FOIA confers jurisdiction on the district courts to enjoin an agency from withholding agency records and to order the production of any agency records improperly withheld.

FACTS: The Tax Division of the U.S. Department of Justice (Department) (D) represents parties in litigation, receives copies of all opinions and orders issued by the courts in such cases, and makes copies of these decisions for the Tax Division's staff attorneys. The original documents are sent to the official files kept by the Department (D). In July 1979, Tax Analysts (P), publisher of a weekly magazine which reports on legislative, judicial, and regulatory developments in the field of federal taxation to a readership largely composed of tax attorneys, accountants, and economists, filed a request under the FOIA asking the Department (D) to make available all district court tax opinions and final orders received by the Tax Division earlier that month. The Department (D) denied the request on the grounds that these decisions were not Tax Division records. The Department (D) appealed a lower court order to comply with the request.

ISSUE: Does the FOIA confer jurisdiction on the district courts to enjoin an agency from withholding agency records and to order the production of any agency records improperly withheld?

HOLDING AND DECISION: (Marshall, J.) Yes. The FOIA confers jurisdiction on the district courts to enjoin an agency from withholding agency records and to order the production of any agency records improperly withheld. Under the Act, "federal jurisdiction is dependent on a showing that an agency had (1) `improperly' (2) `withheld' (3) `agency records.'" Each of these criteria must be met before a district court will have jurisdiction to devise remedies to force an agency to comply with the FOIA's disclosure requirements. The test as to whether requested materials qualify as "agency records" requires two steps. First, the requested materials must have been either "created or obtained" by an agency, and second, the agency must have been in control of the requested materials at the time the FOIA request was made. Under these two tests, the requested district court decisions constituted "agency records." Congress used the word "withheld" only in its usual sense. When a document is under an agency's control, and that agency denies an otherwise valid request for its production, the agency has "withheld" the document, despite public availability of the document outside of the agency. Finally, Congress sought "to insulate its product from judicial tampering and to preserve the emphasis on disclosure by admonishing that the `availability of records to the public' is not limited, `except as specifically stated.'" It follows from the exclusive nature of the exemption scheme in § 552(b) that agency records which do not fall within one of the exemptions are "improperly" withheld. None of the § 552(b) enumerated exemptions protects the district court decisions sought by Tax Analysts (P). Thus, the documents requested by Tax Analysts (P) were agency records improperly withheld by the Department (D), which must comply with the request for production made under the FOIA by Tax Analysts (P).

DISSENT: (Blackmun, J.) Tax Analysts (P) is in the business of selling summaries of these opinions and supplies full texts to major electronic databases. The result of this litigation is to impose the cost of obtaining the court orders and opinions upon the government and thus upon taxpayers generally, rather than on the requesting party.

EDITOR'S ANALYSIS: According to the dissent, the public, as taxpayers, is being asked to pay the cost of providing information to a commercial enterprise. It would appear that Justice Blackmun's fears of the taxpayers' bearing the expense of responding to FOIA requests is not unfounded, since even though the FOIA stipulates that each agency shall promulgate regulations specifying a uniform schedule of fees applicable to all document search and duplication, oftentimes these fees are waived. In his hornbook on Administrative Law, Professor William F. Fox, Jr. reveals that because — in addition to the many agencies that waive fees — fee schedules rarely reflect the actual costs of searching and retrieval, congressional inquiries indicate that the FOIA is costing agencies millions of dollars each year in processing expenses.

[For more information on FOIA, see Casenote Law Outline on Administrative Law, Chapter 11, Openness and Public Control of Processes, § I, Freedom of Information Act.]

NATIONAL PARKS & CONSERVATION ASSOCIATION v. MORTON

Federal agency (D) v. Concessioner (P)

498 F.2d 765 (D.C. Cir. 1974).

NATURE OF CASE: Appeal in connection with non-disclosure of records.

FACT SUMMARY: Morton (P) wanted information about concessions operated by National Parks (D).

CONCISE RULE OF LAW: The Freedom of Information Act may be invoked for the benefit of a person who has provided commercial or financial information if it can be shown that public disclosure is likely to cause substantial harm to his competitive position.

FACTS: Morton (P) sought financial information concerning concessions operated by National Parks (D). The district court held that this information was exempt under the Freedom of Information Act (FOIA), on the ground that this information was of the kind "that would not generally be made available for public perusal." Morton (P) appealed, contending that disclosure could not impair the concessioners' competitive position because they were monopolists and had no competition.

ISSUE: May the Freedom of Information Act be invoked for the benefit of a person who has provided commercial or financial information if it can be shown that public disclosure is likely to cause substantial harm to his competitive position?

HOLDING AND DECISION: (Tamm, J.) Yes. The Freedom of Information Act may be invoked for the benefit of a person who has provided commercial or financial information if it can be shown that public disclosure is likely to cause substantial harm to his competitive position. The district court's conclusion does not, by itself, support application of the financial information exemption of the FOIA. The district court must also inquire into the possibility that disclosure will harm legitimate private or governmental interests in secrecy. While Morton's (P) argument concerning the concessioners' monopoly is very compelling, the court is reluctant to accept it without first providing National Parks (D) the opportunity to develop a fuller record in the district court. It might be shown, for example, that disclosure of information about concession activities will injure the concessioners' competitive position in a noncompetitive enterprise. In that case, disclosure would be improper. [This matter was, therefore, remanded to the district court for the purpose of determining whether public disclosure of the information in question poses the likelihood of substantial harm to the competitive positions of the parties from whom it has been obtained.]

EDITOR'S ANALYSIS: This case came before the court of appeals again in 1976. The court emphasized that the defendant had to prove the possibility of harm, and not its certainty, otherwise, "the costs of obtaining such detailed economic evidence . . . might well preclude a small business from ever seeking to prevent disclosure." Gellhorn, W., Administrative Law, quoting 547 F.2d 673.

[For more information on FOIA exceptions, see Casenote Law Outline on Administrative Law, Chapter 11, Openness and Public Control of Processes, § I, Freedom of Information Act.]

QUICKNOTES

MONOPOLY - A privilege or right conferred upon an individual or entity granting it the exclusive power to manufacture, sell and distribute a particular service or commodity; a market condition in which one or a few companies control the sale of a product or service thereby restraining competition in respect to that article or service.

NOTES:

CRITICAL MASS ENERGY PROJECT v. NUCLEAR REGULATORY COMMISSION

Project (P) v. Federal agency (D)

975 F.2d 871 (D.C. Cir. 1992).

NATURE OF CASE: Appeal from a grant of summary judgment in favor of the defendant in relation to a Freedom of Information Act (FOIA) request.

FACT SUMMARY: Critical Mass Energy Project's (CMEP) (P) FOIA request for information voluntarily provided to the NRC (D) by the Institute for Nuclear Power Operations was denied on the basis that the information was protected from disclosure under the Act's confidential commercial information exemption.

CONCISE RULE OF LAW: Financial or commercial information voluntarily provided to the government is confidential and exempt from disclosure if it would usually not be released to the public by the person who provided it.

FACTS: Critical Mass Energy Project (CMEP) (P) sought to gain access through the FOIA to information voluntarily provided to the NRC (D) pursuant to a non-disclosure agreement by the Institute for Nuclear Power Operations (INPO). CMEP (P) instituted this action after its request was denied on the ground that the information requested was not subject to disclosure under Exemption 4 of the FOIA because it contained confidential commercial information. While recognizing that disclosure might chill strictly voluntary reports, a divided appellate panel reversed and remanded to the district court. "Critical Mass I," 830 F.2d 278. On remand, the district court ruled in favor of the NRC (D), but a different panel reversed and remanded again. After the district court granted summary judgment to the NRC (D), CMEP (P) appealed.

ISSUE: Is financial or commercial information voluntarily provided to the government confidential and exempt from disclosure if it would usually not be released to the public by the person who provided it?

HOLDING AND DECISION: (Buckley, J.) Yes. Financial or commercial information voluntarily provided to the government is confidential and exempt from disclosure if it would usually not be released to the public by the person who provided it. This exemption serves to encourage cooperation with the government by persons having information useful to officials. Unless persons having such information can be assured that it will remain confidential, they may decline to cooperate with officials, and the ability of the government to make intelligent well-informed decisions will be impaired. The above test is objective, and the agency invoking the exemption must meet the burden of proving the provider's custom. So long as the information requested here is provided voluntarily, and so long as it is of a kind that INPO customarily withholds from the public, it must be treated as confidential. Accordingly, our decision in Critical Mass I is vacated, and the district court's grant of summary judgment for the NRC (D) is affirmed.

DISSENT: (Ginsburg, J.) No longer is there to be an independent judicial check on the reasonableness of the provider's custom and the consonance of that custom with the purposes of Exemption 4 and of the Act of which the exemption is part. The FOIA request at issue here is sought to advance public understanding of the nature and quality of the NRC's (D) oversight operations or activities. The public interest that the FOIA was enacted to serve is thus centrally at stake.

EDITOR'S ANALYSIS: Prior to the decision in this case, courts applied a two-part test to determine the applicability of Exemption 4 of the FOIA: whether disclosure was likely to (1) impair the government's ability to obtain information, or (2) cause harm to the supplier's competitive position. While overruling its decision in Critical Mass I, the court of appeals noted that the panel there adopted the First Circuit's conclusion that the exemption also protects a governmental interest in administrative efficiency and effectiveness. However, the court of appeals offered no opinion as to whether any other governmental or private interest might also fall within the exemption's protection.

[For more information on FOIA exemptions, see Casenote Law Outline on Administrative Law, Chapter 11, Openness and Public Control of Processes, § I, Freedom of Information Act.]

NOTES:

CHRYSLER CORPORATION v. BROWN

Auto manufacturer (P) v. Labor department (D)

441 U.S. 281 (1979).

NATURE OF CASE: Appeal of court order mandating disclosure of certain documents.

FACT SUMMARY: Chrysler Corp. (P) contended that certain documents pertaining to it held by the government fell outside the Freedom of Information Act and, therefore, could not be disclosed pursuant to unrelated regulations.

CONCISE RULE OF LAW: The FOIA does not give rise to a private right to prevent disclosure of documents pursuant to unrelated regulations.

FACTS: Pursuant to Executive Order, Chrysler Corp. (P) had to prepare certain reports giving the status of Chrysler's (P) compliance with federal affirmative action programs. The Executive Order and Regulations of the Dept. of Labor (D) allowed for public inspection of these records. The Dept. of Labor (D) informed Chrysler (P) that a request for some of these records had been made. Chrysler (P) argued that the records contained trade secrets and, therefore, fell under Exemption 4 of the FOIA. The court of appeals held the documents subject to disclosure.

ISSUE: Does the FOIA give rise to a private right to prevent disclosure of documents pursuant to unrelated regulations?

HOLDING AND DECISION: (Rehnquist, J.) No. The FOIA does not give rise to a private right to prevent disclosure of documents pursuant to unrelated regulations. The FOIA, by its terms, is exclusively a disclosure statute. This is borne out by its provisions for judicial review, which allow a court to order disclosure but say nothing about withholding disclosure. Also, legislative history makes it clear that the FOIA was designed to create an avenue for disclosure pursuant to other laws. [The Court went on to hold that the Trade Secrets Act may prevent disclosure and remanded to the Court of Appeals for consideration of this issue.]

CONCURRENCE: (Marshall, J.) The Court does not here consider the validity of the Executive Order in question.

EDITOR'S ANALYSIS: This was what had been labeled a "reverse FOIA" suit. Suppliers of information to the government had argued, as did Chrysler (P), that disclosure broader than that allowed by the FOIA was impermissible. The argument was that the FOIA had superseded all other disclosure rules. This decision put that argument to rest.

[For more information on FOIA exemptions, see Casenote Law Outline on Administrative Law, Chapter 11 Openness and Public Control of Processes, § I, Freedom of Information Act.]

QUICKNOTES

FOIA, EXEMPTION 4 - Exempts trade secrets and privileges or confidential financial information from disclosure.

NOTES:

PUBLIC CITIZEN v. U.S. DEPARTMENT OF JUSTICE

Lobby group (P) v. Government agency (D)

491 U.S. 440 (1989).

NATURE OF CASE: Suit alleging violation of the Federal Advisory Committee Act (FACA).

FACT SUMMARY: Public Citizen (P) alleged that the American Bar Association's committees that reviewed the nominations for federal judgeships fell under FACA rules.

CONCISE RULE OF LAW: FACA was not meant to apply to the American Bar Association's review of judicial nominees.

FACTS: The Federal Advisory Committee Act (FACA) was passed by Congress to provide public access and accountability to committees that advise the executive branch. According to FACA, it is to be applied to "any committee, board, commission, . . . established or utilized by one or more agencies in the interest of obtaining advice or recommendations for the President . . ." For many years prior to FACA, the American Bar Association had reviewed potential nominees for appointment as federal judges and reported whether the nominee was qualified. These recommendations were very influential in the appointment process. Public Citizen (P), a public interest lobbying group, filed suit claiming that these ABA committee meetings should be open to the public since they fell within the purview of FACA. The issue reached the Supreme Court.

ISSUE: Was FACA meant to apply to the American Bar Association's review of judicial nominees?

HOLDING AND DECISION: [No judge listed.] No. FACA was not meant to apply to the American Bar Association's review of judicial nominees. According to a straightforward reading of FACA, it is clear that the ABA committees on judicial nominees are "utilized" by the executive branch. However, it does not seem that Congress could have intended that any group of two or more people from which the President seeks advice would have to meet FACA requirements. The principal purpose of FACA was to enhance public accountability of advisory committees that were actually established by the executive branch. This could be done without expanding FACA's coverage to privately organized groups such as the ABA. The legislative history of FACA demonstrates that neither the House nor the Senate intended to bring all private advisory committees within FACA. Given its prominence, it is telling that it was omitted from a list of groups that would be covered by FACA. The words "or utilized" appear to have been added to the final statute in order to make sure that it covered quasi-public organizations. The literal reading of the law would have a far greater reach than Congress intended. Since the constitutionality of FACA would be arguable under a broad reading, it is appropriate to use a construction that will avoid such problems. Therefore, FACA should be read more narrowly and does not encompass such private groups as the ABA.

EDITOR'S ANALYSIS: The Court noted that the district court had declared FACA unconstitutional when it found that it applied to the ABA. Justices Kennedy, Rehnquist and O'Connor also agreed with this position. However, the majority seemed intent on somehow saving the law by looking past a literal reading of the statute.

QUICKNOTES

FEDERAL ADVISORY COMMITTEE ACT - Law intended to open up executive branch advisory groups to the public and make them more accountable.

NOTES:

NORTHWEST FOREST RESOURCE COUNCIL v. ESPY

Trade organization (P) v. Government agencies (D)

846 F. Supp. 1009 (D.D.C. 1994).

NATURE OF CASE: Suit challenging the legality of an advisory committee under FACA.

FACT SUMMARY: The Forest Ecosystem Management Assessment Team (FEMAT) (D) was established by the executive branch to make recommendations with regard to forest uses, but there was a dispute as to whether it was covered by FACA.

CONCISE RULE OF LAW: State employees without federal duties may not be considered officers of the federal government for purposes of FACA.

FACTS: FEMAT (D) was composed of many subteams and subgroups, encompassing as many as 700 people, in order to study uses of federal forests and identify the best solutions. An interagency group, the Forest Conference Executive Committee, was established to direct and supervise the work of FEMAT (D). At least five people who worked for FEMAT (D) were faculty members at state public universities. The Northwest Forest Resource Council (D), a trade group representing the timber industry, claimed that FEMAT (D) was an advisory committee that had to meet the requirements of FACA.

ISSUE: May state employees without federal duties be considered officers of the federal government for purposes of FACA?

HOLDING AND DECISION: (Jackson, J.) No. State employees without federal duties may not be considered officers of the federal government for purposes of FACA. That law defines an advisory committee as any group established by the executive branch to provide advice. There is no doubt that FEMAT (D) meets these general conditions. However, FACA does exempt certain groups if they are composed wholly of full-time officers or employees of the federal government. The agencies involved with FEMAT (D) claim that the outside faculty members should fit within this exception because they are state employees who could have been assigned a federal function. However, it is obvious that their presence precludes FEMAT (D) from fitting within the FACA exception. The argument that FEMAT (D) was not providing policy advice to the President is also clearly wrong. The record shows that the administration looked only at FEMAT (D) proposals in choosing a policy to implement. Therefore, FEMAT (D) was an advisory committee and its use violated FACA.

EDITOR'S ANALYSIS: Other courts have also rejected the contention that FACA should not apply to advisory committees that consist only of technicians who supply data. In another case, a court was faced with the legality of President Clinton's task force on health care reform. That group was composed of all full-time federal employees except for the First Lady. That court decided that the First Lady should be considered a federal employee for FACA purposes.

QUICKNOTES

FEDERAL ADVISORY COMMITTEE ACT - Law intended to open up executive branch advisory groups to the public and make them more accountable.

NOTES:

FEDERAL COMMUNICATIONS COMMISSION v. ITT WORLD COMMUNICATIONS, INC.
Government agency (D) v. International telecommunications company (P)
466 U.S. 463 (1984).

NATURE OF CASE: Review of order challenging international conferences.

FACT SUMMARY: ITT (P) contended that certain international conferences attended by FCC (D) members were covered by the federal Sunshine Act.

CONCISE RULE OF LAW: The Sunshine Act applies only to discussions that effectively predetermine official actions.

FACTS: Three FCC (D) members attended a series of informal conferences with overseas telecommunications regulators. The FCC (D) had participated in the conferences in the hope that an information exchange might persuade European nations to encourage competition. ITT World Communications (P) filed a rulemaking petition with the FCC (D), contending that the meetings were within the scope of the Sunshine Act and should have been held in public. The court of appeals held that the Sunshine Act did apply to the conferences. The Supreme Court granted review.

ISSUE: Does the Sunshine Act apply only to discussions that effectively predetermine agency actions?

HOLDING AND DECISION: (Powell, J.) Yes. The Sunshine Act applies to discussions that effectively predetermine official actions. Section 552 b(a)(2) of the Act defines "meetings" as "the deliberations of at least the number of individual agency members required to take action on behalf of the agency where such deliberations determine or result in the joint conduct or disposition of official agency business." Although the FCC (D) commissioners who attended the conferences did not constitute a quorum, they did have the power to approve common carrier applications, and therefore the Sunshine Act would normally apply to such conferences. However, the conferences did not result in any formal action by the FCC (D) regarding applications, nor did they result in any firm agency positions on any matter before the commissioners. Therefore the conferences were not meetiings "of an agency" since they were not convened by the FCC (D) nor subject to its unilateral control. For these reasons, the Sunshine Act does not apply. Reversed and remanded.

EDITOR'S ANALYSIS: The Sunshine Act strikes a balance between the public's "need to know" and agency process. On the one hand, "meetings" must be open. On the other hand, the term "meetings" is narrowly defined.

[For more information on the Sunshine Act, see Casenote Law Outline on Administrative Law, Chapter 11 Openness and Public Control of Processes, § III, The Sunshine Act.]

QUICKNOTES

SUNSHINE ACT § 552 - Requires that meetings of agencies be open to the public.

NOTES:

Notes

CHAPTER 9
ATTORNEYS FEES

QUICK REFERENCE RULES OF LAW

1. **Equal Access to Justice Act: Eligibility.** Attorney's fees may be awarded against a party whose position was not justified to a degree that would satisfy a reasonable person. (Pierce v. Underwood)

2. **Equal Access to Justice Act: Eligibility.** Private litigants are not entitled to attorney's fees from the government under EAJA if the governing law at the time was unclear or in flux. (Martinez v. Secretary of Health and Human Services)

3. **Equal Access to Justice Act: Eligibility.** A party must show that it was clearly reasonable and well founded in law and fact in order to prove substantial justification for an incorrect legal position in litigation. (Friends of the Boundary Waters Wilderness v. Thomas)

4. **Equal Access to Justice Act: Amount of Award.** Attorneys may not receive more than the statutory rate under the EAJA, unless the court finds that they have some distinctive knowledge or specialized skill particularly needed in the case. (Pierce v. Underwood)

5. **Equal Access to Justice Act: Amount of Award.** Attorneys with distinctive knowledge in a practice specialty are entitled to fees higher than the maximum rate under EAJA where those qualifications are necessary to the litigation and there are no other lawyers to take the case at the statutory rate. (Pirus v. Bowen)

6. **Equal Access to Justice Act: Amount of Award.** The EAJA statutory cap on attorney's fees may be exceeded only in unusual situations where the legal services rendered require specialized training and expertise unattainable by an ordinary competent attorney. (Chynoweth v. Sullivan)

7. **Equal Access to Justice Act: Amount of Award.** Attorney's fees in excess of the EAJA statutory maximum rate are only appropriate in unusual cases where the case requires someone with specialized training and expertise unattainable by a standard competent attorney. (Raines v. Shalala)

PIERCE v. UNDERWOOD (I)

Parties not identified.

487 U.S. 552 (1988).

NATURE OF CASE: Appeal of an award of attorney's fees.

FACT SUMMARY: A district court awarded attorney's fees to a party because it found that the Housing and Urban Development agency had taken a position that was not substantially justified.

CONCISE RULE OF LAW: Attorney's fees may be awarded against a party whose position was not justified to a degree that would satisfy a reasonable person.

FACTS: The Equal Access to Justice Act (EAJA) allows for the awarding of attorney's fees to the prevailing party in litigation when the other party's position was not "substantially justified." In a suit against the Secretary of Housing and Urban Development (D), the case was settled on grounds very unfavorable to the agency and the trial court ruled that the Secretary's (D) position was not substantially justified because of the objective indicia of the case, including the terms of the settlement, and awarded attorney's fees. The Ninth Circuit Court of Appeals affirmed, finding that a position is "substantially justified" if it "had a reasonable basis both in law and fact." The Secretary (D) appealed to the Supreme Court.

ISSUE: May attorney's fees be awarded against a party whose position was not justified to a degree that would satisfy a reasonable person?

HOLDING AND DECISION: (Scalia, J.) Yes. Attorney's fees may be awarded against a party whose position was not justified to a degree that would satisfy a reasonable person. Courts should not try to substitute for the formula that Congress has laid out in the statute. Accordingly, the "substantially justified" test is the only one that matters. There are a few different meanings of the word "substantial" so the test is susceptible to different interpretations. However, in this field of law there are other tests that use similar phrases and we should use them in interpreting the language of the EAJA. It is clear from these other phrases that substantial justification was not meant to mean "justified to a high degree." Rather, it was meant to be interpreted as "justified in substance." This is essentially the same as the Ninth Circuit's formulation of "reasonable basis both in law and fact." The Court is less sure that the district court should have looked only at the objective indicia of the case to determine whether the Secretary's (D) position was substantially justified. The terms of a settlement may be the result of other factors than a poor legal position. It is better to look directly at the merits of the position taken. After considering the merits, the Court can not find that the district court abused its discretion in finding that there was no substantial justification for the Secretary's (D) position. Affirmed.

EDITOR'S ANALYSIS: The Court noted that looking only at settlement terms to determine justification might discourage settlements in the future. The standard of review in looking at the award of attorney's fees is abuse of discretion. Accordingly, it is not easy for an appellate court to overrule the trial court's initial determination.

QUICKNOTES

EQUAL ACCESS TO JUSTICE ACT - Provides for the awarding of attorney's fees to a prevailing party other than the government when the opposing side took a position that was not substantially justified.

NOTES:

MARTINEZ v. SECRETARY OF HEALTH & HUMAN SERVICES

Injured worker (P) v. Government agency (D)

815 F.2d 1381 (10th Cir. 1987).

NATURE OF CASE: Appeal from an award of attorney's fees.

FACT SUMMARY: The government's (D) position in a disability benefits case was against the position adopted in the jurisdiction after the suit was filed.

CONCISE RULE OF LAW: Private litigants are not entitled to attorney's fees from the government under EAJA if the governing law at the time was unclear or in flux.

FACTS: Martinez (P) was injured in a work accident in 1978 and began receiving disability benefits under the Social Security Act. An investigation led to the cessation of the benefits in 1981 and the termination was upheld by an administrative law judge. In 1983, Martinez (P) sought judicial review in district court and argued that termination of the benefits required evidence that his medical condition had improved and that failure to apply that standard commanded reversal. The Secretary of Health and Human Services (D) asserted that this was not the proper test. In 1984, in a separate case, the Tenth Circuit ruled that benefits could not be discontinued without a showing that the claimant's medical condition had improved. Based on this ruling, the district court ruled that Martinez (P) should have his benefits reinstated. Martinez (P) then applied for attorney's fees under the EAJA. The Secretary (D) argued that the medical improvement standard was not adopted until after the litigation and thus, there was substantial justification for their position. The district court agreed and denied attorney's fees. Martinez (P) appealed.

ISSUE: Are private litigants entitled to attorney's fees from the government under EAJA if the governing law at the time was unclear or in flux?

HOLDING AND DECISION: [Per curiam.] No. Private litigants are not entitled to attorney's fees from the government under EAJA if the governing law at the time was unclear or in flux. The more clearly established the governing norms are, the less justified a position in litigation will be. Where there are contrary interpretations by district courts and no clear precedent on a particular issue, it would be unfair to say that one position is not substantially justified because the other position is later adopted as law. In the present case, other circuit courts had adopted the medical improvement standard, but the governing law in this circuit was less certain. There were some intimations that this standard would be used, but some district courts had ruled differently on the issue prior to our definitive 1984 ruling. Accordingly, the Secretary (D) was substantially justified in taking an opposing position in the Martinez (P) litigation, which was prior to the 1984 decision. Therefore, the district court's ruling denying an award of attorney's fees is affirmed.

EDITOR'S ANALYSIS: One judge on the Tenth Circuit deciding this case dissented, finding that the government was not substantially justified. This case stands for the proposition that the governing law must be fairly well settled before a court will find that an opposing position is not justified. Where there is any controversy or ambiguity, parties won't be punished for taking a position later ruled wrong.

QUICKNOTES

EQUAL ACCESS TO JUSTICE ACT - Provides for the awarding of attorney's fees to a prevailing party, other than the government, when the opposing side took a position that was not substantially justified.

JUDICIAL REVIEW - The authority of the courts to review decisions, actions or omissions committed by another agency or branch of government.

NOTES:

FRIENDS OF THE BOUNDARY WATERS WILDERNESS v. THOMAS

Public interest group (P) v. Government agency (D)
53 F.3d 881 (8th Cir. 1995).

NATURE OF CASE: Appeal from denial of attorney's fees.

FACT SUMMARY: The Chief of the United States Forest Service (D) argued that its position in a losing case was justified because a district court had agreed before being reversed on appeal.

CONCISE RULE OF LAW: A party must show that it was clearly reasonable and well founded in law and fact in order to prove substantial justification for an incorrect legal position in litigation.

FACTS: In 1978, Congress passed the Boundary Waters Canoe Wilderness Area Act providing that the termination of existing motor boat transport operations at a certain waterway was required unless it was determined that there was no "feasible" nonmotorized means available. In 1986, the Forest Service authorized continued motor boat operations of various portages because it found that it was not feasible to use nonmotorized portage wheels. The Friends (P) brought an administrative appeal of this ruling and the Chief of the Forest Service (D) affirmed. The Friends (P) filed suit in district court, which found that the Chief's (D) interpretation of the Act was reasonable and also affirmed. The Friends (P) appealed and the court of appeals reversed, finding that the Chief's (D) interpretation was contrary to the definition of "feasible." The Friends (P) applied for an award of attorney's fees under EAJA as the prevailing party, but the district court denied the award, finding that the Chief's (D) position was substantially justified given the ambiguity of the statute. The Friends (P) once again appealed.

ISSUE: Must a party show that it was clearly reasonable and well founded in law and fact in order to prove substantial justification for an incorrect legal position in litigation?

HOLDING AND DECISION: (Gibson, J.) Yes. A party must show that it was clearly reasonable and well founded in law and fact in order to prove substantial justification for an incorrect legal position in litigation. In order for the government's position to be substantially justified, it must be justified to a degree that would "satisfy a reasonable person" and have "a reasonable basis both in law and fact." The most powerful indicator of the reasonableness of an ultimately rejected position is a decision on the merits and the rationale supporting that decision. The decision of the district court and dissenting judges may be considered. However, when the superior appellate court finds that a position was clearly contrary to the law, this must be given greater weight. In this case, this court concluded that the Chief's (D) position was contrary to clear Congressional intent and the plain meaning of "feasible." Given this unequivocal rejection of the Chief's (D) position in the earlier litigation, it cannot now be said that the position was reasonable or well founded. Thus, the district court abused its discretion in concluding that the Chief (D) was substantially justified and the attorney's fees should have been awarded to the Friends (P). Reversed.

EDITOR'S ANALYSIS: The court also noted that the Chief (D) had not always interpreted the statute in the same way prior to the litigation with the Friends (P). One judge dissented from the majority position when the original litigation reached the court of appeals. This decision here is rather biting in that it implies strongly that the dissenting judge took a clearly unreasonable position in the dissent.

QUICKNOTES

EQUAL ACCESS TO JUSTICE ACT - Provides for the awarding of attorney's fees to a prevailing party, other than the government, when the opposing side took a position that was not substantially justified.

ABUSE OF DISCRETION - A determination by an appellate court that a lower court's decision was based on an error of law.

NOTES:

PIERCE v. UNDERWOOD (II)

Parties not identified.

487 U.S. 552 (1988).

NATURE OF CASE: Appeal of an award of attorney's fees.

FACT SUMMARY: The amount of an award of attorney's fees was disputed.

CONCISE RULE OF LAW: Attorneys may not receive more than the statutory rate under the EAJA, unless the court finds that they have some distinctive knowledge or specialized skill particularly needed in the case.

FACTS: The Equal Access to Justice Act (EAJA) allows for the awarding of attorney's fees to the prevailing party in litigation when the other party's position was not "substantially justified." There is a statutory maximum rate for the award unless the court finds a special factor that justifies enhancing the amount. In a suit against the Secretary of Housing and Urban Development (D), the trial court ruled that the Secretary's (D) position was not substantially justified and awarded attorney's fees in excess of the statutory rate because of the "limited availablity of qualified attorneys for the proceedings involved." The court also took into account the customary fees and awards in other cases and the contingent nature of the fee. The Secretary (D) appealed to the Supreme Court.

ISSUE: May attorneys receive more than the statutory rate under the EAJA unless the court finds that they have some distinctive knowledge or specialized skill particularly needed in the case?

HOLDING AND DECISION: (Scalia, J.) No. Attorneys may not receive more than the statutory rate under the EAJA, unless the court finds that they have some distinctive knowledge or specialized skill particularly needed in the case. If the factor relied on by the district court, the "limited availability of qualified attorneys," meant merely that skilled lawyers are in short supply, the statutory maximum rate would be effectively eliminated. The exception to the maximum rate for limited availability must refer to attorneys that are qualified in a specialized sense for the particular litigation. It cannot refer only to general legal competence. Thus, the factors that allow a court to award above the statutory cap must not be broad and of general application. In the present case, the district court's general findings on the special factors reflect generally applicable factors, not the type that command going above the cap. Thus, the award is remanded for proceedings consistent with this opinion.

EDITOR'S ANALYSIS: The Court declined to list other special factors it would find to mandate going outside the maximum rate structure. Under the original EAJA, the rate was $75 an hour if not enhanced. In 1996, it was raised to $125.

QUICKNOTES

EQUAL ACCESS TO JUSTICE ACT - Provides for the awarding of attorney's fees to a prevailing party, other than the government, when the opposing side took a position that was not substantially justified.

NOTES:

PIRUS v. BOWEN

Class representative (P) v. Department of Health and Human Services (D)

869 F.2d 536 (9th Cir. 1989).

NATURE OF CASE: Appeal of an award of attorney's fees.

FACT SUMMARY: The government (D) complained that an award of attorney's fees should not have been enhanced past the statutory maximum rate.

CONCISE RULE OF LAW: Attorneys with distinctive knowledge in a practice specialty are entitled to fees higher than the maximum rate under EAJA where those qualifications are necessary to the litigation and there are no other lawyers to take the case at the statutory rate.

FACTS: Pirus (P) brought a class action against the Secretary of the Department of Health and Human Services (D) on behalf of a class which was denied social security benefits. The district court granted summary judgment to Pirus (P) and the class. Pirus (P) then petitioned for an award of attorney's fees under EAJA. The court awarded the fees and determined that special factors justified an award of fees in excess of the EAJA maximum cap. The factors considered by the court were the attorney's expertise, the lack of other lawyers willing to take the case, and the unique ability of the attorneys in this particular area of the law. The Secretary (D) appealed.

ISSUE: Are attorneys with distinctive knowledge in a practice specialty entitled to fees higher than the maximum rate under EAJA where thoses qualifications are necessary to the litigation and there are no other lawyers to take the case at the lower rate?

HOLDING AND DECISION: (Norris, J.) Yes. Attorneys with distinctive knowledge in a practice specialty are entitled to fees higher than the maximum rate under EAJA where thoses qualifications are necessary to the litigation and there are no other lawyers to take the case at the statutory rate. The Supreme Court has decided that Congress intended for courts to deviate from the statutory cap only if the attorney had some distinctive knowledge or specialized skill needful for the litigation. Although the Supreme Court pointed out patent law as an example of a practice specialty and specialized skill, there is no reason to believe that this standard would not apply to other areas of the law. In the present case, Pirus' (P) attorneys developed a speciality in social security law and had expertise pertaining to the complex statutory scheme of the law. The district court found that this special expertise was needed in the case, which was highly complex and required substantial knowledge about a narrow area of the law. Accordingly, the district court acted properly in awarding an enhanced fee. Affirmed.

EDITOR'S ANALYSIS: The reasoning of this decision would seem to open up fee enhancements to many types of cases. In many, if not most, cases the prevailing party's attorneys will have some expertise in the legal area of the case.

QUICKNOTES

EQUAL ACCESS TO JUSTICE ACT - Provides for the awarding of attorney's fees to a prevailing party, other than the government, when the opposing side took a position that was not substantially justified.

NOTES:

CHYNOWETH v. SULLIVAN

Benefits recipient (P) v. Government agency (D)
920 F.2d 648 (10th Cir. 1990).

NATURE OF CASE: Appeal from denial of enhancement of attorney's fees award.

FACT SUMMARY: Chynoweth (P) claimed her attorneys were entitled to a fee enhancement under EAJA because of their special expertise in Social Security disability law.

CONCISE RULE OF LAW: The EAJA statutory cap on attorney's fees may be exceeded only in unusual situations where the legal services rendered require specialized training and expertise unattainable by an ordinary competent attorney.

FACTS: Chynoweth (P) was awarded attorney's fees under EAJA after a successful lawsuit involving Social Security disability benefits. Chynoweth (P) petitioned the district court for attorneys fees of $150 per hour under EAJA, claiming he was a specialist in Social Security disability benefits law. The district court held that Chynoweth (P) was entitled to attorneys fees since the Secretary's denial of disability benefits was not substantially justified. However, the district court concluded that Chynoweth's (P) attorney was not entitled to a fee enhancement based on the absence of a special factor of any expertise in Social Security benefits law. Chynoweth (P) appealed this aspect of the award.

ISSUE: May the EAJA statutory cap on attorney's fees be exceeded only in unusual situations where the legal services rendered require specialized training and expertise unattainable by an ordinary competent attorney?

HOLDING AND DECISION: (Baldock, J.) Yes. The EAJA statutory cap on attorney's fees may be exceeded only in unusual situations where the legal services rendered require specialized training and expertise unattainable by an ordinary competent attorney. EAJA mandates a maximum rate unless a special factor justifies a higher fee. Expertise in a particular legal field alone does not justify the higher rate. Merely because some scholarly effort or professional experience is required to attain proficiency in a particular practice area does not automatically require a fee enhancement. Social Security law is not beyond the grasp of a typical competent practicing attorney. In the present case, the district court also made no findings that Chynoweth's (P) action was a particularly difficult case or that she would have been unable to obtain other competent representation at the enhanced rate. Affirmed.

EDITOR'S ANALYSIS: Although this case would seem to turn mostly on the court's opinion that expertise with Social Security law is not a specialized skill, there may be more important factors. The court was reviewing the district court's denial of the fee enhancement under an abuse of discretion standard. Also, the district court obviously made no effort to put on the record facts about Chynoweth's (P) case that would make it seem difficult and unique.

QUICKNOTES

EQUAL ACCESS TO JUSTICE ACT - Provides for the awarding of attorney's fees to a prevailing party other than the government when the opposing side took a position that was not substantially justified.

NOTES:

RAINES v. SHALALA

Benefits recipient (P) v. Secretary of Health and Human Services (D)

44 F.3d 1355 (7th Cir. 1995).

NATURE OF CASE: Appeal from award of attorney's fees.

FACT SUMMARY: Raines' (P) attorney was awarded fees in excess of the EAJA statutory cap in a Social Security benefits case.

CONCISE RULE OF LAW: Attorney's fees in excess of the EAJA statutory maximum rate are only appropriate in unusual cases where the case requires someone with specialized training and expertise unattainable by a standard competent attorney.

FACTS: Raines (P) filed suit against Health and Human Services (D) for his entitlement to Social Security disability benefits and prevailed. Raines' (P) petition requested $175 per hour for attorney's fees, claiming that this was the prevailing market rate due to the limited availability of qualified Social Security lawyers. The district court awarded attorney's fees pursuant to EAJA, deciding that special factors were present in order to award fees in excess of the statutory cap. The court found that the attorney had expertise with a complex statutory scheme, familiarity with a particular agency, and understood the needs of a particular class of clients. Health and Human Services (D) appealed, claiming that if such practice specialties were routinely found to be special factors, fee awards subject to the statutory cap would be rare.

ISSUE: Are attorney's fees in excess of the EAJA statutory maximum rate only appropriate in unusual cases where the case requires someone with specialized training and expertise unattainable by a standard competent attorney?

HOLDING AND DECISION: (Ripple, J.) Yes. Attorney's fees in excess of the EAJA statutory maximum rate are only appropriate in unusual cases where the case requires someone with specialized training and expertise unattainable by a standard competent attorney. The Supreme Court has clearly held that a fee enhancement under EAJA can not be based simply on the limited availability of qualified attorneys. The nature of the case must also make it necessary to have an attorney with a specialized skill in an identifiable practice specialty. This special skill requirement means something not easily acquired by a reasonably competent attorney or a special non-legal skill such as knowledge of a foreign language. Additionally, it will be an exceptional or unusual situation when the special factors will apply. The test applied by the district court in the instant case was a bit too lenient. Although Raines' (P) attorney was undoubtedly very proficient in the area of Social Security benefits law, this isn't the type of skill and expertise that is unattainable by a competent attorney through diligent study. Furthermore, the principal issues arising in Raines' (P) case are issues that arise not infrequently in disability litigation. Accordingly, the award in excess of the statutory cap was improper and must be reversed and remanded.

EDITOR'S ANALYSIS: The EAJA also has a provision for cost of living enhancements. It was to be calculated by looking at the Consumer Price Index. The Supreme Court has also found that attorney's fees may be awarded for the time spent in litigating the fee issue and amount.

QUICKNOTES

EQUAL ACCESS TO JUSTICE ACT - Provides for the awarding of attorney's fees to a prevailing party, other than the government, when the opposing side took a position that was not substantially justified.

NOTES:

Notes